Mental Math
in Junior High

Jack A. Hope • Barbara J. Reys • Robert E. Reys

DALE SEYMOUR PUBLICATIONS

Cover design: Rachel Gage
Illustrations: Mitchell Rose

Order number DS01808
ISBN 0-86651-433-3

DALE
SEYMOUR
PUBLICATIONS
P.O. BOX 10888
PALO ALTO, CA 94303

8 9 10 11 12 13 14 15-MA-95 94 93

CONTENTS

PREFACE

Learning to calculate mentally, without the use of external memory aids (including paper and pencil), has many benefits.

1. **Calculating in your head is a practical life skill.** Many types of everyday computation problems can be solved mentally. In fact, practically speaking, many *must* be solved mentally, since we often need to make quick computations when we don't have a calculator or paper and pencil at hand. For example: You are at the airport. The departure board indicates that your flight is scheduled to leave at 3:35. Your watch shows that it's now 2:49. How much time do you have? Enough time to grab a snack? Here's another example: You find tuna fish on sale at the supermarket for 69 cents a can. You would like to stock up now, but you know that you have only $10 with you, and you also need to buy bread and milk. How many cans of tuna could you buy on sale? These and similar situations demonstrate the everyday utility of mental math skills.

2. **Skill at mental math can make written computation easier or quicker.** A student who is dependent on written algorithms might calculate 1000 x 945 this way:

$$\begin{array}{r} 1000 \\ \times\ 945 \\ \hline 5000 \\ 4000 \\ 9000 \\ \hline 945,000 \end{array}$$

Knowing how to "tack on trailing zeros," a mental math skill, can reduce that process to one step: **1000 x 945 = 945,000.** Similarly, faced with the addition of long columns of figures, even with a pencil in hand, the mental math skill "searching for compatible pairs" can simplify the computation. For example, finding numbers that sum to ten makes this addition quicker than taking it step by step:

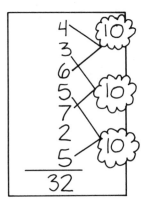

In these and many other ways, mental math skills can streamline students' written work and increase their understanding at the same time.

3. Proficiency in mental math contributes to increased skill in estimation. Estimation has come to be recognized as an important part of the mathematics curriculum. It is essential for checking the reasonableness of an answer obtained through the use of a calculator, and estimation skills are useful in solving many everyday problems as well. Mental calculation provides the cornerstone for all estimation processes, offering a variety of alternative algorithms and nonstandard techniques for finding answers.

4. Mental calculation can lead to a better understanding of place value, mathematical operations, and basic number properties. Students often do written computation mechanically, without a great deal of thought, simply applying the written algorithms with very little sense of what they are *really* doing. Efficient paper-and-pencil calculation demands careful attention to digits and bookkeeping rules and contributes to a fragmentary view of number relationships. Mental computation, on the other hand, forces students to think about numbers and number relationships. As students learn to manipulate numbers in their heads, they develop a keen number sense and experience increased confidence in their mathematical abilities. Such confidence ensures that these students will not have to turn to a machine or pencil and paper for every straightforward calculation they encounter in daily life.

Despite its many attractive benefits, mental calculation has not played a prominent role in most contemporary mathematics programs. Because of this neglect, most people are not very proficient mental calculators. Recent studies have demonstrated that a large majority of children and young adults cannot perform even the simplest mental calculations. For example, the third National Assessment of Educational Progress in mathematics found that less than half of the 13-year-old sample correctly calculated the product of 60 and 70 "in the head" within 9 seconds. According to the same survey, most children were unaware that a mental calculation is often the most convenient method of solution. For example, only 38 percent of the 13-year-olds thought that the exercise 945 x 1000 should be done mentally; the majority claimed that either a pencil and paper or a calculator was needed to determine the solution.

Undoubtedly, this performance reflects the current lack of attention given to mental computation by textbook publishers and curriculum developers. To counter this we offer the *Mental Math* series, a planned program of instruction in mental calculation that complements any current elementary school, middle grades, and junior high mathematics program. We think you will find the lessons fun and easy to teach. Used regularly, with plenty of practice, these materials can turn your whole class into "mentalmathletes."

Jack Hope
Barbara Reys
Robert Reys

INTRODUCTION

About the *Mental Math* Series

Mental Math in Junior High is the last in a series of three books designed to help teach students the techniques of "figuring in your head." None of the books is a prerequisite to those that follow; any students can benefit from the instruction regardless of their prior experience with mental computation.

The first book in the series, *Mental Math in the Primary Grades,* is suited for students in grades one through three and focuses on simple calculation with whole numbers. These lessons help students develop good reasoning strategies to learn and remember the basic facts. Visual aids such as dominoes, a ten frame and counters, and the 100 chart figure prominently in this first book. The second book, *Mental Math in the Middle Grades,* is designed for grades four through six. It introduces a series of strategies emphasizing patterns and shortcuts that help students mentally perform more difficult mental calculations with whole numbers.

This third book, *Mental Math in Junior High,* is intended for grades seven through nine. It extends the strategies introduced at earlier levels—such as finding or making compatible numbers, working from the front-end, and dealing with trailing zeroes—with more advanced lessons that introduce methods of calculating mentally with fractions, decimals, and percents, as well as whole numbers. The most important strategies taught in the preceding book are repeated at the junior high level, usually with extensions into more difficult computation.

Features of This Book

Mental Math in Junior High contains 50 lessons in mental calculation. The book is divided into five units.

Each unit opens with a *Mentalmathletes* page, featuring general interest anecdotes about experts in mental calculation. These pages also divulge some of the tricks used by Mentalmathletes that students can learn as well to increase their own powers of mental calculation. Mentalmathletes pages can be presented on the overhead and then posted on the bulletin board to stimulate student interest and involvement in mental mathematics.

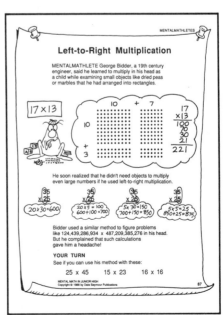

Mentalmathletes Page

There are 10 lessons in each unit, each lesson consisting of two reproducible pages: a *lesson page* that you can use to introduce each new mental math strategy, and a *Power Builder* page with two sets of practice problems.

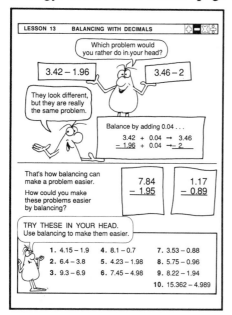

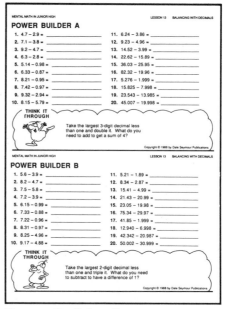

Lesson Page

Power Builder Sets

Mental Math in Daily Life

In each unit, one or two *Mental Math in Daily Life* lessons are included to illustrate how calculating mentally can help in solving problems and in carrying out tasks frequently encountered in everyday affairs. Challenge your students to look through magazines, newspapers, and advertising flyers to find situations that suggest practical uses of mental math. Encourage students to share any experiences in which they needed to calculate mentally. Perhaps working parents will be willing to provide you with examples of on-the-job calculations and estimates that are often handled mentally.

At the close of each unit, a review page focuses class discussion on the strategies presented in that unit, to prepare students for the unit progress test.

A section of teaching notes at the front of the book offers helpful tips for presenting each lesson, plus additional problems to use for oral practice in follow-up work. In addition to the unit progress tests, a cumulative test appears in two forms for use in pre- and post-testing. Answer keys for the Power Builder practice sets and all the tests are included at the back of the book.

Teaching Mental Math

SCHEDULING THE LESSONS

If the *Mental Math* program is to be effective, you must incorporate instruction, discussion, and practice into your daily lesson plans on a regular basis. Here is a suggested schedule, based on one week per lesson:

DAY 1: Present the new lesson, including the "Problems for Oral Practice" that appear with the teaching notes.

DAY 2: Hand out the first practice set (Power Builder A).

DAYS 3 AND 4: Reinforce the new strategy by providing 2–3 minutes of practice using problems similar to the "Problems for Oral Practice."

DAY 5: Hand out the second practice set (Power Builder B).

As a teacher at a single grade level, you are not expected to include all 50 lessons in a year's work; rather, you have the freedom to pick and choose those lessons most appropriate for your students.

PLANNING THE LESSONS

The lesson pages have been set in large-size type for display on the overhead projector, a teaching mode that is especially appropriate for presenting mental math strategies. If you are not comfortable with this approach, you could present the lesson at the board or as a class handout. To prepare for each lesson:

1. Duplicate the appropriate masters, either as transparencies or handouts, as needed—both the lesson page and the Power Builder sets. Power Builder pages are designed to be cut in half for distribution at different times.

2. Preview the lesson and the teaching notes. The notes generally give you the rationale behind the lesson and will alert you to important considerations and occasional pitfalls in the new strategy being presented.

3. Consider collecting a number of problems from the Power Builder sets of previous lessons; these can serve as a brief mental warm-up for the students before you begin a new lesson.

PRESENTING THE LESSONS

Discussion Is Critical

As you teach each new lesson, be sure to spend plenty of time developing and discussing the new strategy. This discussion should continue as you proceed to the "TRY THESE . . ." practice problems in the box at the bottom of the teaching page. The TRY THESE exercises are an important part of the instruction. At this stage you are not working on *speed* in mental calculation; you are working on *understanding*. With each problem, pause to discuss the students' answers and their methods of solution. If there are wrong answers, take time to explore how students got them. Through such discussion, you can quickly diagnose and correct the source of any difficulties.

As you will discover, class discussion is a critical part of teaching mental math because there is no other way for students to "show their work." It's all taking place in their heads, and talking about their thought processes is the only way to find out how well they understand the strategies.

Here's another reason that discussion should play a dominant role in the teaching of mental math skills: there is no single "right" way to do a problem in your head. Several alternative methods may be equally practical and efficient. To develop flexibility in thinking about numbers and number relationships, students should learn to look for and recognize a variety of approaches to the same problem. During discussion, encourage students to share different strategies and talk about the advantages of each. If you are a practiced mental calculator yourself, you may have additional tips for the students based on your own techniques.

Stress Visual Thinking

Another important aspect of teaching mental math is developing mental imagery that helps students perform computation in their heads. Too often, students who are asked to do a mental computation simply try to envision the problem as if they were working with pencil and paper. This is often accompanied by physical motions, so that you might see, for example, students using their fingers to "write" the problem in the air or on the desk. Such dependence on familiar paper-and-pencil methods is awkward and ignores many number properties than can simplify mental calculation.

Use concrete materials such as *place value charts* and *money,* which can suggest new ways of thinking about and visualizing computation problems. *Number lines* are often helpful in visualizing addition and subtraction, and *rectangular arrays* or *repeating patterns* can help students visualize multiplication. As you discuss the mental math strategies, encourage students to share the way they "see" a problem in their mind's eye.

Help Students Take "Thinking Shortcuts"

Students are often inclined to approach computation problems on a laborious digit-by-digit basis, methodically plodding along in certain rote patterns. Teach them that they need not say (or think) to themselves every digit and every step of the computation process.

That is, faced with a problem of column addition like the one shown here, they should not have to think to themselves:
"4 plus 6 is 10, plus 7 is 17, plus 2 is 19. . . . "
Instead, they should be able to look at the numbers (ones digits) and think simply:
"10 . . . 17 . . . 19 . . ." and so forth.
Often the teaching pages demonstrate such "thinking shortcuts"; model this shortcut thinking for the students as often as you can.

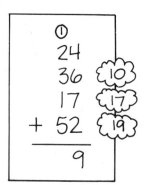

PRACTICING THE STRATEGIES

The two sets of Power Builder exercises with each lesson provide independent practice with specific strategies. As you move from group discussion to independent work, continue to insist that the problems be done *mentally*. When working on the Power Builders, students will need pencils to record their answers, but that is *all* the pencils should be used for.

At first, you may want to circulate around the classroom to enforce the "in your head" rule while students are working on the practice sets. You might also set a time limit so that students won't have time for paper-and- pencil computation. Push them to complete each Power Builder set as rapidly as possible. Three or four minutes is a reasonable target time, but you may need to adjust this to the difficulty of the problems and the abilities of your students. The best timing standards can be determined by experimenting with your class. You might allow more time for Power Builder A sets than for Power Builder B.

At the end of each Power Builder set is a problem called "Think It Through." These problems are generally more difficult than the practice problems, but students still should be able to solve them using mental math. These are to be done *after* the practice problems, and need not be completed within the time limit you have set. Note that a "Think It Through" problem does not necessarily involve the mental math strategy taught in that particular lesson.

OFFERING RELATED PRACTICE

Regular drill of the basic facts of addition, subtraction, multiplication, and division should be used to complement the *Mental Math* program. A daily three-minute oral drill helps students master these important number combinations. Such a drill can serve as a brief warm-up before you teach a *Mental Math* lesson. Include such extensions of the basic facts as $30 + 40$, $18,000 - 9000$, 800×70, and $4200 \div 70$.

Encourage students to use mental calculation whenever the opportunity arises in a regular mathematics lesson. Try not to discourage them from using shortcut mental methods to eliminate steps in written calculations. Instead, challenge them to use mental techniques to solve all or part of a problem before they reach for a pencil or a calculator.

Demonstrate the power and usefulness of mental math in making estimates. You might also show how mental calculation can often be used to improve the accuracy of a first rough estimate.

Some students will catch on to mental math strategies more quickly than others in your class. Encourage these more able calculators to extend the strategies to more difficult problems. While these students are working independently, you can slow your lesson pace to help the less able mental calculators in your class.

You may want to become familiar with the lower level book in this series, *Mental Math in the Middle Grades*. The lessons in that book provide a valuable foundation for the strategies explored in this volume. Such background will be helpful for students who are experiencing difficulties with any of the lessons in *Mental Math in Junior High*.

USING THE TESTS

The tests for *Mental Math in Junior High* include a cumulative test that comes in two parallel forms. Administer Form A before you start instruction in mental math and Form B after you have completed the program. Unless they have had prior instruction in mental computation, students are likely to perform very poorly on the pre-test (Form A). Caution them that these exercises may seem very hard, and ask them simply to do the best they can. Comparing the results of the two tests (Form A and Form B) will demonstrate the improvement in students' ability to calculate mentally.

In addition, there are five progress tests for use throughout the school year, one at the end of each unit. Each progress test provides mixed practice of mental computation strategies that were developed in that unit. Administer the appropriate test shortly after a unit has been taught and practiced. Regular testing reminds students that mental computation is important and something you value.

Be sure to prepare students for these progress tests with a thorough review of the strategies presented in the preceding unit. The review page for each unit can serve as a starting point for class discussion. In most of their other practice, students will have been concentrating on one operation and one clearly identified strategy at a time. In order to perform with reasonable speed on the progress tests, they will need practice with mixed groups of problems, learning to quickly identify an efficient solution strategy.

If there is material within a unit that you have not presented because it seems too difficult for your class, you will need to take this into account when interpreting the test results. You might prefer to modify the tests, eliminating inappropriate items. The same applies to the use of Form B as a post-test.

Timing is an important consideration. Since emphasis is placed on quick and efficient mental computation strategies, you will need to monitor test time carefully. For example, the amount of time allowed for each form of the cumulative tests should be the same. This will enable students to observe improvement not only in the number of correct answers they give, but also in the total number of mental computation problems they were able to complete in the allotted time. There are a number of ways that each test can be presented and timed:

1. **As a handout.** Duplicate and distribute a copy of the test to each student. To time the students, you can write the elapsed time every 10 seconds on the board or an overhead transparency. When a student completes the test, he or she records the most recent elapsed time on the test paper. Alternative ways of presenting elapsed time to a classroom of students are to display cards with easily seen numbers (such as 10 seconds, 20 seconds, and so forth) or to cross out numbers that you have written on a transparency or the board.

2. **As an oral test.** Read aloud each problem on the test, presenting them at a fixed rate (for example, one every 10 seconds). A tape player is an effective way of presenting a test orally because you can carefully control the time per question and you are free during the test to circulate around the classroom. When you give a test orally, students can write their answers on notebook paper.

3. **As a visual presentation.** You might present a test one item at a time, using an overhead transparency or flash cards with easily read figures. In this method, you control the timing by displaying each problem for a brief period (such as 10 seconds), then going on to the next one. Again, students will use a blank sheet of notebook paper to record their answers.

Just before giving any test, remind the students to use only *mental* methods to calculate their answers. You might tap your forehead periodically throughout the test and say "In your head" as a gentle reminder.

Mental Math in Junior High

TEACHING NOTES

LESSON 1 ADDING FROM THE LEFT

Mental math skill: Adding whole numbers and decimals by starting with the front-end digits (when regrouping is required)

This first lesson demonstrates that, for mental math, the way we approach a problem may differ significantly from what we do in written work. With this strategy, students learn to start on the left (with the "front-end" digits) and move to the right as they compute sums. As a warm-up exercise, dictate two-step problems such as: "Add 40 + 40, now add this sum to 6 + 7."

As you present the lesson, ask a volunteer to explain how adding from left to right works with larger numbers, like 453 + 38 (the example shown on the lesson page); that is, by thinking "450 + 30 = 480, 3 + 8 = 11, and 480 + 11 = 491." Before proceeding with decimal addition, you might want to ensure that your students can quickly add tenths, such as 0.7 + 0.9 = 16 tenths = 1.6.

This is a powerful strategy that often works for the addition of multidigit numbers as well as decimals. Although some students will feel confident with this strategy, others may still try to use the familiar right-to-left written algorithm as they work sums in their heads. Encourage students to talk about how they mentally compute. For instance, for TRY THESE problem 5 (329 + 36), a student might say, "I thought *three hundred twenty-nine plus thirty is three fifty-nine, plus six is three hundred sixty-five.*" Sharing a solution orally will likely raise questions such as "Where did the thirty come from?" or "Are there other ways to do the calculation?" The ensuing discussion provides insight to other students into how a mental computation is performed.

Problems for Oral Practice
1. 25 + 26
2. 75 + 75
3. 54 + 39
4. 62 + 28
5. 145 + 25
6. 125 + 35
7. 115 + 18
8. 225 + 65
9. 4.5 + 1.5
10. 8.5 + 2.5
11. 3.6 + 1.9
12. 19.3 + 2.7

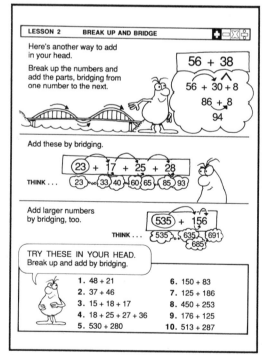

Page 41

LESSON 2 BREAK UP AND BRIDGE

Mental math skill: Adding whole numbers from the front end by using expanded form

Adding multidigit numbers in your head can be easier if you expand or "break up" one of the numbers and add the parts one step at a time. The visual imagery introduced with this strategy suggests that we "connect" the parts, step by step, by *bridging* from one to the next.

As a warm-up to this lesson, ask students to mentally add 350 and 400. When they have an answer, say "Now add 30 (pause), and now add 8." Point out that they have just mentally computed 350 + 438, but it was easier because the second number (438) was broken up into 400 + 30 + 8.

This lesson focuses on expanding the second addend. However, bridging can also be done by expanding the first addend instead of the second, as you can demonstrate with examples from the TRY THESE problems. For instance, for problem 1 (48 + 21), you might think: "40 plus 21 is 61, plus 8 is 69."

Note that students accustomed to familiar written algorithms for addition will often try to use that approach in their heads. That is, a student might think "Add 56 + 38 . . . 6 plus 8 is 14, write 4, carry 1, 5 plus 1 is 6, plus 3 is 9 . . . write 9, answer is 94." Obviously the problem can be done that way, but it is not efficient. This lesson demonstrates an alternative way of thinking about such computations— a way that works much better for mental math.

Problems for Oral Practice
1. 45 + 30 + 5
2. 79 + 20 + 9
3. 58 + 30 + 8
4. 156 + 40 + 9
5. 156 + 100 + 50 + 3
6. 250 + 100 + 50 + 7
7. 55 + 35
8. 145 + 25
9. 280 + 180
10. 285 + 185
11. 315 + 515
12. 1250 + 250

Page 43

LESSON 3   BRIDGING DECIMALS

Mental math skill: Adding decimals from the front end by using expanded form

This lesson applies the "break up and bridge" strategy introduced in the preceding lesson to problems involving decimals and money.   For example:

To add: 1.5   +   2.6   +   3.7

Break up: 1.5   +   2   +   .6   +   3   +   .7

Think: 1.5   3.5   4.1   7.1 and 7.8

Use the "bridging" arrows to show how we think about just one part at a time, creating partial sums until a total is found. With this strategy, remind students that it's important to pay close attention to place value as they add the individual digits of the numbers, especially in problems containing varying numbers of digits.

This technique helps students think about the parts (whole number and decimal) of mixed numbers.   It is particularly useful for mentally computing sums of money.

Encourage students to check their answers by adding first in one direction, then in the other.   That is, to check the answer for the example shown above, add from right to left: 3.7 plus 2 is 5.7, plus 0.6 is 6.3, plus 1 is 7.3, plus 0.5 is 7.8.

Problems for Oral Practice
1. 2.4 + 1 + 0.8
2. 3.5 + 2 + 0.5
3. 4.5 + 3 + 0.8 + 2
4. 2.8 + 6 + 0.9 + 5
5. $1.50 + $2 + $0.56
6. $8.45 + $4 + $0.35
7. 6.5 + 2.5
8. 3.8 + 1.7
9. 10.8 + 2.5
10. $5.50 + $3.75
11. $10.75 + $5.25
12. $1.75 + $1.50 + $1.75

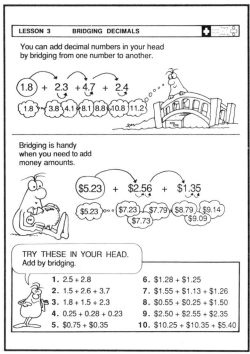

Page 45

LESSON 4   SUBTRACTING FROM THE LEFT

Mental math skill: Subtracting whole numbers and decimals from the front end (when regrouping is not required)

This lesson focuses on the "front-end" or "start at the left" strategy as it applies to subtraction.   After students are comfortable with this strategy for addition, they will readily see that it also works well for subtraction problems when regrouping is not needed.

Ask for volunteers to complete the two decimal examples on the lesson page before going on to the TRY THESE.   In order to decide if the front end strategy will work for a given problem, students need to recognize when a problem requires regrouping.   You may want to provide some practice with this, particularly with problems involving decimals.   For example, write the following problems on the board, asking students to decide for each one if the computation would be easy to do mentally:

    A. 4.23 – 1.86   (no)   D. 6.02 – 1.8   (no)
    B. 7.45 – 3.34   (yes)   E. 4.27 – 1.13   (yes)
    C. 8.14 – 6.01   (yes)   F. 5.06 – 1.05   (yes)

Although some students may be able to do all of them mentally, discussion should bring out that B, C, E, and F are much easier to do in the head because no regrouping is required and the front-end approach can be used.

Problems for Oral Practice
1. 76 – 51
2. 98 – 36
3. 75 – 25
4. 288 – 77
5. 455 – 32
6. 267 – 54
7. 987 – 186
8. 525 – 124
9. 5.8 – 4.7
10. 6.6 – 2.5
11. 2.75 – 1.25
12. 5.45 – 3.41

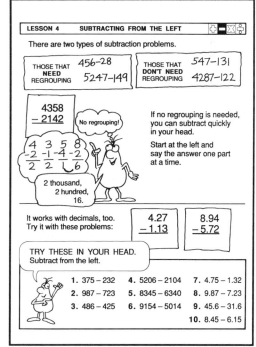

Page 47

9

LESSON 5   SUBTRACTING IN PARTS

Mental math skill: Using expanded form to subtract whole numbers and decimals from the front end (when regrouping is required)

When a subtraction problem requires regrouping, the paper-and-pencil approach is *not* suitable as a mental technique; it's too easy to lose track of the digits. In this lesson, students learn to expand the subtrahend to make such subtraction problems easier to do in their heads. As a warm-up, ask them to subtract 30 from 190. When they have an answer, say "Now subtract 8." Point out that they have just subtracted 38 from 190 by subtracting in parts (after expanding 38 to 30 and 8).

TRY THESE problems such as 1000 – 475 and 500 – 125 may be easier for some students to mentally compute by thinking of and making compatible numbers (a strategy introduced in *Mental Math in the Middle Grades,* lessons 15 and 16). Accept any such variations in technique; students should be allowed to use whatever approach works best for them.

Notice that this expanding strategy can be used in making estimates. For example, we can very quickly estimate 14,000 – 5,856 as being between 8000 and 9000 by subtracting parts from the front end.

Problems for Oral Practice

1. 80 – 30 – 6
2. 90 – 28
3. 165 – 80 – 6
4. 170 – 95
5. 1000 – 500 – 50 – 5
6. 1000 – 625
7. 136 – 89
8. 500 – 135
9. 10 – 1 – 0.5
10. 8 – 2.5
11. $10 – $5 – $0.75
12. $10 – $3.85

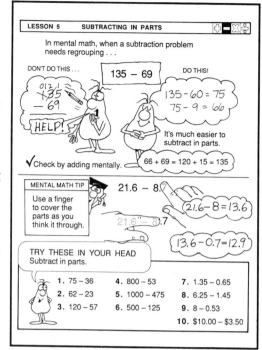

LESSON 5   SUBTRACTING IN PARTS

In mental math, when a subtraction problem needs regrouping . . .

DON'T DO THIS . . .   135 – 69   DO THIS!

135 – 60 = 75
75 – 9 = 66

HELP!

It's much easier to subtract in parts.

✓ Check by adding mentally.   66 + 69 = 120 + 15 = 135

MENTAL MATH TIP
Use a finger to cover the parts as you think it through.

21.6 – 8.7

21.6 – 8 = 13.6

21.6 – 8.7

13.6 – 0.7 = 12.9

TRY THESE IN YOUR HEAD
Subtract in parts.

1. 75 – 36
2. 62 – 23
3. 120 – 57
4. 800 – 53
5. 1000 – 475
6. 500 – 125
7. 1.35 – 0.65
8. 6.25 – 1.45
9. 8 – 0.53
10. $10.00 – $3.50

LESSON 6   SEARCHING FOR COMPATIBLES

Mental math skill: Identifying compatible numbers for multiples of 10 and 100

Many techniques of mental computation make use of *compatible numbers,* that is, numbers that are easy to mentally compute. Lessons 6–11 introduce the concept and help students develop skill in using compatibles in addition problems involving both whole numbers and decimals. Although the emphasis is on addition, recognizing that the compatibles 45 and 55 equal 100 will help find 100 – 55 or 100 – 45, so that developing skill in adding compatible numbers will quickly pay off in subtraction, too.

Invite students to share how they go about their search for compatibles. For example, to find the mate of 140, you would look for a number ending in 60, thus choosing 360.

Give extra practice in a money context. Say, "I'm going to tell you how much money I have. You tell me how much more I need to make a dollar." Then name various amounts: 75¢, 32¢, 91¢, 40¢, 28¢, 52¢. Show how this technique can be used to determine the change from a purchase. For example: 32-cent purchase, pay with one dollar, change is 68 cents (a compatible number). Continue with practice problems using common denominations such as $2.00, $5.00, $10.00 and $20.00. (Figuring change will be handled further in lesson 10.)

Problems for Oral Practice

1. 35 + ? = 100
2. 65 + ? = 100
3. 25 + ? = 100
4. 75 + ? = 200
5. 150 + ? = 500
6. 150 + ? = 1000
7. 775 + ? = 1000
8. 63 + ? = 100
9. 21 + ? = 100
10. 81 + ? = 100
11. 136 + ? = 200
12. 155 + ? = 300

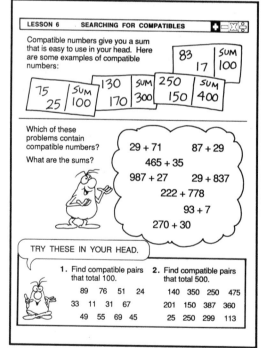

LESSON 6   SEARCHING FOR COMPATIBLES

Compatible numbers give you a sum that is easy to use in your head. Here are some examples of compatible numbers:

83 | 17 | SUM 100
75 | 25 | SUM 100
130 | 170 | SUM 300
250 | 150 | SUM 400

Which of these problems contain compatible numbers? What are the sums?

29 + 71   87 + 29
465 + 35
987 + 27   29 + 837
222 + 778
93 + 7
270 + 30

TRY THESE IN YOUR HEAD.

1. Find compatible pairs that total 100.

89 76 51 24
33 11 31 67
49 55 69 45

2. Find compatible pairs that total 500.

140 350 250 475
201 150 387 360
25 250 299 113

LESSON 7   MAKE YOUR OWN COMPATIBLES

Mental math skill: Expanding or using compensation to make compatible pairs for adding

Before trying this lesson, students should be able to readily identify compatible numbers and to use the expanding or "break it up" strategy introduced in Lesson 2. Here they will combine the two concepts, breaking up one or more numbers in a problem to *make* compatibles for easier mental addition. This is a natural but powerful process that helps us use things we know to do mental computation very quickly.

As a warm-up, tell students, "Add 125 to 75 (pause), now add 2." Point out that they have just added 77 to 125 by making compatible numbers to add, then adjusting.

Sometimes students find it easier to make compatibles in a money context. Name an amount of money, such as 54 cents, and ask students to name coins that total that amount. Many answers are possible, but the point is to find the simplest breakdown. In this case a half dollar and 4 pennies, or 2 quarters and 4 pennies, would be reasonable answers. Show how this breakdown could help them mentally add $1.25 and $0.54.

Be sure students understand the adjusting process. Whether they add or subtract a number from the total of the compatible pairs depends on what they did to the original number in order to make compatibles. For example, in an alternative approach to the problem on the lesson page, 750 + 275 can be reasoned as 750 + 300 = 1050, *minus* 25 = 1025 (*minus* 25 because that's what we added to 275 to make 300).

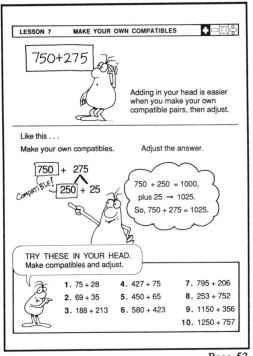

Page 53

Problems for Oral Practice

1. 50 + 50 + 6	**5.** 165 + 38	**9.** 25 + 176
2. 50 + 156	**6.** 550 + 50 + 8	**10.** 465 + 37
3. 50 + 256	**7.** 550 + 153	**11.** 550 + 453
4. 165 + 35 + 2	**8.** 63 + 38	**12.** 163 + 39

LESSON 8   SEARCHING FOR COMPATIBLE DECIMALS

Mental math skill: Recognizing pairs of decimal numbers whose sums equal whole numbers

This lesson extends to decimals the basic "compatibles" strategy taught in lesson 6. Although the mental computation skills used with problems involving decimals are exactly the same as for problems involving money, many students seem to be unaware of—or forget—this relationship. It is not unusual to find students who do mental computation very well with money but who become confused when the money context is changed to ordinary decimals. Reminding students of the similarities is good anticipatory teaching.

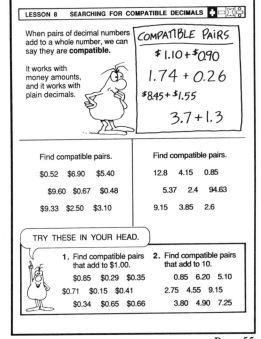

Problems for Oral Practice

What decimal is needed to make a sum of 1?

1. 0.25	**3.** 0.85	**5.** 0.47
2. 0.78	**4.** 0.19	**6.** 0.22

What amount of money is needed to make a sum of $5.00?

7. $4.25	**9.** $3.50	**11.** $0.85
8. $2.95	**10.** $1.98	**12.** $2.93

Page 55

Mental Math in Daily Life
LESSON 9   DIFFERENCES IN TIME
Mental math skill: Applying "adding on" and compatible numbers in time-telling situations

Determining the duration of time "from now till then" is a very practical and common use of mental math. Although it might seem that subtraction is the way to find differences in time, in fact, adding on is often much easier. This lesson demonstrates how to "add on" or "count on," a skill that involves the use of compatible numbers that sum to 60 (for seconds and minutes), or to 12 (for hours). Knowing the appropriate compatible pairs is crucial to mentally computing time with ease. Thus, to find the duration of time from 6:55 to 9:00, knowing that 55 + 5 = 60 allows us to think "6:55, 7:55, 8:55, 9:00; that's 2 hours and 5 minutes," or alternatively, "6:55, 7:00, 8:00, 9:00."

For problems in which the first number is an even hour (see oral practice problems 1–6), counting on need not involve compatibles at all. The same is true for problems with identical ending digits (such as 8:25 to 11:25). Students need to choose the best approach based on the given times. Encourage students to think about the problem before carrying out a solution.

Discuss possible alternative solutions, such as adding on past the ending time, then subtracting the extra minutes to adjust the answer. For example: "1:45 to 3:40 . . . that's 1:45 to 3:45 is 2 hours, less 5 minutes is 1 hour 55 minutes."

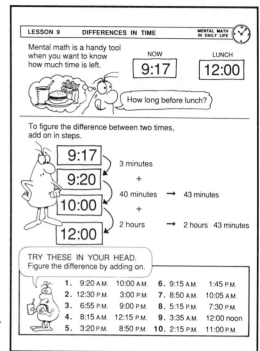

Problems for Oral Practice
How long is it from 8:00 A.M. to . . .

1. 10:00 A.M.	**3.** 2:00 P.M.	**5.** 5:30 P.M.
2. 11:30 A.M.	**4.** 5:00 P.M.	**6.** 9:45 P.M.

How long is it from 4:15 P.M. to . . .

7. 7:30 P.M.	**9.** 9:05 P.M.	**11.** 12:30 A.M.
8. 8:15 P.M.	**10.** 6:35 P.M.	**12.** 4:00 A.M.

Mental Math in Daily Life
LESSON 10   CHECKING YOUR CHANGE
Mental math skill: Applying "adding on" and compatible numbers in exchanges of money

Most of us buy something with cash on nearly a daily basis. When we pay cash, it's a good idea to check mentally to be sure that we are not shortchanged. Although our first inclination might be to subtract ($10.00 – $4.65 = ??), the fact that we generally offer a round amount in payment (a $1, $5, $10, or $20 bill) makes such subtraction difficult to do mentally.

As a warm-up to this lesson, say, "I will tell you how much money I have. You tell me how much money I need to make a dollar." Then name various amounts: 45¢, 89¢, 17¢. Ask students how this way of thinking might be helpful in figuring change. Also ask how compatible numbers are involved.

The lesson illustrates two ways of mentally checking change. In the first approach, we "count on" from the amount of purchase; in the second, we make an estimate and then refine it. Both rely on a knowledge of compatible numbers. There are other ways to make and figure change, and you might want to ask students to share specific techniques they have used.

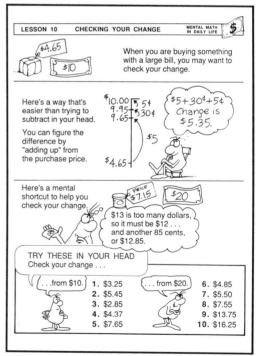

Problems for Oral Practice
1. I hand over $1 for a purchase costing _____. What is my change?
   (Substitute these amounts: $0.25; $0.45; $0.10; $0.78; $0.57)

2. I hand over $5 for a purchase costing _____. What is my change?
   (Substitute these amounts: $4.25; $0.98; $2.55; $1.95; $3.80)

UNIT ONE REVIEW

To prepare students for the Unit One progress test, help them review the mental math strategies of lessons 1–10. Go over the mental math techniques listed in the box at left, working through the sample problems together. In the numbered review exercises, encourage discussion of different strategies that could be used for the same problem.

Students will need to pick up speed with the new strategies if they are to succeed on the timed test. Plan to give them some timed practice with problems you select at random from the Power Builder sets for lessons 1–10. You can present these orally or write them on the board, erasing them after a set length of time. Gradually shorten the time you allow for selecting a strategy and computing the answer.

UNIT ONE REVIEW	(CLASS DISCUSSION)

Mental Math Techniques	Do the problems below in your head. Tell which techniques you find useful for each one.
• ADD FROM THE LEFT. 245 + 138 = 300 + 70 + 13	1. 527 + 36
• SUBTRACT FROM THE LEFT. 5.78 − 3.45	2. 2 − 1.95
• BREAK IT UP. 140 + 285 = 140 + 200 + 80 + 5	3. 965 − 342
• BREAK UP AND BRIDGE. 4.5 + 2.7 = 6.5 + 0.7	4. 1000 − 350
• USE COMPATIBLES. 3.85 + 1.99 = 3.84 + 2	5. 145 + 38 + 56
	6. 100 − 73
	7. 0.15 + 0.65
	8. 4.37 + 0.48 + 0.16
	9. 457 + 298
	10. 350 + 455

Talk about each problem below. What's an easy way to do it in your head? Tell how you would think it through.

1. 1000 − 475
2. 636 + 48
3. 465 + 236
4. 344 + 38 + 76
5. 4275 − 3160

6. 14.6 + 3.8 + 6.7
7. $4 − $2.27
8. 857 + 498
9. 1.55 + 3.45
10. 100 − 87

Page 61

UNIT ONE PROGRESS TEST

This progress test checks students' proficiency in the strategies presented in lessons 1–10. See the Introduction, page 6, for suggestions for presenting this as a timed test.

MENTAL MATH PROGRESS TEST
UNIT ONE LESSONS 1–10

1. 150 + 172 = _____
2. 8.1 − 2.9 = _____
3. 375 + 226 = _____
4. 10 − 0.77 = _____
5. The difference in time from 9:15 A.M. to 12:30 P.M. = _____
6. 325 + 265 = _____
7. 74 − 35 = _____
8. 348 + 155 = _____
9. The difference in time from 8:00 A.M. to 11:45 A.M. = _____
10. 6.7 − 4.3 = _____
11. $10.00 − $4.69 = _____
12. 5 − 1.36 = _____
13. $20 − $15.50 = _____
14. 355 + 38 = _____
15. 476 − 125 = _____
16. 1000 − 829 = _____
17. $10 − $4.37 = _____
18. The difference in time from 11:15 A.M. to 7:30 P.M. = _____
19. 545 + 128 = _____
20. $0.65 + $0.25 = _____
21. 100 − 67 = _____
22. $20 − $1.78 = _____
23. 5.5 + 1.7 = _____

24. 23.7 + 5.5 = _____
25. 2.6 + 0.6 + 1.3 = _____
26. 500 − 275 = _____
27. 3 − 1.254 = _____
28. $1.45 + $0.25 + $1.30 + $1.15 = _____
29. 47 + 26 = _____
30. 1 − 0.67 = _____
31. 1000 − 455 = _____
32. The difference in time from 2:35 P.M. to 9:30 P.M. = _____
33. 9150 + 275 = _____
34. 800 − 445 = _____
35. 595 + 308 = _____
36. 9 + 16 + 25 + 18 = _____
37. 4.75 − 1.35 = _____
38. $100 − $75.88 = _____
39. 369 − 36 = _____
40. 75 + 27 = _____

Page 62

13

LESSON 11   MAKING COMPATIBLE DECIMALS

Mental math skill: Expanding or using compensation to make compatible pairs for adding decimals

Before doing this lesson, students should be able to readily identify compatible numbers as introduced in lesson 6; they should be comfortable with the "break it up" strategy (expanding one of the addends) introduced in lesson 2; and they should be successful with "making your own compatibles" as discussed in lesson 7. Here we extend the techniques of lesson 7 to problems with decimals, including money.

As in lesson 7, be sure students understand the adjusting step. Whether we add or subtract a number from the total of our compatible pairs depends on what we have done to the original numbers in order to make the compatible pair. If we expanded, we need to add the "leftover" digits. If we used compensation, we need to subtract the amount we first added to make compatibles.

Problems for Oral Practice

1. 0.25 + 0.27	**5.** 1.75 + 0.16	**9.** $1.49 + $1.49
2. 0.55 + 0.26	**6.** 1.28 + 0.25	**10.** $2.49 + $3.49
3. 0.65 + 0.37	**7.** $2.15 + $0.27	**11.** $4.95 + $0.95
4. 0.98 + 0.47	**8.** $2.59 + $1.38	**12.** $2.85 + $1.17

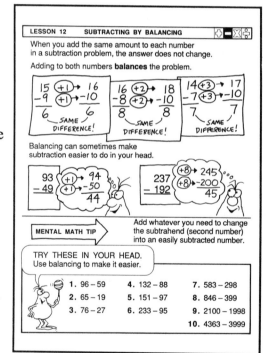

Page 65

LESSON 12   SUBTRACTING BY BALANCING

Mental math skill: Simplifying subtraction by "balancing" (adding a constant to both the subtrahend and minuend)

To introduce this lesson, write on the board a subtraction problem such as 52 – 17. Calculate the difference (35). Then add 1 to 52 (the minuend) and to 17 (the subtrahend), and calculate this difference (35). Continue with a few more examples until the students understand that adding a constant to both the subtrahend and minuend will *not* affect the difference. However, by carefully choosing the number that we add, we can greatly simplify a subtraction problem.

In order to be comfortable with this strategy, students need to understand the following specific relationships:

A. 52 – 17 = 35
B. 53 – 18 = 35
C. 54 – 19 = 35
D. 55 – 20 = 35

In general, this means that for any two numbers x and y ($x > y$), if $x - y = d$, then $(x + a) - (y + a) = d$. This is a powerful principle that we often use in mental computation. It allows us to do simple computation (like D), instead of more tedious computation (like A, B, or C), and still get the same result. You might want to point out how this is a subtle variation of working with compatible numbers.

Emphasize that the constant we choose must be one that will change the subtrahend into an easy number to subtract—generally a number ending in zero.

Students who are already comfortable with the strategy may discover the variation of *subtracting* a constant from the subtrahend to balance, as would be appropriate in problems such as 50 – 11, 180 – 52, 500 – 304, and 400 – 202.

Problems for Oral Practice

1. 18 – 9	**5.** 93 – 39	**9.** 387 – 199
2. 27 – 8	**6.** 44 – 27	**10.** 326 – 195
3. 46 – 19	**7.** 125 – 36	**11.** 500 – 293
4. 85 – 29	**8.** 243 – 124	**12.** 400 – 288

Page 67

14

LESSON 13 BALANCING WITH DECIMALS
Mental math skill: Using balancing to simplify subtraction of decimals

This lesson extends the "balancing" notion introduced in lesson 12 to problems involving subtraction of decimals. To remind students of the power of this technique, you might want to write these problems on a transparency or the board:

Group A	Group B
4.2 – 1.9	4.3 – 2
5.76 – 1.97	5.79 – 2
7.43 – 2.85	7.58 – 3

Ask half the class to do Group A and the other half to do Group B. Time the students and discuss which group took longer. Were their answers the same? Which problems would they *rather* do? This warm-up provides a motivation for "balancing decimals" and helps students appreciate the value of making problems easier for mental computation.

Problems for Oral Practice
1. 3.5 – 0.6
2. 1.4 – 0.8
3. 3.2 – 0.7
4. 9.2 – 1.3
5. 8.3 – 3.8
6. 4.5 – 1.7
7. 4 – 0.74
8. 5 – 0.39
9. 6.1 – 2.9
10. 5.1 – 8.6
11. 8.6 – 2.7
12. 7 – 0.88

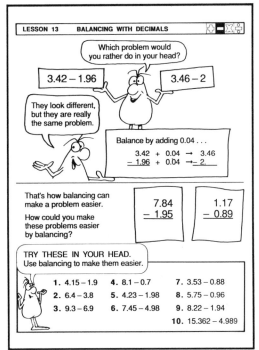

LESSON 14 Tack on Trailing Zeros
Mental math skill: Multiplying by multiples of powers of ten when the product is less than one million

This lesson presents a very basic mental computation strategy which was also treated in *Mental Math in the Middle Grades*. You might emphasize the idea of "cutting off" zeros by covering them with a mask or a grease pencil, thereby isolating the other digits . Then uncover them (or rub off the grease pencil) to call attention to the zeros that must be "tacked on" to the answer.

One common error in using this strategy arises when the leading numbers yield a product that ends in zero itself. For example, in the problem 50 x 20, we cut off the trailing zeros, multiply 5 x 2 = 10, and then tack on the zeros again. Sometimes the zero in the 10 gets lost in the mental process and students give the answer 100 rather than 1000. If students have this problem, work through some additional problems that involve an "extra" zero (such as 40 x 50, 800 x 50, 500 x 600), emphasizing the number of zeros that must be "tacked on" to the product of the leading digits.

Problems for Oral Practice
1. 5 x 50
2. 7 x 40
3. 8 x 50
4. 4 x 700
5. 2 x 800
6. 5 x 400
7. 3 x 2000
8. 4 x 9000
9. 5 x 6000
10. 50 x 100
11. 20 x 10
12. 30 x 60

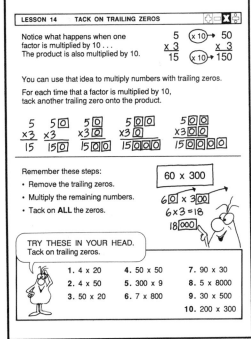

LESSON 15   FRONT-END MULTIPLICATION

Mental math skill: Multiplying from the front end by expanding a two- or three-digit factor

This lesson discusses the front-end multiplication strategy (also presented in *Mental Math in the Middle Grades* at a simpler level). It provides a good opportunity to compare written and mental algorithms. Our written multiplication starts at the right (back-end digit) and moves to the left, whereas our mental algorithm begins at the left (front-end digit) and moves to the right. Both algorithms use the distributive property, but the mental algorithm eliminates the need to remember any carried numbers. Show students how to help keep track of their calculation by covering some of the digits with a finger.

There are different ways to "break up" numbers to apply the front end strategy. For example, 4 x 28 might be viewed as 4 x (20 + 8), or as 4 x (25 + 3). Similarly, 3 x 415 might be viewed as 3 x (400 + 10 + 5), or 3 x (410 + 5), or 3 x (400 + 15). Any of these is perfectly acceptable; students should be encouraged to share different possibilities to discover which seems easiest for them to use.

When you work through the TRY THESE problems as a group, ask students how they would "break up" the numbers in each problem. Emphasize that there is no single "right" way and encourage variations.

Problems for Oral Practice

1. 4 x 21	**5.** 4 x 24	**9.** 4 x 225
2. 3 x 32	**6.** 3 x 34	**10.** 3 x 126
3. 2 x 44	**7.** 2 x 46	**11.** 2 x 354
4. 5 x 31	**8.** 5 x 35	**12.** 6 x 125

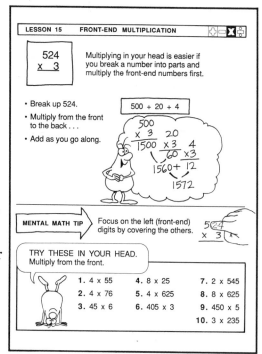

Mental Math in Daily Life
LESSON 16   CALCULATING COSTS

Mental math skill: Applying front-end multiplication to consumer situations

This lesson presents a practical application of the front-end multiplication strategy developed in the previous lesson. When shopping, we often buy several of the same thing (such as two dozen doughnuts, four record albums, two bicycle tubes). For most students, it is natural to multiply the dollars first and then calculate the rest. This common-sense approach is consistent with front-end multiplication and should be encouraged. As an extension, show how this strategy can be used to estimate costs (that is, by focusing on the most significant front-end digits).

Problems for Oral Practice

1. If oranges are 6 for $1.25, what will you pay for 12? 18? 24?
2. If peaches are $0.75 each, what will you pay for 2? 3? 4? 5? 10?
3. If milk costs $0.65 a glass, what will you pay for 2 glasses? 4? 6? 10?

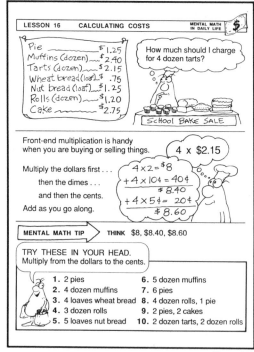

LESSON 17 TACK ON TRAILING ZEROS

Mental math skill: Dividing by one- or two-digit divisors when there are trailing zeros in the dividend

Students who have learned to use the "tack on trailing zeros" strategy in mental multiplication, as discussed in lesson 14, should have little trouble using it in mental division. To help students form a mental image of the process of "cutting off" zeros and "tacking" them back on, use a grease pencil, a mask, a Post-it note, or your finger to physically cover up and later expose the zeros.

In the TRY THESE problems, have the students multiply to check their answers. Since mental multiplication is generally easier than mental division, checking by multiplying is always a good policy. In this checking step, we check to see that we tacked on the correct number of zeros.

Problems for Oral Practice

1. 80 ÷ 2	**5.** 6300 ÷ 3	**9.** 650 ÷ 10
2. 480 ÷ 4	**6.** 5000 ÷ 5	**10.** 2000 ÷ 20
3. 250 ÷ 5	**7.** 2400 ÷ 6	**11.** 460 ÷ 10
4. 180 ÷ 3	**8.** 3200 ÷ 4	**12.** 3000 ÷ 30

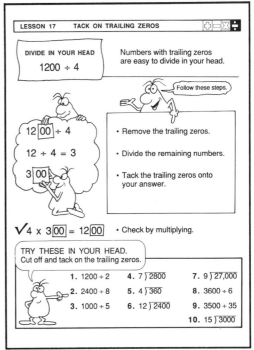

LESSON 18 CANCEL COMMON TRAILING ZEROS

Mental math skill: Dividing when there are trailing zeros in both the divisor and dividend

To get things started you might write on the board the following problems:

24 ÷ 6   240 ÷ 60   2400 ÷ 600   24,000 ÷ 6000

Ask students to tell you what patterns they see in the problems and in the answers. Then ask them to generate similar "families" for 35 ÷ 7. This experience should help students recognize that "canceling common zeros" is the same as dividing both numbers by 10, 100, or 1000, or multiplying both by 1/10, 1/100, or 1/1000.

Be sure students understand they can cancel only *common* or *shared* trailing zeros. For example, even though both numbers in the problem 505 ÷ 50 have a zero, they are not *common* zeros. Also, in the problem 42,000 ÷ 60, we cancel only one zero from 42,000 because that's all the two numbers share. You may need to show several different examples to be sure students can identify the common zeros in division problems.

For the first few TRY THESE problems, ask students how many zeros can be canceled. As with other mental division, students should check their answers by multiplying.

Problems for Oral Practice

1. 300 ÷ 10	**5.** 6000 ÷ 3000	**9.** 3500 ÷ 700
2. 400 ÷ 100	**6.** 8000 ÷ 4000	**10.** 3500 ÷ 500
3. 8000 ÷ 2000	**7.** 12,000 ÷ 6000	**11.** 4800 ÷ 600
4. 8000 ÷ 20	**8.** 24,000 ÷ 8000	**12.** 4800 ÷ 800

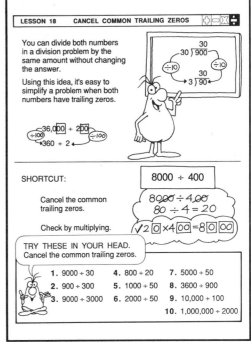

Mental Math in Daily Life
LESSON 19   TIME AND SPEED
Mental math skill: Applying division of compatible numbers with trailing zeros in a travel context

This lesson demonstrates a natural application of the mental division techniques presented in this program. Real-world problems involving division and units of measure abound. One common use is in figuring unit prices at the supermarket. Another practical application—the context of the problems in this lesson—is determining how long it will take to get somewhere, traveling at a given average speed.

After students have solved some problems like $300 \div 50 = 6$ and $300 \div 60 = 5$, ask what a good estimate of $300 \div 55$ would be. Such mental math experiences are typical in solving everyday problems and can help students develop some number sense and estimation skills as well.

Problems for Oral Practice
How long will it take to go:

1. 12 mi at 4 mph? **5.** 160 mi at 40 mph? **9.** 800 mi at 400 mph?
2. 12 mi at 3 mph? **6.** 250 mi at 50 mph? **10.** 800 mi at 40 mph?
3. 55 mi at 55 mph? **7.** 400 mi at 40 mph? **11.** 1200 mi at 300 mph?
4. 100 mi at 50 mph? **8.** 440 mi at 40 mph? **12.** 1200 mi at 40 mph?

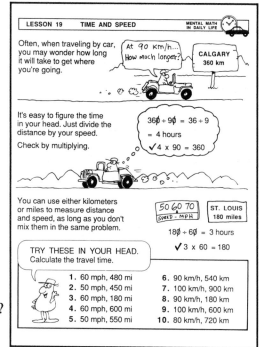

Page 81

Mental Math in Daily Life
LESSON 20   WORKING WITH PRICES
Mental math skill: Applying mental math techniques to addition, subtraction, and multiplication of common prices

Students are likely aware that consumer items are frequently priced just under a whole dollar or half-dollar amount, such as $4.99, $15.98, $1.49, and so on. These prices are based on marketing research results that indicate people are more likely to make a purchase if the prices follow this pattern.

Such prices provide a natural environment for developing mental math skills. Whether the problem is addition (total of several prices), subtraction (change due from a purchase), or multiplication (multiple quantities of the same item), the underlying strategy is "round to make compatibles, then adjust." For addition problems, we round up to the nearest even amount, then adjust the total downward. For subtraction, we round the subtrahend, then adjust the difference upward by the same amount. (Balancing might also be used, with the minuend adjusted by the same amount as the subtrahend before subtracting.) In multiplication, we again round up, then adjust the total downward.

In TRY THESE problems 7–10, help the students decide on the amount that needs to be subtracted after the multiplication has been carried out. This often proves to be the most difficult step in the procedure.

Page 83

Problems for Oral Practice
1. $2.70 + $0.99 **5.** $5.00 − $2.99 **9.** 4 at $0.79
2. $4.98 + $0.99 **6.** $5.00 − $1.99 **10.** 3 at $0.98
3. $3.99 + $2.50 **7.** $10.00 − $3.98 **11.** 5 at $2.99
4. $5.98 + $3.48 **8.** $20.00 − $2.49 **12.** 4 at $1.98

UNIT TWO REVIEW

To prepare students for the Unit Two progress test, help them review the mental math strategies of lessons 11–20. Go over the mental math techniques listed in the box at left, working through the sample problems together. In the numbered review exercises, encourage discussion of different strategies that could be used for the same problem.

Students will need to pick up speed with the new strategies if they are to succeed on the timed test. Plan to give them some timed practice with problems you select at random from the Power Builder sets for lessons 11–20. You can present these orally or write them on the board, erasing them after a set length of time. Gradually shorten the time you allow for selecting a strategy and computing the answer.

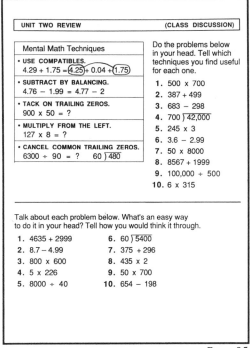

UNIT TWO REVIEW	(CLASS DISCUSSION)

Mental Math Techniques

- **USE COMPATIBLES.**
  4.29 + 1.75 = 4.25 + 0.04 + 1.75
- **SUBTRACT BY BALANCING.**
  4.76 − 1.99 = 4.77 − 2
- **TACK ON TRAILING ZEROS.**
  900 x 50 = ?
- **MULTIPLY FROM THE LEFT.**
  127 x 8 = ?
- **CANCEL COMMON TRAILING ZEROS.**
  6300 ÷ 90 = ?   60)480

Do the problems below in your head. Tell which techniques you find useful for each one.

1. 500 x 700
2. 387 + 499
3. 683 − 298
4. 700)42,000
5. 245 x 3
6. 3.6 − 2.99
7. 50 x 8000
8. 8567 + 1999
9. 100,000 ÷ 500
10. 6 x 315

Talk about each problem below. What's an easy way to do it in your head? Tell how you would think it through.

1. 4635 + 2999
2. 8.7 − 4.99
3. 800 x 600
4. 5 x 226
5. 8000 ÷ 40
6. 60)5400
7. 375 + 296
8. 435 x 2
9. 50 x 700
10. 654 − 198

Page 85

UNIT TWO PROGRESS TEST

This progress test checks students' proficiency in the strategies presented in lessons 11–20. See the Introduction, page 6, for suggestions for presenting this as a timed test.

MENTAL MATH PROGRESS TEST	UNIT TWO LESSONS 11–20

1. 2.75 + 1.28 = _____
2. 323 − 89 = _____
3. 4.6 − 2.9 = _____
4. 8 x 90 = _____
5. 4 x 82 = _____
6. Total cost for 2 at $0.95 each = _____
7. 3500 ÷ 7 = _____
8. 2400 ÷ 60 = _____
9. Time to travel 480 miles at 60 mph = _____
10. 457 + 199 = _____
11. 40 x 70 = _____
12. Total cost for 5 at $1.19 each = _____
13. 1.49 + 2.49 = _____
14. 6 x 225 = _____
15. 500)40,000 = _____
16. 426 − 198 = _____
17. 825 − 399 = _____
18. 6)540 = _____
19. 7.3 − 4.8 = _____
20. 3.65 + 1.37 = _____
21. Time to travel 1500 km at 500 km/h = _____
22. 45.04 − 20.95 = _____
23. Total cost for 4 at $2.49 each = _____
24. 4 x 127 = _____
25. 2.88 + 4.15 = _____
26. 3000 x 60 = _____
27. 90)6300 = _____
28. Time to travel 1500 miles at 50 mph = _____
29. 542 − 295 = _____
30. 5 x 600 = _____
31. 9543 − 2985 = _____
32. Total cost for 3 at $7.29 each = _____
33. $6.00 − $4.98 = _____
34. Time to travel 4500 km at 90 km/h = _____
35. 15.32 − 1.88 = _____
36. 8)7200 = _____
37. 8 x 725 = _____
38. 2800 ÷ 2 = _____
39. $4.98 + $2.99 = _____
40. 48,000 ÷ 800 = _____

Page 86

LESSON 21   ADDING SPECIAL FRACTIONS

Mental math skill: Adding fractions for which a common denominator is easily determined

Because of the number of steps involved, most problems requiring the addition of fractions are more efficiently done with paper and pencil. Sometimes, though, they *can* be done mentally; this lesson addresses those instances. We refer to them as "special" fractions because they are limited in number and generally have the special characteristic that one denominator is a multiple of the other. To help students judge which problems can easily be done mentally, you might present examples like these:

3/4 + 1/2   1/2 + 1/10   5/6 + 2/7   4 1/4 + 1/2   3/4 + 7/16

Ask students which problems they think would be easiest to do mentally, and why. Students will likely disagree about the relative difficulty of each problem. This discussion will reveal some individual preferences and remind everyone that what is a simple mental calculation for one person may not be so simple for another.

Some review of mixed numbers will be helpful and can serve as a good warm-up. In particular, you might want to offer some preliminary oral work such as: "What is two and one-half plus one-half? What is three-fourths plus three-fourths?"

Problems for Oral Practice

At this point it is too difficult for most students to find common denominators when working orally; instead, have them practice adding fractions that already share a common denominator.

1. 1/2 + 1/2   **5.** 2/3 + 1/3   **9.** 2 1/3 + 2/3
2. 3/8 + 1/8   **6.** 3/5 + 3/5   **10.** 1 1/4 + 1/4
3. 1/3 + 1/3   **7.** 4/7 + 5/7   **11.** 3 1/2 + 1/2
4. 1/10 + 3/10   **8.** 3/10 + 7/10   **12.** 1 1/8 + 1 3/8

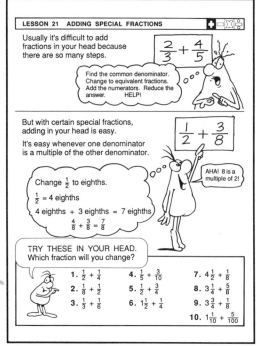

Page 89

LESSON 22   SUBTRACTING SPECIAL FRACTIONS

Mental math skill: Subtracting fractions for which a common denominator is easily determined

This lesson extends the principle of lesson 21 to subtraction of fractions. In order to add or subtract fractions mentally, students must be fluent in working with equivalent fractions. A good warm-up for this lesson might focus on equivalent fractions. For example, you name a fraction, such as 1/4, and ask students to name two equivalent fractions. Continue with thirds, fifths, sixths, eighths, and tenths.

Once again emphasize that this mental technique works with a very limited number of fractions, and help students recognize those problems that can be subtracted mentally.

Problems for Oral Practice

As in lesson 21, most of the oral practice for this lesson should deal with fractions that already share a common denominator.

1. 3/4 − 1/4   **5.** 5/6 − 1/6   **9.** 5/8 − 1/2
2. 3/8 − 1/8   **6.** 7/8 − 3/8   **10.** 7/8 − 1/2
3. 5/8 − 3/8   **7.** 9/10 − 3/10   **11.** 3/4 − 1/2
4. 2/3 − 1/3   **8.** 4/5 − 3/5   **12.** 7/10 − 1/2

Page 91

20

LESSON 23 TAKING PARTS FROM WHOLES
Mental math skill: Subtracting a fractional part from a whole number

As a warm-up to this lesson on subtracting fractions from whole numbers, draw a diagram of a pizza on the board or on a transparency:  Then ask: "If I divide this pizza into five equal pieces and eat one piece, how many pieces will be left? What fractional part have I eaten? What fractional part remains? What if I eat two pieces? three? Suppose I have two pizzas, each cut into five equal pieces, and I eat one piece. How many pieces are left? What fractional part remains?"

    The pizza model provides the foundation for complements: $1/5 + 4/5 = 1$, so $1 - 1/5 = 4/5$, and $1 - 4/5 = 1/5$. This is a nice extension of the notion of compatible numbers to fractions. Encourage students to visualize the pizza model as they work with fractions and whole numbers. Thinking of a familiar, concrete model leads them to use common sense in doing subtraction mentally.

Problems for Oral Practice

1. $1 - 1/8$
2. $1 - 3/8$
3. $1 - 7/8$
4. $1 - 1/4$
5. $1 - 3/4$
6. $1 - 1/3$
7. $1 - 2/3$
8. $1 - 3/8$
9. $2 - 1/2$
10. $2 - 1/4$
11. $2 - 1/3$
12. $2 - 7/8$

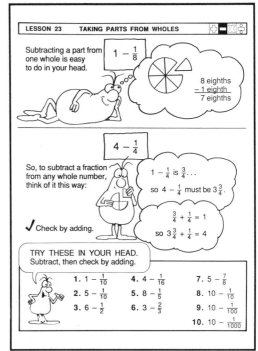

Page 93

LESSON 24 SUBTRACTING MIXED NUMBERS
Mental math skill: Subtracting a mixed number from a whole number

Here we integrate the skills developed in the three preceding lessons to helps students mentally subtract a mixed number from a whole number. For written work with fractions, students may have learned to deal with a problem like $3 - 1\ 2/7$ by renaming the whole number using an improper fraction (that is, 3 becomes $2\ 7/7$). When doing such a problem mentally, we can skip the renaming step by simply "breaking up" the mixed number and subtracting in parts—whole numbers first, and then the fractional part. You may want to illustrate these two steps with concrete models such as subdivided circles or rulers divided into fractional units. Show how these problems can also be solved by adding on to the subtrahend instead of subtracting.

Problems for Oral Practice

1. $2 - 1\ 1/2$
2. $2 - 1\ 1/8$
3. $2 - 1\ 1/4$
4. $2 - 1\ 1/3$
5. $3 - 2\ 3/4$
6. $3 - 2\ 2/3$
7. $3 - 2\ 7/8$
8. $3 - 2\ 5/6$
9. $5 - 2\ 1/2$
10. $5 - 3\ 1/3$
11. $5 - 3\ 2/3$
12. $5 - 1\ 1/2$

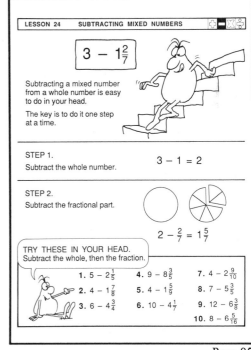

Page 95

Mental Math in Daily Life
LESSON 25   CUTTING LENGTHS OF LUMBER
Mental math skill: Applying mental subtraction of mixed numbers from whole numbers in a carpentry context

Carpentry and sewing are two real-life applications for mental subtraction of mixed numbers. This lesson focuses on cutting lumber.

The lumber we buy often comes in fixed lengths, such as 8, 12, 16, and 24 feet. Many times, we don't need a board exactly as long as the original length; we need to cut shorter lengths from it. When we cut off a given length, sometimes we need to know how much is left of the original board. The lesson illustrates two approaches: (1) subtracting by breaking up the mixed number into parts, and (2) adding on in steps. Encourage students to share different strategies they find useful. You may want to illustrate these techniques using scale models (paper) of these lengths of lumber.

Have students who are interested in sewing make up similar problems involving lengths of fabric and trimmings. For example:

You have a remnant with 12 yards of fabric. You use 5 3/8 yards to make a costume. Is there enough left to make a second costume?

Problems for Oral Practice

1. 12 − 5 1/2	**5.** 12 − 2 1/5	**9.** 12 − 4 3/4
2. 12 − 5 1/4	**6.** 12 − 4 1/4	**10.** 12 − 7 3/8
3. 12 − 5 1/3	**7.** 12 − 7 1/8	**11.** 12 − 8 2/3
4. 12 − 5 1/2	**8.** 12 − 9 1/10	**12.** 12 − 6 3/4

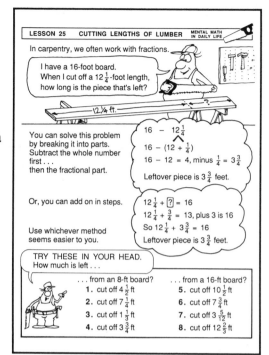

Page 97

LESSON 26   COMPATIBLE FRACTIONS
Mental math skill: Recognizing compatible fractions as an aid to adding and subtracting mixed numbers

Compatible or complementary fractions are pairs that sum to a whole number. Being able to recognize such pairs at a glance can help in subtracting fractions and mixed numbers. As a warm-up exercise, state a mixed number and have students write or state the fraction needed to make a whole number sum. For example, if you say 4 1/4, they name the compatible fraction 3/4, for the sum of 5.

Remind students that solving 10 − 4 1/2 = ? is equivalent to solving 4 1/2 + ? = 10. Thus, with problems involving mixed numbers, students can think in terms of either addition or subtraction. Encourage them to use whichever process they find easiest.

Problems for Oral Practice

1. 1 4/5 + 2 1/5	**5.** 5 1/10 + 2 9/10	**9.** 1 3/4 + 2 1/4
2. 4 5/7 + 1 2/7	**6.** 3 4/9 + 1 5/9	**10.** 4 7/12 + 1 5/12
3. 5/6 + 3 1/6	**7.** 2/3 + 4 1/3	**11.** 8/9 + 2 1/9
4. 2 5/8 + 2 3/8	**8.** 4 7/10 + 2 3/10	**12.** 3 2/7 + 1 5/7

Page 99

22

LESSON 27   MAKING COMPATIBLE FRACTIONS

Mental math skill: Using equivalent forms to make compatible pairs for adding fractions

Making your own compatible fractions to simplify a problem is both a challenging and creative task. To be successful, students need to understand fully the concept of compatible fractions introduced in the preceding lesson, and they need to be fluent with equivalent fractions.

As a warm-up, you might review both ideas with some oral exercises. Remind students that compatible fractions are pairs that sum to a whole number. Then state a variety of fractions, asking students to name the complementary fraction (to make a compatible pair); for example: 5/8 (3/8); 3/4 (1/4); 3/16 (13/16); 7/8 (1/8); 11/16 (5/16).

To review equivalent fractions, ask: "Three-fourths equals how many eighths? Four and one-fourth equals four and how many eighths? Three and five-sixteenths equals three and how many thirty-seconds? Seven and three-eighths equals seven and how many sixteenths?"

Consider using a ruler subdivided into fractional parts of an inch as a visual aid in this lesson, to help clarify the relationship of compatible fractions.

In each TRY THESE problem, ask students to describe which addend they will break up, and how, and what compatible pair they will make to solve the problem.

Problems for Oral Practice
Keep in mind that this strategy is difficult for students to do without being able to see the fractions. These oral exercises may be a real challenge.

1. 1 5/8 + 7/8	**5.** 3 3/4 + 1 5/12	**9.** 7 9/10 + 1 2/5
2. 2 2/3 + 4 2/3	**6.** 6 1/4 + 15/16	**10.** 3 7/10 + 4 1/2
3. 1 3/4 + 1 3/8	**7.** 7 7/16 + 1 15/16	**11.** 2 1/3 + 1 11/12
4. 2 7/8 + 5 1/4	**8.** 2 7/9 + 4 1/3	**12.** 1 5/6 + 4 1/2

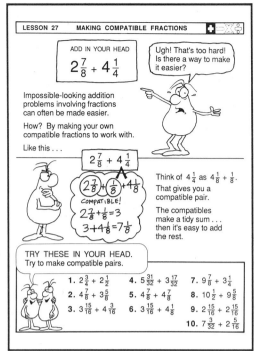

Page 101

LESSON 28   BALANCING WITH FRACTIONS

Mental math skill: Using balancing to simplify subtraction of mixed numbers

The concept of "balancing" or compensating in subtraction of whole numbers and decimals, developed in lessons 12 and 13, is extended here to problems with fractions.

To demonstrate the value of this technique, write these problems on the board or overhead:

Group A	Group B
7/8 − 1/2	1 − 5/8
2 1/2 − 2/3	2 5/6 − 1
5 1/8 − 2 3/8	5 3/4 − 1

Ask half the class to do Group A and the other half to do Group B. Are their answers the same? Why? Which group of problems is easier to mentally compute? Bring out in the discussion that making either the minuend or subtrahend a whole number often makes the computation easier.

Students who are adept at using the compatible fractions strategies (lesson 26 and 27) may observe that some of these subtraction problems are easily solved by thinking of compatible pairs. For example, consider the first problem in TRY THESE (5 − 2 4/5). We might think: "2 4/5 plus 1/5 makes 3, plus 2 makes 5. The difference is 2 1/5." As always, students should be encouraged to use whichever approach is easier for them.

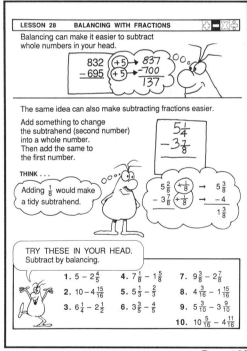

Page 103

Problems for Oral Practice

1. 4 − 2 3/8	**5.** 4 1/3 − 2	**9.** 2 3/5 − 1/2
2. 5 − 1 5/6	**6.** 6 3/4 − 3	**10.** 1 7/8 − 1/4
3. 3 − 1 1/3	**7.** 2 1/2 − 2	**11.** 3 5/6 − 1/2
4. 2 − 7/8	**8.** 5 1/3 − 3	**12.** 4 1/7 − 5/7

23

LESSON 29   FINDING FRACTIONAL PARTS
Mental math skill: Finding fractional parts of whole numbers

This lesson demonstrates two slightly different ways of thinking about the same type of problem. Most students will have been taught the rote rule, "divide by the denominator, then multiply by the numerator," but many forget it or get it confused. This lesson helps students understand (and therefore remember) the rule, leading them through a more intuitive approach to finding fractional parts.

Computing fractional parts mentally works best when the denominator of the fraction is a factor of the whole quantity—making the two numbers compatible. So, for example, 5/8 of 32 is easy to mentally compute; 5/8 of 36 is not so easy. To demonstrate, you might write problems like these on the board or overhead:

1/2 of 16   1/3 of 40   1/5 of 150   1/6 of 20   1/9 of 36   1/12 of 100

Ask students to decide which problems contain compatible numbers, and why. This will help them decide if a problem can be approached through the strategy outlined in this lesson.

In this two-step strategy, we focus first on a unit fraction, regardless of the fractional part we have to find in the end. Dividing the whole number by the denominator of the fraction gives us one fractional part. That is, 1/2 of 8 is 8 ÷ 2 = 4; 1/3 of 15 is 15 ÷ 3 = 5. Some people remember this first step by a mnemonic: *denominator* and *divide* both begin with the letter *d*. Once that step is complete, we go to step two: multiply the result by the numerator. For practice in recalling the steps, conduct oral exercises based on this pattern:

> To find 2/3 of 9 apples, take 1/3 of 9 (or divide by 3), then multiply by 2.
> To find 5/6 of 24 eggs, take ____ of 24 (or divide by ____), then multiply by ____.
> To find 3/8 of 40 people, take ____ of 40 (or divide by ____), then multiply by ____.

In the TRY THESE problems, encourage students to think out loud and describe their solution process.

Problems for Oral Practice

1. 1/8 of 24	**5.** 1/7 of 28	**9.** 1/4 of 80
2. 1/6 of 24	**6.** 2/7 of 28	**10.** 3/4 of 80
3. 1/4 of 24	**7.** 1/3 of 150	**11.** 1/5 of 30
4. 1/3 of 24	**8.** 2/3 of 150	**12.** 3/5 of 30

LESSON 30   Comparing Prices
Mental math skill: Applying mental math techniques in making price comparisons

One of the most practical and most frequently used applications of mental math skills is comparing prices of consumer items. This lesson illustrates only one of several methods. In class discussion you might cover other techniques for determining the better buy, such as comparing unit prices. One advantage of the method used in this lesson is that it tells you how much your savings amounts to.

The second example in the lesson shows how mental calculation with fractions can help in price comparison. Some students may find it difficult to see the relationship between two amounts in fractional terms, so this point may need extra discussion. TRY THESE problem 3 sets up a similar situation.

Problems for Oral Practice
For oral practice, price comparison is impractical because of the difficulty in remembering all the relevant product information. Instead, you might offer related practice with doubling prices, tripling them, halving them, and so forth.

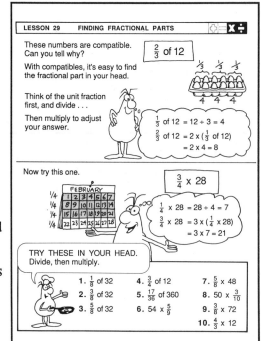

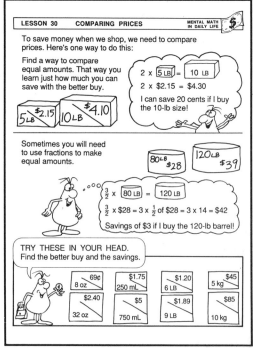

UNIT THREE REVIEW

To prepare students for the Unit Three progress test, help them review the mental math strategies of lessons 21–30. Go over the mental math techniques listed in the box at left, working through the sample problems together. In the numbered review exercises, encourage discussion of different strategies that could be used for the same problem.

Students will need to pick up speed with the new strategies if they are to succeed on the timed test. Plan to give them some timed practice with problems you select at random from the Power Builder sets for lessons 21–30. You can present these orally or write them on the board, erasing them after a set length of time. Gradually shorten the time you allow for selecting a strategy and computing the answer.

UNIT THREE REVIEW	(CLASS DISCUSSION)

Mental Math Techniques

Do the problems below in your head. Tell which techniques you find useful for each one.

- **CHANGE SPECIAL FRACTIONS TO ADD OR SUBTRACT.**
  $\frac{1}{2} + \frac{1}{4} = ?$ $\frac{7}{8} - \frac{1}{2} = ?$
- **SUBTRACT FRACTIONS FROM WHOLE NUMBERS.**
  $3 - \frac{1}{4} = ?$ $3 - 1\frac{3}{4} = ?$
- **USE COMPATIBLE FRACTIONS.**
  $4\frac{1}{2} + 2\frac{1}{2} = ?$
- **BALANCE TO SUBTRACT FRACTIONS.**
  $5\frac{1}{2} - 3\frac{7}{8} = ?$ (add $\frac{1}{8}$ to balance)
- **DIVIDE, THEN MULTIPLY, TO FIND FRACTIONAL PARTS.**
  $\frac{2}{3}$ of $12 = ?$ $\frac{3}{4} \times 24 = ?$

1. $8 - \frac{7}{8}$
2. $12 - 1\frac{3}{4}$
3. $4\frac{1}{4} - 1\frac{7}{8}$
4. $\frac{2}{3}$ of 18
5. $\frac{1}{2} + \frac{3}{4}$
6. $\frac{1}{2} + \frac{3}{4} - \frac{1}{8}$
7. $2\frac{1}{2} + 1\frac{1}{2} + 1\frac{3}{4}$
8. $5\frac{1}{16} - 2\frac{15}{16}$
9. $18 - 4\frac{1}{2}$
10. $\frac{3}{8} \times 48$

Talk about each problem below. What's an easy way to do it in your head? Tell how you would think it through.

1. $3\frac{1}{4} + 4\frac{3}{4}$
2. $11\frac{3}{8} - 3\frac{7}{8}$
3. $4\frac{1}{8} + 5\frac{7}{8}$
4. $\frac{1}{4} \times 48$
5. $20 - 4\frac{9}{10}$
6. $1\frac{7}{8} - \frac{1}{4}$
7. $12 - 5\frac{3}{8}$
8. $\frac{5}{6}$ of 24
9. $4\frac{3}{4} + 2\frac{1}{4} + 3\frac{5}{16}$
10. $\frac{1}{2} + \frac{1}{4} + \frac{1}{8}$

UNIT THREE PROGRESS TEST

This progress test checks students' proficiency in the strategies presented in lessons 21–30. See the Introduction, page 6, for suggestions for presenting this as a timed test.

MENTAL MATH PROGRESS TEST   **UNIT THREE LESSONS 21–30**

1. $\frac{1}{2} - \frac{1}{10} =$ _____
2. $12 - 2\frac{9}{10} =$ _____
3. $6 - 4\frac{7}{8} =$ _____
4. $\frac{1}{2} + \frac{1}{3} =$ _____
5. $1\frac{1}{4} + 2\frac{3}{8} =$ _____
6. $\frac{1}{7}$ of 35 = _____
7. $8 \text{ ft} - 4\frac{1}{3} \text{ ft} =$ _____
8. $4 - \frac{4}{5} =$ _____
9. Which is the better buy: 4 for $3.49 or 8 for $6.89? _____
10. $8 - 4\frac{5}{8} =$ _____
11. $\frac{1}{2} + \frac{1}{8} =$ _____
12. $1 - \frac{5}{9} =$ _____
13. $16 \text{ ft} - 2\frac{3}{4} \text{ ft} =$ _____
14. $6\frac{11}{12} + 1\frac{1}{2} =$ _____
15. Which is the better buy: 5 for $0.39 or 10 for $0.85? _____
16. $\frac{3}{4} - \frac{1}{8} =$ _____
17. $6 - 1\frac{3}{8} =$ _____
18. $\frac{3}{10}$ of 90 = _____
19. $2\frac{1}{2} + \frac{3}{4} =$ _____
20. $4\frac{1}{8} - 1\frac{7}{8} =$ _____

21. $24 \text{ ft} - 16\frac{2}{3} \text{ ft} =$ _____
22. Which is the better buy: 6 for $1.20 or 9 for $1.67? _____
23. $5\frac{1}{4} - 2\frac{1}{3} =$ _____
24. $\frac{7}{10} - \frac{1}{5} =$ _____
25. $5 - 2\frac{1}{8} =$ _____
26. $4\frac{1}{3} - 1\frac{7}{12} =$ _____
27. $\frac{3}{10} + \frac{1}{5} =$ _____
28. $7 - 3\frac{2}{5} =$ _____
29. $6\frac{3}{10} - 1\frac{7}{10} =$ _____
30. $\frac{2}{3} - \frac{1}{2} =$ _____
31. $1 - \frac{3}{8} =$ _____
32. $3 - \frac{2}{3} =$ _____
33. $4 - 1\frac{2}{3} =$ _____
34. $10 \text{ ft} - 4\frac{3}{8} \text{ ft} =$ _____
35. $4 - 2\frac{4}{7} =$ _____
36. $2\frac{5}{8} + 4\frac{1}{3} =$ _____
37. $4\frac{1}{8} - 1\frac{5}{8} =$ _____
38. $\frac{2}{5}$ of 15 = _____
39. Which is the better buy: 8 for $4.00 or 12 for $6.99? _____
40. $\frac{5}{8}$ of 40 = _____

LESSON 31   MULTIPLYING MIXED NUMBERS

Mental math skill: Using the distributive property to multiply a mixed number by a whole number

This lesson demonstrates a two-step process for multiplying a mixed number by a whole number. If students have any difficulty, you might compare this approach to the techniques we use to find the product of whole numbers, such as 4 x 98. Using expanded form, we can see the problem as 4 x (90 + 8) = (4 x 90) + (4 x 8). Or, expanding with subtraction, we can think of it as (4 x 100) – (4 x 2)= 400 – 8 = 392. Either way is fine; each is an example of the distributive property in action.

In the oral exercises, you might want to "pace" the parts, at least in the beginning. For example, you might say "four times three," then pause before saying "plus four times one-half."

Problems for Oral Practice

1. 4 x 3 1/2	**5.** 2 x 3 1/6	**9.** 4 x 2 1/4
2. 2 x 1 1/5	**6.** 3 x 2 1/3	**10.** 8 x 2 1/4
3. 3 x 2 2/7	**7.** 6 x 5 1/3	**11.** 4 x 2 1/4
4. 5 x 3 1/7	**8.** 3 x 2 1/2	**12.** 3 x 5 2/3

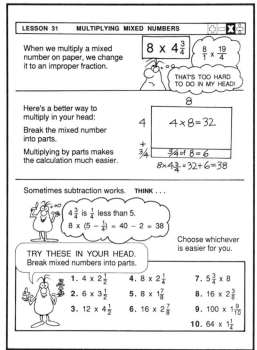

Mental Math in Daily Life
LESSON 32   INCREASING RECIPES

Mental math skill: Applying techniques for multiplying fractions and mixed numbers in a recipe

Here students have a chance to apply the skills developed in lessons 29 and 31. Most recipes contain only commonly used fractions, such as 1/4, 1/3, 1/2, 2/3, and 3/4. You might ask students to bring in and share a favorite recipe. Ask them how they would change the recipe to serve twice as many; to serve half as many.

Note that in the TRY THESE and Power Builder exercises, some answers involve many teaspoons—8 tsp vanilla, 12 tsp salt, 9 1/3 tsp soy sauce, and so forth. As a practical matter, when measuring the actual ingredients, it is useful to know that 3 teaspoons = 1 tablespoon. Clearly, it is more efficient to measure 4 T of salt than 12 tsp. When appropriate, alternative answers (with teaspoons converted to tablespoons) are provided in the Power Builder answer key.

Problems for Oral Practice

Double each ingredient . . . then triple each.

1. 3/4 cup oil	**5.** 2 1/2 tsp salt	**9.** 2 1/4 tsp cinnamon
2. 1/3 cup molasses	**6.** 1 2/3 cups milk	**10.** 1 3/4 tsp baking soda
3. 1 1/4 cups sugar	**7.** 3 3/4 cups flour	**11.** 3 1/4 cups broth
4. 1/8 tsp nutmeg	**8.** 1 1/2 tsp ginger	**12.** 2 2/3 cups cooked rice

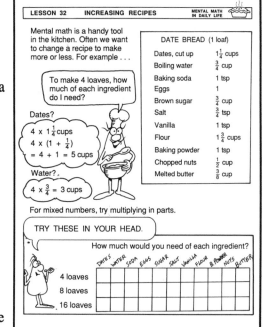

LESSON 33   HALVING AND DOUBLING

Mental math skill: Multiplying by halving one factor and doubling the other

This lesson demonstrates a handy way to make a multiplication problem easier to compute mentally. Like balancing in subtraction, "halving and doubling" in multiplication is a way of changing a problem to numbers that are easier to work with in your head.

As a warm-up, give students practice in doubling various 1-, 2-, and 3-digit numbers and halving 2-, 3-, and 4-digit even numbers. You might also pick a number and see how long it takes students to double it several times. For example: 25, 50, 100, 200, 400, and so on. (Research suggests that good mental calculators practice doubling and halving numbers on their own.)

In the TRY THESE problems, help students recognize when a problem needs more than one halving and doubling step to make it easy to compute mentally.

Problems for Oral Practice

1. Double 53	5. Half of 64	9. 2 x 89
2. Double 420	6. Half of 38	10. 2 x 56
3. Double 29	7. Half of 230	11. 4 x 35
4. Double 58	8. Half of 850	12. 4 x 75

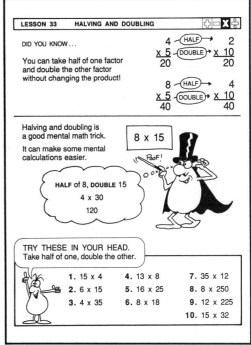

Page 117

LESSON 34   HALVING AND DOUBLING DECIMALS

Mental math skill: Multiplying decimals by halving one factor and doubling the other

This lesson extends the previous lesson to situations where one of the factors is a decimal. It uses the same techniques but requires students to keep the location of the decimal point in mind. As a warm-up, give students a decimal number, then ask them to double it and keep doubling until it exceeds a certain number. For example, take 0.12 and keep doubling it until it is greater than one. Ask students to keep track of the number of times it must be doubled to exceed 1.0 (that is, 0.12, 0.24, 0.48, 0.96, 1.92 . . . doubled four times).

Problems for Oral Practice

1. Double 0.75	5. 4 x 0.75	9. 8 x 0.45
2. Double 1.25	6. 4 x 0.35	10. 4 x 0.75
3. Double 2.15	7. 2 x 0.55	11. 8 x 1.50
4. Double 4.25	8. 5 x 0.42	12. 8 x 0.125

Page 119

LESSON 35   THINK MONEY

Mental math skill: Multiplying any number by a factor of 5, 25, or 50.

This lesson introduces a powerful strategy sometimes called "aliquot parts," reformulating a factor in terms of its multiple (that is, 5 in terms of 10, 25 and 50 in terms of 100). To introduce this strategy, create and distribute pictorial charts with nickels arranged in rows of two, quarters arranged in rows of four, and half dollars arranged in rows of two. Students can use these charts initially as a calculation aid. For example, 12 x 25 can be seen as 3 rows of 4 quarters, or 3 x $1.00 = $3.00; hence 12 x 25 = 300.

When students are proficient with this visual aid, lead them to the short cut of "dividing one factor and then multiplying by tacking on zeros." For example, to multiple 36 x 25, think: "36 ÷ 4 = 9; tack on 2 trailing zeros; so 36 x 25 = 900." This strategy can be easily extended to problems that involve multiplying by 250 (or 1/4 of 1000) and by 500 (or 1/2 of 1000). Additionally, this strategy is useful in making estimates. For example, 23 x 27 is close to 24 x 25, or about 600.

Challenge the more capable students to find strategies for calculating mentally difficult products like the following:

17 x 25   (16 x 25 = 400, plus 25 equals 425)
125 x 64 (125 = 1/8 of 1000, 1/8 of 64 = 8, 8 x 1000 = 8000)
75 x 12   (25 x 12 = 300, 3 x 300 = 900)
2.5 x 48 (2.5 = 1/4 of 10, 1/4 of 48 = 12, 10 x 12 = 120)

Problems for Oral Practice

1. 48 nickels = ? dimes = ? cents
2. 66 nickels = ? dimes = ? cents
3. 24 quarters = ? dollars = ? cents
4. 88 quarters = ? dollars = ? cents
5. 22 half dollars = ? dollars = ? cents
6. 120 half dollars = ? dollars = ? cents
7. 14 x 5
8. 28 x 5
9. 28 x 25
10. 32 x 50
11. 14 x 50
12. 44 x 25

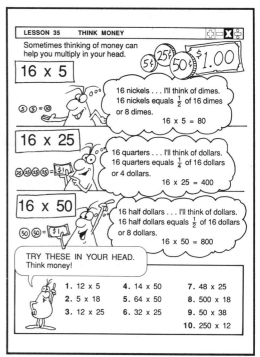

LESSON 36   COMPATIBLE FACTORS

Mental math skill: Combining compatible factors to simplify multi-step multiplication.

Compatible numbers in multiplication are those factors that yield a "nice" product—one that's easy to work with—usually a multiple of a power of 10. When a problem to be done mentally has several factors, combining compatible factors may help simplify it.

Point out that in any one problem, there may be several ways to combine compatible factors. For example, in the problem on the lesson page, we can rearrange the factors either as (25 x 2) x (5 x 4) x 9, or as (25 x 4) x (5 x 2) x 9. Though the arrangements are different, the products are the same. Challenge students to find different arrangements whenever possible.

Because of the hazard of dropping or repeating one factor in the process of rearranging, warn the students to keep track of the numbers that have been and that remain to be multiplied, possibly by crossing out each of the factors as it is used.

Problems for Oral Practice

The strategy presented in this lesson does not lend itself to oral practice, because to locate compatibles, students need to be able to see all the factors at once. However, the following problems can give students practice in handling compatible factors:

1. 5 x 2 x 7
2. 5 x 4 x 6
3. 5 x 6 x 9
4. 5 x 12 x 7
5. 4 x 25 x 9
6. 2 x 25 x 7
7. 8 x 25 x 12
8. 25 x 4 x 13
9. 4 x 50 x 9
10. 8 x 500 x 7
11. 4 x 250 x 13
12. 2 x 150 x 6

LESSON 37   MAKING COMPATIBLE FACTORS

Mental math skill: Factoring and rearranging to simplify multiplication problems

As a warm-up to this lesson, have the students name the factors of 2-digit numbers such as 25, 27, 32, 36, 48, and so on.

With this strategy, it's important that students look for a variety of ways to rearrange factors, both to be sure they don't overlook the most efficient arrangement and to check their work. Thus, the problem on the lesson page (28 x 25) might be seen in any of these ways:

$7 \times 4 \times 25 = 7 \times 100 = 700$ (as shown)

$7 \times 4 \times 5 \times 5 = 7 \times 20 \times 5 = 7 \times 100 = 700$

$5 \times 28 \times 5 = 140 \times 5 = 700$ (not especially easy)

$14 \times 2 \times 25 = 14 \times 50$ (from here, use "think money" or "halving and doubling" to get 700)

For the first few TRY THESE problems, help students select factors that form compatible pairs. For example, in problem 1, 8 x 15 can be reasoned as 4 x 30, 2 x 60, 40 x 3, or 24 x 5. Encourage alternative solutions, reminding students that there is no "right" way. Whichever numbers are easiest for them to multiply is the best way for them.

Problems for Oral Practice
This oral practice will challenge your students because it is difficult to rearrange factors mentally.

1. 4 x 150	**5.** 25 x 8	**9.** 25 x 12
2. 4 x 25	**6.** 8 x 35	**10.** 15 x 8
3. 35 x 4	**7.** 8 x 45	**11.** 16 x 5
4. 8 x 15	**8.** 12 x 5	**12.** 25 x 16

LESSON 38   DECIMAL POINT: SLIDE TO THE RIGHT

Mental math skill: Multiplying a decimal number by a power of 10

Although multiplying and dividing a decimal number by a power of 10 appear to be straightforward and easily learned skills, a surprising number of students are not aware of the important shortcut rules. Consequently, explicit instruction and practice are generally beneficial. Lessons 38 (multiplying) and 39 (dividing) are designed for this purpose.

This lesson translates the decimal number to a fractional expression to demonstrate *why* the slide-to-the-right rule for multiplying works. If students understand the reasoning behind a rote rule, they are more likely to remember it, or to be able to recreate it should they forget it.

A calculator with a constant multiplier can provide a visual illustration of the sliding decimal point. For example, enter 10 x 1.2345678. Each time the = key is pressed, the number will be multiplied by 10, and the decimal point will appear to slide to the right on the display. (NOTE: The manner in which a constant multiplier is entered can vary from calculator to calculator.)

Problems for Oral Practice

1. 1.2 x 10	**5.** 25.3 x 100	**9.** 100 items @ $15.73
2. 1.2 x 100	**6.** 0.23 x 10	**10.** 10 x 15.5
3. 1.2 x 1000	**7.** 10 items @ $1.73	**11.** 100 x 2.54
4. 1.56 x 10	**8.** 100 items @ $0.53	**12.** 1000 x 1.6

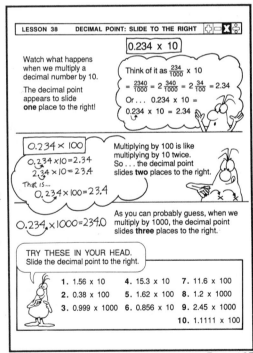

LESSON 39   DECIMAL POINT: SLIDE TO THE LEFT
Mental math skill: Dividing a decimal number by a power of 10

Here a problem is worked out with the quotient expressed in fractional amounts to demonstrate why the slide-to-the-left rule works.

As discussed in the preceding lesson, a calculator can provide a useful visual demonstration of a sliding decimal point. For example, after 12345678 ÷ 10 is entered, the 12345678 will be divided by 10 each time the = key is pressed and the decimal point will appear to slide to the left on the display. Alternatively, the same sliding effect can be seen by entering 0.1 as a constant multiplier (0.1 x 12345678). Have the students reconstruct the original number by reversing the procedure and multiplying by a constant 10.

Some students may be confused by lessons 38 and 39 if they try to generalize the rules to "multiply = slide to the right and divide = slide to the left," because these oversimplified rules do not apply for multiplying or dividing by 0.1, 0.01, and 0.001. Use the fractional expression of these decimals (1/10, 1/100, and 1/1000) to help students see why multiplying by 0.1 is the same as dividing by 10 (and so forth).

For further practice with these concepts, have the students carry out a series of calculations presented orally. For example: "Multiply 1.23 by 10; now multiply the product by 10; now divide by 100. What is the answer?" (1.23)

Problems for Oral Practice
1. 25 ÷ 10	**5.** 0.1 x 36	**9.** 1/100 of $450.00
2. 25 ÷ 100	**6.** 0.01 x 360	**10.** 0.1 x 2.55
3. 25 ÷ 1000	**7.** 1/10 of $45.00	**11.** 0.01 x 456
4. 2.5 ÷ 10	**8.** 1/10 of $4.75	**12.** 0.001 x 12,345

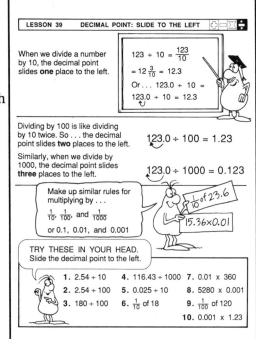

Page 129

Mental Math in Daily Life
LESSON 40   METRIC UNITS OF LENGTH
Mental math skill: Converting one linear metric unit to another

Although the United States still relies heavily on customary units of measure, people in many professions have a need to know and work with the metric system: carpenters, plumbers, electricians, mechanics, architects, engineers, museum curators, industrial designers—the list is endless. This lesson is a real-world application of lessons 38 and 39.

Conduct a brief review of the SI (metric) units of length if necessary, especially the names and number values of the common prefixes:

    1 decimeter = 0.1 meter
    1 centimeter = 0.01 meter
    1 millimeter = 0.001 meter

As a visual aid, a meter stick subdivided into the smaller units should be prominently displayed and used initially as the students convert units. For example, to convert 250 cm to meters, use the meter stick to construct a line of 250 cm, subdividing this line into lengths of 1 m + 1 m + 0.5 m, or 2.5 m.

Problems for Oral Practice
Change to meters:
1. 100 cm	**7.** 1.25 m
2. 150 cm	**8.** 0.85 m
3. 1250 mm	**9.** 2.5 m
4. 750 mm	**10.** 15.55 m
5. 50 cm	**11.** 150 mm
6. 50 mm	**12.** 5 mm

Change to centimeters:

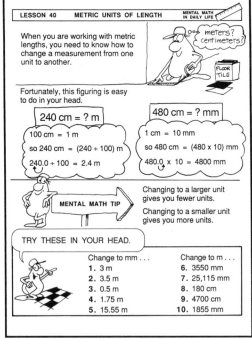

Page 131

UNIT FOUR REVIEW

To prepare students for the Unit Four progress test, help them review the mental math strategies of lessons 31–40. Go over the mental math techniques listed in the box at left, working through the sample problems together. In the numbered review exercises, encourage discussion of different strategies that could be used for the same problem.

Students will need to pick up speed with the new strategies if they are to succeed on the timed test. Plan to give them some timed practice with problems you select at random from the Power Builder sets for lessons 31–40. You can present these orally or write them on the board, erasing them after a set length of time. Gradually shorten the time you allow for selecting a strategy and computing the answer.

UNIT FOUR REVIEW (CLASS DISCUSSION)

Mental Math Techniques	Do the problems below in your head. Tell which techniques you find useful for each one.

- **BREAK MIXED NUMBERS INTO PARTS.**
  $4 \times 2\frac{1}{2} = ?$
- **HALVE ONE, DOUBLE THE OTHER.**
  $8 \times 15 = ?$ $12 \times 1.5 = ?$
- **THINK MONEY.**
  $16 \times 25 = ?$ $18 \times 50 = ?$
- **USE COMPATIBLE FACTORS.**
  $25 \times 7 \times 4 = ?$
  $8 \times 15 = 120$, so $24 \times 15 = ?$
- **SLIDE THE DECIMAL POINT.**
  $0.152 \times 100 = ?$
  $2.13 \div 100 = ?$

1. 8×25
2. $6 \times 2\frac{1}{3}$
3. 16×15
4. 15×12
5. 0.369×1000
6. $12.56 \div 1000$
7. $25 \times 13 \times 2 \times 2$
8. 25×32
9. 50×64
10. 16×35

Talk about each problem below. What's an easy way to do it in your head? Tell how you would think it through.

1. 12.3×100
2. 5×48
3. 500×45
4. $14 \times 25 \times 8$
5. 35×18
6. $8 \times 5\frac{1}{2}$
7. $100.01 \div 10$
8. 25×64
9. $0.356 \div 100$
10. 250×12

Page 133

UNIT FOUR PROGRESS TEST

This progress test checks students' proficiency in the strategies presented in lessons 31–40. See the Introduction, page 6, for suggestions for presenting this as a timed test.

MENTAL MATH PROGRESS TEST   **UNIT FOUR LESSONS 31–40**

1. Double $2\frac{2}{3}$ = _____
2. 100×3.4 = _____
3. $6 \times 2 \times 50$ = _____
4. 8×6.5 = _____
5. 50×36 = _____
6. Change to meters:
   105 cm = _____ m
7. 1000×5.021 = _____
8. $6 \times 3\frac{1}{3}$ = _____
9. 4×85 = _____
10. Triple $\frac{1}{3}$ = _____
11. $7 \times 6 \times 25 \times 4$ = _____
12. $53.4 \div 100$ = _____
13. 8×450 = _____
14. 5×66 = _____
15. Change to meters:
   246.3 mm = _____ m
16. 22×35 = _____
17. $8 \times 4\frac{1}{4}$ = _____
18. $5 \times 18 \times 20$ = _____
19. 16×1.75 = _____
20. 10×0.46 = _____
21. 12×25 = _____
22. $1\frac{3}{4} \times 12$ = _____
23. Change to meters:
   4256.1 cm = _____ m
24. 14×35 = _____
25. 25×4.40 = _____
26. 100×0.0415 = _____
27. $4 \times 3 \times 9 \times 25$ = _____
28. Double $\frac{3}{4}$ = _____
29. Change to meters:
   40,000 mm = _____ m
30. 15×18 = _____
31. $15 \times 2\frac{2}{3}$ = _____
32. $\$1.25 \times 16$ = _____
33. 0.01×5.27 = _____
34. 50×12.80 = _____
35. Triple $1\frac{1}{3}$ = _____
36. 125.6×0.001 = _____
37. 16×42 = _____
38. 45×12 = _____
39. 0.1×42.73 = _____
40. 8×0.45 = _____

Page 134

31

Mental Math in Daily Life
LESSON 41   COPING WITH TWELVES

Mental math skill: Using successive factoring to multiply and divide by 12 for work with dozens/units and feet/inches

As a warm-up to this lesson, give students several series of oral calculations that involve multiplying and dividing by 3 and by 2. For example: "Think of the number 15. Triple it (pause) . . . then double that answer (pause) . . . double again (pause) . . . take one-third of that answer. What number do you end up with?"

When discussing the first example on the lesson page, ask students how they perform the mental math of each tripling and doubling step in determining how many inches in 16 feet. That is, to triple 16, they might use front-end multiplication, thinking $3 \times 16 = 30 + 18 = 48$. Or, they might use halving and doubling, and think $3 \times 16 = 6 \times 8 = 48$.

Problems for Oral Practice

Because of the number of steps involved in this strategy, oral exercises are not recommended for most students. As an alternative approach for additional practice in working with twelves, write the following equations on the board or overhead:

A. _____ x 3 x 2 x 2 =

B. _____ ÷ 3 ÷ 2 ÷ 2 =

C. _____ x 1/3 x 1/2 x 1/2 =

Students should try to determine the answers as quickly as possible as you write different numbers in the blanks. For equations B and C, choose numbers that are multiples of 12.

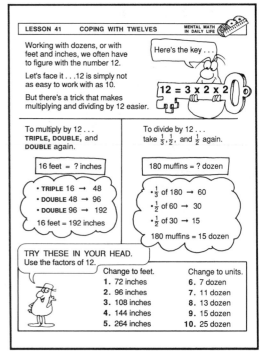

Page 137

LESSON 42   BREAKING UP THE DIVIDEND

Mental math skill: Dividing by expanding the dividend into multiples of the divisor

The strategy in this lesson is similar to the way we approach written division, left to right, except that we think about *groups* of digits in the dividend instead of one digit at a time, and subtraction is eliminated. As a warm-up, provide some oral drill on dividing and multiplying a power of 10 by a single digit factor. For example: "Divide 500 by 5. Multiply 800 by 3. Divide 3000 by 3."

Students will need to recognize that there is more than one way to expand the dividend. Encourage them to choose the expansion that gives them compatible numbers (the easiest numbers to divide). For example, the problem discussed on the lesson transparency ($515 \div 5$) could be thought of as $510 + 5$, but if we think of it as $500 + 15$, it is easier to divide by 5.

For the first few TRY THESE problems, ask students to find different ways to break up the dividend and decide which way makes it easier to divide. Emphasize that each answer should be double-checked using a mental multiplication strategy such as front-end multiplication.

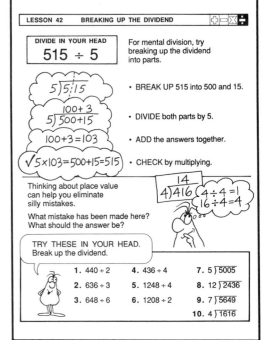

Page 139

Problems for Oral Practice

1. $88 \div 4$	5. $159 \div 3$	9. $355 \div 5$
2. $124 \div 4$	6. $822 \div 2$	10. $246 \div 6$
3. $124 \div 2$	7. $155 \div 5$	11. $369 \div 3$
4. $606 \div 3$	8. $505 \div 5$	12. $488 \div 8$

LESSON 43   MAKING COMPATIBLES IN DIVISION

Mental math skill: Dividing by rearranging the dividend into multiples of the divisor

The "making compatibles" technique developed here is a more complex variation of the division strategy presented in lesson 42. Initial discussion should center on the various productive and unproductive ways to expand the dividend before dividing is begun. Again, students should be encouraged to use the expansion that is most convenient for them to work with. Remind them to double-check their answers using a mental multiplication method.

Problems for Oral Practice
Caution the students that this strategy can be difficult to use when the problems are presented orally.

1. $45 \div 3$
2. $38 \div 2$
3. $52 \div 4$
4. $65 \div 5$
5. $48 \div 3$
6. $78 \div 6$
7. $125 \div 5$
8. $132 \div 2$
9. $175 \div 5$
10. $105 \div 3$
11. $225 \div 5$
12. $416 \div 4$

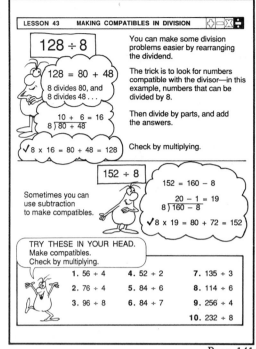

LESSON 44   DIVIDING BY BALANCING

Mental math skill: Simplifying division by multiplying both the dividend and divisor by a constant

This lesson is based on the equal factors principle; that is, multiplying or dividing both the dividend and divisor by a non-zero constant leaves the quotient unchanged.   Emphasize that when the divisor is multiplied by a number, the dividend must be multiplied by the *same* number to ensure that the answer remains the same. Encourage your students to find a number of different ways to simplify the TRY THESE exercises. For example, $3 \div 0.2$ could be simplified as $15 \div 1 = 15$ (multiplying each number by 5) or as $30 \div 2 = 15$ (multiplying each number by 10).

Problems for Oral Practice
1. $2 \div 0.5$
2. $4 \div 1/2$
3. $3 \div 1/4$
4. $5 \div 1/10$
5. $8 \div 0.1$
6. $8 \div 0.01$
7. $12 \div 25$
8. $800 \div 50$
9. $1800 \div 50$
10. $500 \div 25$
11. $160 \div 50$
12. $12 \div 0.25$

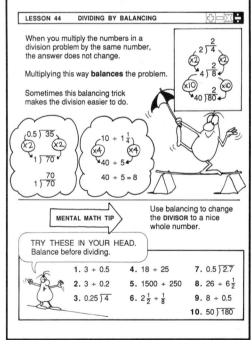

LESSON 45   PERCENTS AND DECIMALS

Mental math skill: Converting decimals to percents and percents to decimals

Make sure your students have a good understanding of the meaning of *percent* before you introduce this lesson on shorthand conversion rules. If necessary, provide a brief review using a 10-by-10 grid to illustrate the relationship between decimals and percents. For example, shade 10 of the 100 squares, then point out the equivalence of 10%, 10/100, 0.10, and even 1/10. A brief review of lessons 38 and 39 (sliding the decimal point) may also be helpful.

The conversion process can be reduced to two rules:
1. To change a percent to a decimal, slide the decimal point two places to the left.
2. To change a decimal to a percent, slide the decimal point two places to the right.

Because it is easy to get these two rules mixed up, this lesson works at developing an understanding of the principles underlying the rules.

Problems for Oral Practice

Express as a decimal:
1. 10%
2. 18%
3. 36%
4. 50.5%
5. 0.5%
6. 125%

Express as a percent:
7. 0.5
8. 0.39
9. 0.85
10. 0.805
11. 0.001
12. 2.56

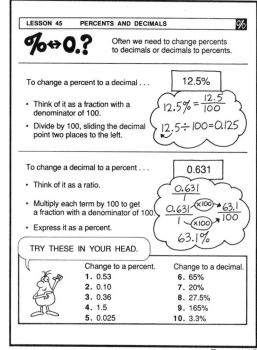

LESSON 46   USING FRACTIONS TO FIGURE PERCENTS

Mental math skill: Figuring 50%, 33 1/3%, 10%, and 1% by recalling fractional equivalents

It's fairly easy to figure the fractional amounts 1/2, 1/3, 1/10, and 1/100 in our heads, and we can use this knowledge to work percent problems with 50%, 33 1/3%, 10%, and 1%. It is important for later practical work that the students eventually memorize these and the other fractional equivalents of common percents worked out in the following lessons.

As new equivalents are introduced, add them to a large chart displayed prominently in the classroom. For daily review, give a few practical problems based on the equivalences on the chart; for example, mentally calculate the annual interest on a $50 loan at a 10% rate.

Use a 10-by-10 grid to illustrate the relationships between the percents and corresponding basic unit fractions introduced in this lesson. That is, to show that 1/2 = 0.50 = 50%, shade half of the 100 squares on the grid.

Problems for Oral Practice

Change to a percent:
1. 1/2
2. 1/100
3. 1/3
4. 1/10
5. 1 1/10
6. 1 1/2

Calculate the amount:
7. 10% of $50
8. 33 1/3% of $60
9. 50% of $48
10. 1% of $150
11. 50% of $14.50
12. 10% of $13.50

LESSON 47   WORKING FROM BASIC EQUIVALENTS

Mental math skill: Figuring percents by reasoning with fractional equivalents

This lesson builds directly onto lesson 46, asking students to work out various percents by thinking in terms of four percents and their fractional equivalents: 50% (1/2), 33 1/3% (1/3), 10% (1/10), and 1% (1/100). Before starting this lesson, review the relationship between proper fractions and unit fractions: that is, a/b = a x 1/b. This will help students to understand such equivalences as 60% = 6 x 10% = 6 x 1/10 = 6/10.

Problems for Oral Practice

Change to a percent:

1. 6/10
2. 1/2
3. 3/10
4. 1/3
5. 2/3
6. 144/100

Calculate the amount:

7. 20% of $40
8. 30% of $40
9. 40% of $40
10. 55% of $200
11. 66 2/3% of $48
12. 2% of $150

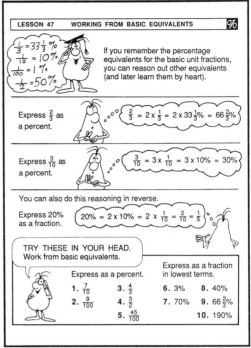

LESSON 48   WORKING OUT DIFFICULT EQUIVALENTS

Mental math skill: Figuring percents by reasoning with fractional equivalents

This lesson focuses on the percentage equivalents for 1/4, 1/8, 1/16, and 1/5 (and multiples thereof). You might work out these equivalents initially on the 10-by-10 grid and later place them on a chart for reference. (Illustrate the percentage equivalents for 1/4, 1/8, and 1/16 by successively halving the square grid: 1/2 = 50/100 = 50%; 1/4 = 1/2 of 1/2 = 25/100 = 25%; 1/8 = 1/2 of 1/4 = 12.5/100 = 12.5%; and so on.)

Once students have learned these equivalents, they can use the 10-by-10 grid to reason out and later memorize the equivalents for many proper and improper fractions whose denominators are a power of 2. For example, the grid can be used to show that 7/8 = 3/4 + 1/8 = 75% + 12.5% = 87.5%.

Again, provide students with regular practice solving practical problems that involve the use of these particular equivalents.

Show students how they can estimate some calculations by recalling a percentage equivalent: for example, 38% of $78.89 can be estimated as 37.5% of $80 = 3/8 of 80 = $30.

Problems for Oral Practice

Change to a percent:

1. 1/2
2. 1/4
3. 1/8
4. 1/16
5. 5/8
6. 3/4

Calculate the amount:

7. 50% of $50
8. 25% of $50
9. 25% of $48
10. 12.5% of $48
11. 75% of $160
12. 37.5% of $160

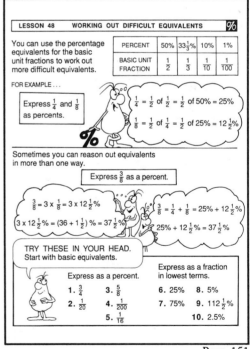

LESSON 49   USING A KNOWN PERCENT
Mental math skill: Simplifying problems by relating unwieldy percents to more easily handled percents

Each of the problems treated on the lesson transparency can be illustrated by shading regions of a suitably chosen rectangular diagram. For example, the calculation 90% of 150 = ? can be illustrated on a 10-by-15 rectangle by dividing the 150 squares into regions of 15 and 135 squares, representing 10% and 90% of 150 respectively.

As was shown in the preceding lesson, many percents can be figured more than one way. For example, 45% might be figured either as 50% − 1/2 of 10%, as 4 x 10% + 1/2 of 10%, or as 50% − 1/10 of 50%. Students should look for efficiency in choosing related percents, but may use whatever works well for them.

Ask students to suggest a shortcut rule for finding 55% of a number; for finding 22% of a number; for finding 18% of a number.

While doing the TRY THESE problems together, ask students what known percent they worked from in each case.

Problems for Oral Practice
Calculate the amount:

1. 10% of $50
2. 90% of $50
3. 110% of $50
4. 50% of $80
5. 40% of $80
6. 45% of $80
7. 50% of $120
8. 60% of $120
9. 55% of $120
10. 125% of $48
11. 200% of $150
12. 190% of $150

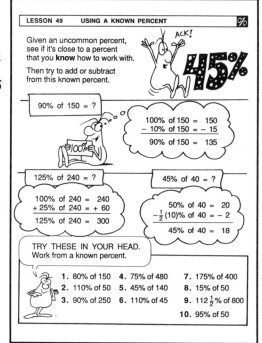

Page 153

Mental Math in Daily Life
LESSON 50   PERCENTS AND MONEY
Mental math skill: Handling percents commonly seen in practical situations

This lesson leads students to consider situations that call for an application of the techniques introduced in lessons 45–49. Whenever possible, use newspapers or advertising flyers to provide students with real-world practice in handling commonly used percents.

For the second example, help students find the 15% tip. Suggest that they round the bill to $47, then think of 15% as 10% plus 5%. Working it through: 10% of $47 is $4.70; 5% of $47 is half of $4.70 or $2.35. So 15% would be $4.70 + $2.35, or $7.05. A tip of $7 would be about right. Be sure students understand why rounding is acceptable in this instance, as it is in so many everyday situations requiring mental math.

In the TRY THESE problems, ask students what fraction equivalent(s) or what known percents they used in each case. You might want to discuss some of the terms used in the TRY THESE and Power Builder exercises (*duty, profit, commission, royalty,* and so on) before assigning these problems.

Problems for Oral Practice
Think of 10% of $35 to start with.

1. 20% of $35
2. 5% of $35
3. 15% of $35
4. 30% of $35
5. 35% of $35
6. 2.5% of $35

Think of 50% of $480 to start with.

7. 25% of $480
8. 75% of $480
9. 150% of $480
10. 12.5% of $480
11. 6.25% of $480
12. 5% of $480

Page 155

36

UNIT FIVE REVIEW

To prepare students for the Unit Five progress test, help them review the mental math strategies of lessons 41–50. Go over the mental math techniques listed in the box at left, working through the sample problems together. In the numbered review exercises, encourage discussion of different strategies that could be used for the same problem.

Students will need to pick up speed with the new strategies if they are to succeed on the timed test. Plan to give them some timed practice with problems you select at random from the Power Builder sets for lessons 41–50. You can present these orally or write them on the board, erasing them after a set length of time. Gradually shorten the time you allow for selecting a strategy and computing the answer.

UNIT FIVE REVIEW	(CLASS DISCUSSION)

Mental Math Techniques

- USE FACTORS OF 12 (3 x 2 x 2).
  8 x 12 = ?   60 ÷ 12 = ?
- BREAK UP THE DIVIDEND.
  515 ÷ 5 = (500 + 15) ÷ 5 = ?
- MAKE COMPATIBLES TO DIVIDE.
  128 ÷ 8 = (80 + 48) ÷ 8 = ?
- BALANCE BEFORE DIVIDING.
  16 ÷ 0.25 = ?
- USE FRACTIONAL EQUIVALENTS OF PERCENTS.
  10% of $17.50 = ?
  $\frac{1}{4}$ = 25%, so $\frac{3}{4}$ = ? %
- USE SIMPLE PERCENTS TO FIGURE HARDER ONES.
  10% of $15 = $1.50,
  so 5% of $15 = ?

Do the problems below in your head. Tell which techniques you find useful for each one.

1. 10% of $135
2. 5% of $135
3. 15% of $135
4. 95% of $135
5. 12 x 14
6. 636 ÷ 6
7. 20 ÷ 0.25
8. 25 ÷ $\frac{1}{5}$
9. $\frac{1}{4}$ = ? %
10. $\frac{3}{8}$ = ? %

Talk about each problem below. What's an easy way to do it in your head? Tell how you would think it through.

1. 144 ÷ 12
2. 4848 ÷ 8
3. 85 ÷ 5
4. 75% of $120
5. $\frac{2}{3}$ = ? %
6. 15% of $24
7. 15 ÷ 0.25
8. 110% of $50
9. 45% of $50
10. 33$\frac{1}{3}$% of $24.36

Page 157

UNIT FIVE PROGRESS TEST

This progress test checks students' proficiency in the strategies presented in lessons 41–50. See the Introduction, page 6, for suggestions for presenting this as a timed test.

MENTAL MATH PROGRESS TEST

UNIT FIVE
LESSONS 41–50

1. 72 ÷ 6 = _____
2. 10% of $60 = _____
3. 250 ⟌ 1200 _____
4. 0.43 = _____ %
5. 30% of $55 = _____
6. 636 ÷ 6 = _____
7. 8 dozen eggs = _____ eggs
8. $\frac{1}{8}$ = _____ %
9. 3% of $45.00 = _____
10. 9009 ÷ 3 = _____
11. 0.9 = _____ %
12. 3% of $1500 = _____
13. 2 ÷ 0.25 = _____
14. 25% of $84 = _____
15. 848 ÷ 4 = _____
16. 13 feet = _____ inches
17. 99% of $200 = _____
18. 50% of $260 = _____
19. 3.2 ÷ 0.5 = _____
20. 1.3 = _____ %
21. 12.5% of $56 = _____
22. 315 ÷ 5 = _____
23. 4242 ÷ 7 = _____
24. 1% of $39 = _____
25. 15% of $12 = _____

26. 112.5% of $16 = _____
27. 66$\frac{2}{3}$% of $600 = _____
28. 288 ÷ 9 = _____
29. 720 inches = _____ feet
30. 101% of $85 = _____
31. $\frac{3}{16}$ = _____ %
32. 33$\frac{1}{3}$ of $75 = _____
33. 1$\frac{1}{3}$ + $\frac{1}{3}$ = _____
34. 84 ÷ 7 = _____
35. 20% of $50 = _____
36. 110% profit on $54 = _____
37. 0.025 = _____ %
38. 72 rolls = _____ dozen rolls
39. 9% loss on $700 = _____
40. 250% of $18 = _____

Page 158

37

Memorizing π

MENTALMATHLETES often like to challenge their numerical memory. One perfect challenge is found in the decimal digits of π (pi).

The decimal expansion of π never ends or repeats itself, so people like to see how many digits of π they can memorize.

MENTALMATHLETE Hans Eberstark memorized π to 11,944 digits, but his record was beaten by Creighton Carvello, the present record-holder, with 20,013 digits!

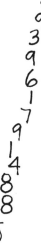

3.14159265358979323846264338327950288419716939937510

YOUR TURN

Challenge your friends to see who can memorize the most digits of π. Here are the first 50 digits:

3. 14159　26535　89793　23846　26433
　 83279　50288　41971　69399　37510

Here's a memory aid for the first 8 digits. The number of letters in each word corresponds to a digit of π.

MAY I HAVE A LARGE CONTAINER OF COFFEE?
3. 1 4 1 5 9 2 6

MENTAL MATH IN JUNIOR HIGH
Copyright © 1988 by Dale Seymour Publications

Memorizing Pi

Having a good memory for numbers is obviously an important part of being a successful Mentalmathlete. Memorizing the decimal digits of pi is a "just for fun" activity through which students can test their number memories.

Here are some interesting tidbits about pi that you might want to share with your students:

1. Even after the German mathematician Lambert proved in 1761 that the decimal expansion of pi would never repeat, many mathematicians continued to calculate pi to numerous decimal places. For example, William Shanks spent 15 years calculating pi to 707 places; he held the record until 1949, when the ENIAC computer found an error in his calculation in the 528th decimal place.

2. Fractions like 22/7 are only approximations of pi. The fraction 355/113 is the best approximation of pi that can be expressed as a reasonably simple common fraction. You might want to have your students use calculators to evaluate the accuracy of these two fractional approximations of pi.

3. Although computers have calculated the decimal expansion of pi to several thousand places, there is rarely a practical need for digits beyond 9 or 10 places. To demonstrate this point, ask your students to use a calculator and the formula $C = \pi d$ to determine the circumference of the earth with a diameter of 8000 miles. Have them use various values of pi to create a table like the one below:

Value of pi	Circumference	Difference in estimates
3.1	24,800 miles	
3.14	25,120 miles	680 miles
3.141	25,128 miles	8 miles
3.1415	25,132 miles	4 miles
3.14159	25,132.72 miles	3800 feet
3.141592	25,132.736 miles	84 feet
3.1415926	25,132.740 miles	21 feet

Students can readily see, by examining the completed table, that increasing the decimal expansion of pi beyond 4 or 5 digits adds relatively little to the accuracy of the estimate.

Some students might be interested in library research into the number pi. One inexpensive source of number lore is *Asimov's Numbers*, written by Isaac Asimov and published by Pocket Books.

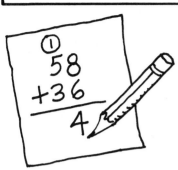

In paper-and-pencil computation, we usually start at the right and work toward the left.

To add in your head, start at the **left.**

THINK . . .

$58 + 36$

50 plus 30 is 80, and 8 plus 6 is 14 . . . 80 plus 14 is 94.

It works with larger numbers, too . . .

$453 + 38$

It also works with decimals.

THINK . . .

$1.7 + 3.6$

$1 + 3 = 4$
7 tenths + 6 tenths = 1 and 3 tenths
$4 + 1$ and 3 tenths $= 5.3$

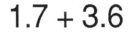

TRY THESE IN YOUR HEAD.
Add from the left.

1. $22 + 39$ **4.** $526 + 48$ **7.** $4.5 + 2.5$

2. $45 + 38$ **5.** $329 + 36$ **8.** $6.4 + 1.8$

3. $56 + 37$ **6.** $236 + 120$ **9.** $26.5 + 2.7$

                                   10. $43.8 + 10.8$

POWER BUILDER A

1. 38 + 46 = _____
2. 57 + 25 = _____
3. 44 + 39 = _____
4. 64 + 18 = _____
5. 68 + 35 = _____
6. 268 + 35 = _____
7. 417 + 58 = _____
8. 545 + 228 = _____
9. 624 + 239 = _____
10. 356 + 517 = _____

11. 4.7 + 2.8 = _____
12. 3.8 + 1.5 = _____
13. 5.7 + 2.5 = _____
14. 8.3 + 4.7 = _____
15. 5.4 + 3.8 = _____
16. 12.6 + 6.7 = _____
17. 23.6 + 5.9 = _____
18. 45.8 + 3.8 = _____
19. 37.8 + 11.2 = _____
20. 45.9 + 12.8 = _____

THINK IT THROUGH

December 22 is the first day of winter. March 21 is the last day of winter. How many days does winter offically have?

POWER BUILDER B

1. 46 + 28 = _____
2. 47 + 25 = _____
3. 66 + 19 = _____
4. 24 + 58 = _____
5. 48 + 35 = _____
6. 437 + 55 = _____
7. 638 + 29 = _____
8. 345 + 227 = _____
9. 462 + 219 = _____
10. 456 + 338 = _____

11. 5.2 + 3.9 = _____
12. 5.8 + 1.5 = _____
13. 3.7 + 4.6 = _____
14. 2.9 + 5.3 = _____
15. 2.8 + 6.4 = _____
16. 14.6 + 4.9 = _____
17. 43.4 + 4.6 = _____
18. 53.7 + 5.4 = _____
19. 33.6 + 12.5 = _____
20. 65.8 + 12.2 = _____

THINK IT THROUGH

June 22 is the first day of summer. September 21 is the last day of summer. How many days does summer officially have?

Here's another way to add in your head.

Break up the numbers and add the parts, bridging from one number to the next.

$$56 + 38$$

$$56 + 30 + 8$$

$$86 + 8$$

$$94$$

Add these by bridging.

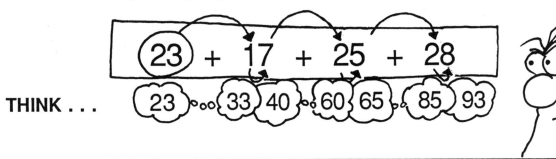

THINK . . .

$23 + 17 + 25 + 28$

23   33   40   60   65   85   93

Add larger numbers by bridging, too.

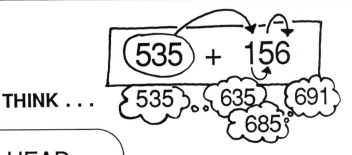

$535 + 156$

THINK . . .

535   635   691

685

TRY THESE IN YOUR HEAD.
Break up and add by bridging.

1. $48 + 21$
2. $37 + 46$
3. $15 + 18 + 17$
4. $18 + 25 + 27 + 36$
5. $530 + 280$

6. $150 + 83$
7. $125 + 186$
8. $450 + 253$
9. $176 + 125$
10. $513 + 287$

POWER BUILDER A

1. 48 + 25 = _____
2. 35 + 47 = _____
3. 56 + 38 = _____
4. 74 + 19 = _____
5. 63 + 27 = _____
6. 15 + 12 + 25 = _____
7. 44 + 17 + 28 = _____
8. 9 + 24 + 19 + 23 = _____
9. 23 + 17 + 28 + 14 = _____
10. 34 + 9 + 17 + 34 = _____

11. 450 + 180 = _____
12. 270 + 540 = _____
13. 654 + 253 = _____
14. 437 + 190 = _____
15. 140 + 686 = _____
16. 275 + 126 = _____
17. 415 + 285 = _____
18. 639 + 263 = _____
19. 8250 + 875 = _____
20. 4265 + 435 = _____

THINK IT THROUGH

The sum of the squares of 5 consecutive whole numbers is 90. What are the five numbers?

POWER BUILDER B

1. 57 + 24 = _____
2. 45 + 37 = _____
3. 39 + 57 = _____
4. 55 + 38 = _____
5. 64 + 26 = _____
6. 14 + 17 + 34 = _____
7. 24 + 18 + 13 = _____
8. 8 + 23 + 25 + 34 = _____
9. 25 + 16 + 21 + 38 = _____
10. 45 + 6 + 28 + 19 = _____

11. 540 + 290 = _____
12. 160 + 750 = _____
13. 752 + 155 = _____
14. 339 + 280 = _____
15. 596 + 330 = _____
16. 376 + 225 = _____
17. 135 + 465 = _____
18. 344 + 457 = _____
19. 7275 + 725 = _____
20. 5184 + 416 = _____

THINK IT THROUGH

The sum of the ages in a family of four is 110. The mother and father are the same age. The older child is twice the age of the younger, and all the ages are multiples of 5. What are the ages?

You can add decimal numbers in your head
by bridging from one number to another.

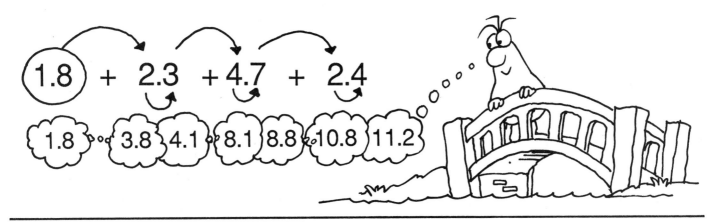

(1.8) + 2.3 + 4.7 + 2.4

1.8   3.8 4.1 8.1 8.8 10.8 11.2

Bridging is handy
when you need to add
money amounts.

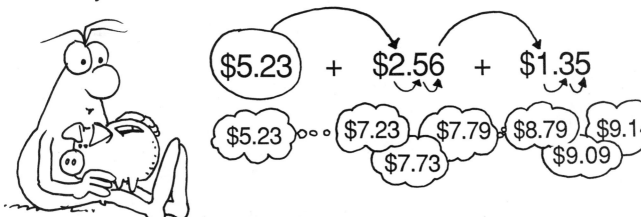

$($5.23$)$ + $2.56 + $1.35

$5.23 $7.23 $7.79 $8.79 $9.14
          $7.73 $9.09

TRY THESE IN YOUR HEAD.
Add by bridging.

1. 2.5 + 2.8

2. 1.5 + 2.6 + 3.7

3. 1.8 + 1.5 + 2.3

4. 0.25 + 0.28 + 0.23

5. $0.75 + $0.35

6. $1.28 + $1.25

7. $1.55 + $1.13 + $1.26

8. $0.55 + $0.25 + $1.50

9. $2.50 + $2.55 + $2.35

10. $10.25 + $10.35 + $5.40

POWER BUILDER A

1. 2.4 + 1.8 = _____
2. 12.7 + 3.9 = _____
3. 4.2 + 2.8 = _____
4. 3.8 + 4.5 = _____
5. 6.5 + 2.7 = _____
6. 1.6 + 0.7 + 2.4 = _____
7. 2.7 + 1.8 + 4.4 = _____
8. 0.27 + 0.35 + 0.14 = _____
9. 0.54 + 0.17 + 0.25 = _____
10. 0.25 + 0.09 + 0.18 + 0.36 = _____

11. $0.55 + $0.35 = _____
12. $0.45 + $0.25 = _____
13. $1.55 + $2.35 = _____
14. $2.75 + $4.25 = _____
15. $1.55 + $1.15 + $1.30 = _____
16. $2.15 + $0.25 + $4.35 = _____
17. $4.30 + $0.45 + $2.60 = _____
18. $1.55 + $0.25 + $3.30 + $1.20 = _____
19. $4.20 + $1.35 + $2.15 + $0.85 = _____
20. $2.35 + $1.45 + $2.25 + $1.65 = _____

THINK IT THROUGH

Begin with 6000. Add one-third of 3000.
Add half of 1000. Add one-fourth of 500.
What is the total?

POWER BUILDER B

1. 3.5 + 1.6 = _____
2. 11.8 + 6.4 = _____
3. 3.7 + 1.9 = _____
4. 5.6 + 2.6 = _____
5. 7.3 + 1.7 = _____
6. 1.5 + 0.8 + 3.6 = _____
7. 1.8 + 2.9 + 4.3 = _____
8. 0.32 + 0.19 + 0.37 = _____
9. 0.33 + 0.28 + 0.24 = _____
10. 0.23 + 0.08 + 0.26 + 0.85 = _____

11. $0.45 + $0.15 = _____
12. $0.55 + $0.45 = _____
13. $1.45 + $2.35 = _____
14. $3.25 + $2.75 = _____
15. $1.45 + $1.25 + $1.50 = _____
16. $3.25 + $0.25 + $4.75 = _____
17. $3.35 + $0.65 + $1.65 = _____
18. $1.45 + $0.55 + $2.75 + $1.15 = _____
19. $3.25 + $1.10 + $2.25 + $1.65 = _____
20. $1.35 + $2.45 + $1.70 + $1.45 = _____

THINK IT THROUGH

Begin with 2000. Add half of 1000. Add half of 500.
Add half of 250. What is the total?

There are two types of subtraction problems.

THOSE THAT **NEED** REGROUPING

456−28

5247−149

THOSE THAT **DON'T NEED** REGROUPING

547−131

4287−122

$$4358 - 2142$$

No regrouping!

$$\begin{array}{cccc} 4 & 3 & 5 & 8 \\ -2 & -1 & -4 & -2 \\ \hline 2 & 2 & 1 & 6 \end{array}$$

2 thousand, 2 hundred, 16.

If no regrouping is needed, you can subtract quickly in your head.

Start at the left and say the answer one part at a time.

It works with decimals, too. Try it with these problems:

$$4.27 - 1.13$$

$$8.94 - 5.72$$

TRY THESE IN YOUR HEAD.
Subtract from the left.

1. 375 − 232   **4.** 5206 − 2104   **7.** 4.75 − 1.32

2. 987 − 723   **5.** 8345 − 6340   **8.** 9.87 − 7.23

3. 486 − 425   **6.** 9154 − 5014   **9.** 45.6 − 31.6

10. 8.45 − 6.15

POWER BUILDER A

1. 427 – 315 = _____
2. 876 – 550 = _____
3. 736 – 524 = _____
4. 945 – 540 = _____
5. 697 – 346 = _____
6. 8275 – 4160 = _____
7. 5260 – 4160 = _____
8. 9854 – 3421 = _____
9. 8547 – 5034 = _____
10. 95,476 – 82,153 = _____

11. 4.95 – 1.23 = _____
12. 6.04 – 4.02 = _____
13. 9.57 – 3.54 = _____
14. 6.24 – 2.13 = _____
15. 7.54 – 5.04 = _____
16. 11.27 – 1.15 = _____
17. 19.88 – 8.77 = _____
18. 51.47 – 30.25 = _____
19. 83.59 – 43.56 = _____
20. 75.75 – 25.20 = _____

THINK IT THROUGH

The difference between the squares of two consecutive even numbers is 36. What are the numbers?

POWER BUILDER B

1. 359 – 224 = _____
2. 668 – 330 = _____
3. 845 – 223 = _____
4. 835 – 230 = _____
5. 786 – 135 = _____
6. 6484 – 2150 = _____
7. 4480 – 2180 = _____
8. 7654 – 2533 = _____
9. 7458 – 4247 = _____
10. 89,753 – 57,412 = _____

11. 6.84 – 2.63 = _____
12. 5.07 – 3.05 = _____
13. 7.84 – 5.82 = _____
14. 8.07 – 7.04 = _____
15. 8.87 – 5.66 = _____
16. 12.57 – 2.54 = _____
17. 19.89 – 9.77 = _____
18. 27.56 – 12.34 = _____
19. 51.37 – 41.36 = _____
20. 89.67 – 35.40 = _____

THINK IT THROUGH

The difference between the squares of two consecutive even numbers is 44. What are the numbers?

In mental math, when a subtraction problem needs regrouping . . .

DON'T DO THIS . . .

$$135 - 69$$

DO THIS!

$$135 - 60 = 75$$
$$75 - 9 = 66$$

HELP!

It's much easier to subtract in parts.

✓ Check by adding mentally.

$$66 + 69 = 120 + 15 = 135$$

MENTAL MATH TIP

Use a finger to cover the parts as you think it through.

$$21.6 - 8.7$$

21.6 — 8.7

$$21.6 - 8 = 13.6$$

$$13.6 - 0.7 = 12.9$$

TRY THESE IN YOUR HEAD
Subtract in parts.

1. 75 – 36   **4.** 800 – 53   **7.** 1.35 – 0.65

2. 62 – 23   **5.** 1000 – 475   **8.** 6.25 – 1.45

3. 120 – 57   **6.** 500 – 125   **9.** 8 – 0.53

                                   10. $10.00 – $3.50

POWER BUILDER A

1. 56 − 38 = _____
2. 80 − 44 = _____
3. 65 − 36 = _____
4. 50 − 29 = _____
5. 83 − 35 = _____
6. 90 − 36 = _____
7. 9.0 − 3.6 = _____
8. 8.2 − 1.9 = _____
9. 5.4 − 2.6 = _____
10. 9 − 7.8 = _____

11. 400 − 125 = _____
12. 534 − 225 = _____
13. 800 − 275 = _____
14. 775 − 485 = _____
15. 900 − 355 = _____
16. 1000 − 825 = _____
17. 6.35 − 2.55 = _____
18. 8.37 − 4.38 = _____
19. $20.00 − $3.75 = _____
20. $10.00 − $8.63 = _____

THINK IT THROUGH

The difference between two numbers is 25. If the numbers are tripled, what is the difference between the numbers?

POWER BUILDER B

1. 45 − 27 = _____
2. 60 − 33 = _____
3. 84 − 55 = _____
4. 70 − 38 = _____
5. 93 − 46 = _____
6. 80 − 49 = _____
7. 8.0 − 2.5 = _____
8. 7.8 − 2.9 = _____
9. 7.5 − 2.6 = _____
10. 6 − 3.7 = _____

11. 400 − 150 = _____
12. 627 − 418 = _____
13. 543 − 244 = _____
14. 1000 − 650 = _____
15. 800 − 450 = _____
16. 1000 − 735 = _____
17. 8.25 − 3.45 = _____
18. 9.45 − 3.46 = _____
19. $10.00 − $2.25 = _____
20. $20.00 − $6.55 = _____

THINK IT THROUGH

The difference between two numbers is 19. If the numbers are doubled, what is the difference between the numbers?

Compatible numbers give you a sum that is easy to use in your head. Here are some examples of compatible numbers:

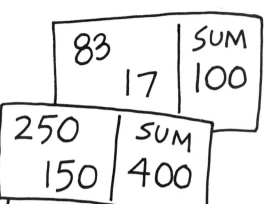

83 17	SUM 100

75 25	SUM 100

130 170	SUM 300

250 150	SUM 400

Which of these problems contain compatible numbers?

What are the sums?

$29 + 71$ $87 + 29$

$465 + 35$

$987 + 27$ $29 + 837$

$222 + 778$

$93 + 7$

$270 + 30$

TRY THESE IN YOUR HEAD.

1. Find compatible pairs that total 100.

89	76	51	24
33	11	31	67
49	55	69	45

2. Find compatible pairs that total 500.

140	350	250	475
201	150	387	360
25	250	299	113

POWER BUILDER A

1. 45 + _____ = 100
2. 73 + _____ = 100
3. 19 + _____ = 100
4. 58 + _____ = 100
5. 37 + _____ = 100
6. 350 + _____ = 1000
7. 275 + _____ = 1000
8. 635 + _____ = 1000
9. 876 + _____ = 1000
10. 444 + _____ = 1000

11. 125 + _____ = 400
12. 239 + _____ = 300
13. 544 + _____ = 700
14. 199 + _____ = 500
15. 436 + _____ = 800
16. 275 + _____ = 500
17. 143 + _____ = 300
18. 333 + _____ = 600
19. 45 + _____ = 200
20. 685 + _____ = 900

THINK IT THROUGH

A 10-m tape breaks at the 565 mm mark.
How much of the tape is left?

POWER BUILDER B

1. 55 + _____ = 100
2. 76 + _____ = 100
3. 29 + _____ = 100
4. 43 + _____ = 100
5. 68 + _____ = 100
6. 250 + _____ = 1000
7. 375 + _____ = 1000
8. 445 + _____ = 1000
9. 759 + _____ = 1000
10. 666 + _____ = 1000

11. 275 + _____ = 400
12. 149 + _____ = 300
13. 233 + _____ = 700
14. 299 + _____ = 500
15. 634 + _____ = 800
16. 175 + _____ = 500
17. 134 + _____ = 300
18. 444 + _____ = 600
19. 35 + _____ = 200
20. 258 + _____ = 900

THINK IT THROUGH

In a 10-km run, Jack quit after 2500 m.
What distance was he from the finish?

$750+275$

Adding in your head is easier when you make your own compatible pairs, then adjust.

Like this . . .

Make your own compatibles.　　　Adjust the answer.

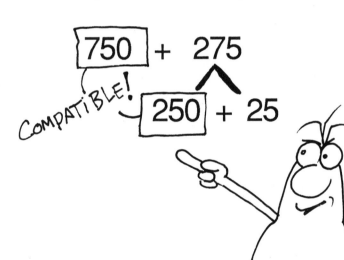

750 + 250 = 1000,

plus 25 → 1025.

So, 750 + 275 = 1025.

TRY THESE IN YOUR HEAD.
Make compatibles and adjust.

1. 75 + 28　　　**4.** 427 + 75　　　**7.** 795 + 206

2. 69 + 35　　　**5.** 450 + 65　　　**8.** 253 + 752

3. 188 + 213　　**6.** 580 + 423　　　**9.** 1150 + 356

　　　　　　　　　　　　　　　　　　　10. 1250 + 757

POWER BUILDER A

1. 25 + 79 = _____

2. 45 + 57 = _____

3. 18 + 85 = _____

4. 75 + 28 = _____

5. 68 + 33 = _____

6. 159 + 42 = _____

7. 125 + 277 = _____

8. 468 + 35 = _____

9. 109 + 393 = _____

10. 254 + 349 = _____

11. 435 + 568 = _____

12. 295 + 706 = _____

13. 455 + 456 = _____

14. 263 + 738 = _____

15. 375 + 526 = _____

16. 276 + 727 = _____

17. 459 + 544 = _____

18. 2500 + 501 = _____

19. 425 + 176 = _____

20. 725 + 277 = _____

THINK IT THROUGH

If 867 + 133 = 1000, what is 867 + 135?
868 + 132? 8.67 + 1.33?

POWER BUILDER B

1. 75 + 26 = _____

2. 35 + 67 = _____

3. 19 + 82 = _____

4. 27 + 75 = _____

5. 65 + 38 = _____

6. 143 + 58 = _____

7. 275 + 127 = _____

8. 235 + 67 = _____

9. 362 + 139 = _____

10. 155 + 249 = _____

11. 345 + 659 = _____

12. 307 + 695 = _____

13. 285 + 717 = _____

14. 155 + 846 = _____

15. 518 + 485 = _____

16. 475 + 426 = _____

17. 365 + 337 = _____

18. 4246 + 555 = _____

19. 425 + 376 = _____

20. 525 + 478 = _____

THINK IT THROUGH

If 655 + 1345 = 2000, what is 655 + 1355?
645 + 1355? 6.55 + 13.45?

When pairs of decimal numbers add to a whole number, we can say they are **compatible.**

It works with money amounts, and it works with plain decimals.

COMPATIBLE PAIRS

$1.10 + $0.90

1.74 + 0.26

$8.45 + $1.55

3.7 + 1.3

Find compatible pairs.

$0.52 $6.90 $5.40

$9.60 $0.67 $0.48

$9.33 $2.50 $3.10

Find compatible pairs.

12.8   4.15   0.85

5.37   2.4   94.63

9.15   3.85   2.6

TRY THESE IN YOUR HEAD.

1. Find compatible pairs that add to $1.00.

$0.85 $0.29 $0.35

$0.71 $0.15 $0.41

$0.34 $0.65 $0.66

2. Find compatible pairs that add to 10.

0.85   6.20   5.10

2.75   4.55   9.15

3.80   4.90   7.25

POWER BUILDER A

1. $0.52 + _____ = $1.00
2. $0.69 +_____ = $1.00
3. _____ + 0.36 = 1
4. _____ + 0.88 = 1
5. 0.41 + _____ = 1
6. $2.45 +_____ = $10.00
7. $4.51 + _____ = $10.00
8. 9.38 + _____ = 10
9. _____ + 3.69 = 10
10. _____ + 5.74 = 10

11. $4.95 + _____ = $5.00
12. $3.69 + _____ = $5.00
13. _____ + 1.63 = 5
14. 1.7 + _____ = 5
15. 8.2 + _____ = 10
16. _____ + 4.4 = 10
17. _____ + 17.64 = 20
18. 0.74 + _____ = 10
19. 9.345 + _____ = 10
20. _____ + 4.745 = 5

THINK IT THROUGH

Megan has only dimes and quarters. She has the same number of quarters as dimes. If she has $3.85, how many quarters does she have?

POWER BUILDER B

1. $0.64 + _____ = $1.00
2. $0.73 + _____ = $1.00
3. _____ + $0.44 = $1.00
4. _____ + 0.77 = 1
5. 0.39 + _____ = 1
6. $3.35 + _____ = $10.00
7. $6.52 + _____ = $10.00
8. 8.28 + _____ = 10
9. _____ + 4.59 = 10
10. _____ + 6.68 = 10

11. $3.72 + _____ = $5.00
12. $3.57 + _____ = $5.00
13. _____ + 1.59 = 5
14. 2.6 + _____ = 5
15. 7.3 + _____ = 10
16. _____ + 5.5 = 10
17. _____ + 18.38 = 20
18. 0.74 + _____ = 10
19. 9.125 + _____ = 10
20. _____ + 4.085 = 5

THINK IT THROUGH

Josh has only dimes and quarters. He has the same number of quarters as dimes. The total value of the quarters is 75¢ more than the total value of the dimes. How much money does he have?

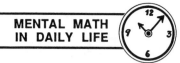

Mental math is a handy tool
when you want to know
how much time is left.

NOW
9:17

LUNCH
12:00

How long before lunch?

To figure the difference between two times,
add on in steps.

9:17
9:20
10:00
12:00

3 minutes

+

40 minutes　→　43 minutes

+

2 hours　→　2 hours　43 minutes

TRY THESE IN YOUR HEAD.
Figure the difference by adding on.

1.	9:20 A.M.	10:00 A.M.	**6.**	9:15 A.M.	1:45 P.M.
2.	12:30 P.M.	3:00 P.M.	**7.**	8:50 A.M.	10:05 A.M.
3.	6:55 P.M.	9:00 P.M.	**8.**	5:15 P.M.	7:30 P.M.
4.	8:15 A.M.	12:15 P.M.	**9.**	3:35 A.M.	12:00 noon
5.	3:20 P.M.	8:50 P.M.	**10.**	2:15 P.M.	11:00 P.M.

POWER BUILDER A

1. From 9:00 A.M. to 10:40 A.M. = _____
2. From 7:30 P.M. to 10:40 P.M. = _____
3. From 2:10 P.M. to 9:25 P.M. = _____
4. From 8:25 A.M. to 11:45 A.M. = _____
5. From 12:15 P.M. to 6:30 P.M. = _____
6. From 11:20 A.M. to 4:30 P.M. = _____
7. From 7:35 A.M. to 11:45 A.M. = _____
8. From 1:05 P.M. to 8:55 P.M. = _____
9. From 3:15 P.M. to 9:45 P.M. = _____
10. From 7:45 A.M. to 10:55 A.M. = _____

11. From 2:45 P.M. to 5:20 P.M. = _____
12. From 3:30 P.M. to 8:45 P.M. = _____
13. From 5:10 A.M. to 11:05 A.M. = _____
14. From 7:35 P.M. to 8:20 P.M. = _____
15. From 5:25 P.M. to 11:10 P.M. = _____
16. From 7:20 A.M. to 8:15 A.M. = _____
17. From 11:30 A.M. to 2:25 P.M. = _____
18. From 8:50 A.M. to 7:50 P.M. = _____
19. From 9:15 P.M. to 12:05 A.M. = _____
20. From 8:45 A.M. to 3:25 P.M. = _____

THINK IT THROUGH

Juan started a marathon race at 9:15 A.M. and finished the race 2 hours and 47 minutes later. At what time did Juan finish the race?

POWER BUILDER B

1. From 8:00 P.M. to 11:40 P.M. = _____
2. From 5:30 P.M. to 11:40 P.M. = _____
3. From 4:10 P.M. to 8:30 P.M. = _____
4. From 7:15 A.M. to 10:35 A.M. = _____
5. From 12:25 P.M. to 7:45 P.M. = _____
6. From 11:25 A.M. to 3:45 P.M. = _____
7. From 6:45 A.M. to 11:55 A.M. = _____
8. From 2:05 P.M. to 9:45 P.M. = _____
9. From 2:20 P.M. to 8:40 P.M. = _____
10. From 5:35 P.M. to 11:55 P.M. = _____

11. From 1:40 P.M. to 3:20 P.M. = _____
12. From 5:20 A.M. to 7:45 A.M. = _____
13. From 4:15 A.M. to 8:10 A.M. = _____
14. From 6:25 P.M. to 9:20 P.M. = _____
15. From 4:15 P.M. to 11:10 P.M. = _____
16. From 6:15 P.M. to 8:05 P.M. = _____
17. From 11:40 A.M. to 3:25 P.M. = _____
18. From 7:40 A.M. to 8:35 A.M. = _____
19. From 8:15 A.M. to 12:10 P.M. = _____
20. From 8:25 P.M. to 7:30 A.M. = _____

THINK IT THROUGH

Sarah ran a marathon race in 3 hours and 19 minutes. If the race started at 10:45 A.M., at what time did she finish?

When you are buying something with a large bill, you may want to check your change.

Here's a way that's easier than trying to subtract in your head.

You can figure the difference by "adding up" from the purchase price.

$$\$10.00 5¢$$
$$9.95 30¢$$
$$9.65$$
$$\$5$$
$$\$4.65$$

$5 + 30¢ + 5¢
Change is
$5.35.

Here's a mental shortcut to help you check your change.

PRICE $7.15

$20

$13 is too many dollars, so it must be $12 . . . and another 85 cents, or $12.85.

TRY THESE IN YOUR HEAD
Check your change . . .

. . .from $10.

1. $3.25
2. $5.45
3. $2.85
4. $4.37
5. $7.65

. . . from $20.

6. $4.85
7. $5.50
8. $7.55
9. $13.75
10. $16.25

POWER BUILDER A

What is your change?

1. Have $10, spend $3.75 = _____
2. Have $10, spend $1.87 = _____
3. Have $10, spend $7.45 = _____
4. Have $10, spend $4.98 = _____
5. Have $10, spend $0.78 = _____
6. Have $20, spend $14.35 = _____
7. Have $20, spend $9.75 = _____
8. Have $20, spend $12.34 = _____
9. Have $20, spend $2.69 = _____
10. Have $20, spend $19.43 = _____

11. Have $15, spend $12.46 = _____
12. Have $5, spend $2.26 = _____
13. Have $30, spend $26.84 = _____
14. Have $40, spend $32.95 = _____
15. Have $15, spend $10.81 = _____
16. Have $20, spend $14.44 = _____
17. Have $50, spend $43.49 = _____
18. Have $80, spend $77.77 = _____
19. Have $100, spend $54.86 = _____
20. Have $100, spend $73.65 = _____

THINK IT THROUGH

What is the least number of coins you need
to pay, in exact change, any amount less than
one dollar?

POWER BUILDER B

What is your change?

1. Have $10, spend $4.28 = _____
2. Have $10, spend $2.93 = _____
3. Have $10, spend $6.55 = _____
4. Have $10, spend $5.04 = _____
5. Have $10, spend $0.89 = _____
6. Have $20, spend $9.85 = _____
7. Have $20, spend $14.55 = _____
8. Have $20, spend $12.47 = _____
9. Have $20, spend $3.59 = _____
10. Have $20, spend $19.37 = _____

11. Have $15, spend $13.07 = _____
12. Have $5, spend $1.79 = _____
13. Have $30, spend $27.18 = _____
14. Have $40, spend $31.86 = _____
15. Have $15, spend $10.81 = _____
16. Have $20, spend $13.33 = _____
17. Have $50, spend $44.44 = _____
18. Have $80, spend $16.66 = _____
19. Have $100, spend $51.48 = _____
20. Have $100, spend $89.69 = _____

THINK IT THROUGH

What is the least number of coins you need
to pay, in exact change, any amount less than
one half dollar?

Mental Math Techniques
• **ADD FROM THE LEFT.** $245 + 138 = 300 + 70 + 13$
• **SUBTRACT FROM THE LEFT.** $5.78 - 3.45$
• **BREAK IT UP.** $140 + 285 = 140 + 200 + 80 + 5$
• **BREAK UP AND BRIDGE.** $4.5 + 2.7 = 6.5 + 0.7$
• **USE COMPATIBLES.** $3.85 + 1.99 = 3.84 + 2$

Do the problems below in your head. Tell which techniques you find useful for each one.

1. $527 + 36$
2. $2 - 1.95$
3. $965 - 342$
4. $1000 - 350$
5. $145 + 38 + 56$
6. $100 - 73$
7. $0.15 + 0.65$
8. $4.37 + 0.48 + 0.16$
9. $457 + 298$
10. $350 + 455$

Talk about each problem below. What's an easy way to do it in your head? Tell how you would think it through.

1. $1000 - 475$
2. $636 + 48$
3. $465 + 236$
4. $344 + 38 + 76$
5. $4275 - 3160$
6. $14.6 + 3.8 + 6.7$
7. $\$4 - \$2.27$
8. $857 + 498$
9. $1.55 + 3.45$
10. $100 - 87$

1. $150 + 172 =$ _____

2. $8.1 - 2.9 =$ _____

3. $375 + 226 =$ _____

4. $10 - 0.77 =$ _____

5. The difference in time from 9:15 A.M. to 12:30 P.M. = _____

6. $325 + 265 =$ _____

7. $74 - 35 =$ _____

8. $348 + 155 =$ _____

9. The difference in time from 8:00 A.M. to 11:45 A.M. = _____

10. $6.7 - 4.3 =$ _____

11. $\$10.00 - \$4.69 =$ _____

12. $5 - 1.36 =$ _____

13. $\$20 - \$15.50 =$ _____

14. $355 + 38 =$ _____

15. $476 - 125 =$ _____

16. $1000 - 829 =$ _____

17. $\$10 - \$4.37 =$ _____

18. The difference in time from 11:15 A.M. to 7:30 P.M. = _____

19. $545 + 128 =$ _____

20. $\$0.65 + \$0.25 =$ _____

21. $100 - 67 =$ _____

22. $\$20 - \$1.78 =$ _____

23. $5.5 + 1.7 =$ _____

24. $23.7 + 5.5 =$ _____

25. $2.6 + 0.6 + 1.3 =$ _____

26. $500 - 275 =$ _____

27. $3 - 1.254 =$ _____

28. $\$1.45 + \$0.25 + \$1.30 + \$1.15 =$ _____

29. $47 + 26 =$ _____

30. $1 - 0.67 =$ _____

31. $1000 - 455 =$ _____

32. The difference in time from 2:35 P.M. to 9:30 P.M. = _____

33. $9150 + 275 =$ _____

34. $800 - 445 =$ _____

35. $595 + 308 =$ _____

36. $9 + 16 + 25 + 18 =$ _____

37. $4.75 - 1.35 =$ _____

38. $\$100 - \$75.88 =$ _____

39. $369 - 36 =$ _____

40. $75 + 27 =$ _____

The "Teens" Times Table

Most of us learn the multiplication tables so well that when we are asked "6 times 5," we immediately say "30."

MENTALMATHLETES learn to multiply larger numbers so quickly that they can give the answer as fast as if they had memorized it.

Here's a way to multiply the "teens" numbers in your head so rapidly that people will think you know them by heart.

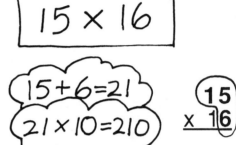

1. Add one teens number to the ones digit of the other.

2. Multiply that sum by 10.

3. Multiply the ones digits.

4. Add this to your answer above.

$$15 + 6 = 21$$
$$21 \times 10 = 210$$
$$6 \times 5 = 30$$
$$210 + 30 = 240$$

$$\begin{array}{r} 15 \\ \times\ 16 \end{array}$$

$$\begin{array}{r} 15 \\ \times\ 16 \end{array}$$

With a bit of practice, no one will be able to tell whether you're figuring or remembering!

YOUR TURN
Use this method to construct a teens times table.

X	11	12	13	14	15	16	17	18	19
11									
12									
13									
.									
.									
.									
19									

The "Teens" Times Table

To demonstrate why this rule works, expand each "teen" number as illustrated below:

$$
\begin{array}{r}
15 \\
\times 16 \\
\hline
\end{array}
\rightarrow
$$

$$
\begin{array}{r}
15 \times \quad 10 \times 10 \\
5 \times 10 \\
+ \ 6 \times \quad 6 \times 10 \\
\hline
\longrightarrow (21) \times 10 = 210 \\
6 \times 5 = \ \underline{30} \\
240
\end{array}
$$

Encourage students to develop other shortcut rules to complete the teens times table. For example, here are two of many other ways to think as you multiply 15 and 16:

$$
\begin{array}{r}
15 \\
\times 16 \\
\hline
\end{array}
\rightarrow
\begin{array}{r}
15 \\
\times 10 \times 6 \\
\hline
150 \\
+ \ 90 \\
\hline
240
\end{array}
$$

$$
\begin{array}{r}
15 \\
\times 16 \quad (=4 \times 4)
\end{array}
\qquad
\begin{array}{r}
15 \\
\times 4 \\
\hline
60 \\
\times 4 \\
\hline
240
\end{array}
$$

$2.75 + 4.26$

That's hard to do in my head!

With an addition problem involving decimals, you can often make it easier. Just make your own compatible pairs.

Make it easier, then adjust.

THINK . . .

2.75 + 4.26
(4.25) + 0.01

2.75 + 4.25 = 7

7 + 0.01 = 7.01

← ADD COMPATIBLES →

← NOW ADJUST →

OR, YOU MIGHT THINK . . .

2.75 + 4.26
(0.25) + 4.01

2.75 + 0.25 = 3

3 + 4.01 = 7.01

There are often several different compatible pairs.
Pick whichever numbers work well for you.

TRY THESE IN YOUR HEAD.
Make compatibles and adjust.

1. 3.27 + 2.75   **4.** 1.28 + 1.28   **7.** $2.55 + $3.54

2. 8.92 + 4.09   **5.** 4.85 + 1.19   **8.** $1.75 + $2.79

3. 3.57 + 3.57   **6.** 8.29 + 1.75   **9.** $15.27 + $15.29

10. $4.57 + $3.56

POWER BUILDER A

1. 1.75 + 3.28 = _____
2. 1.65 + 2.37 = _____
3. 2.45 + 3.56 = _____
4. 4.49 + 4.49 = _____
5. 2.27 + 1.27 = _____
6. $3.85 + $2.19 = _____
7. $4.29 + $2.75 = _____
8. $2.75 + $1.76 = _____
9. $3.08 + $4.93 = _____
10. $4.69 + $1.34 = _____

11. 2.27 + 2.28 = _____
12. 4.55 + 2.47 = _____
13. 3.56 + 3.56 = _____
14. 1.77 + 2.78 = _____
15. 2.58 + 3.44 = _____
16. $1.16 + $2.85 = _____
17. $15.27 + $3.75 = _____
18. $1.77 + $4.77 = _____
19. $12.07 + $13.95 = _____
20. $5.47 + $8.49 = _____

THINK IT THROUGH

Kim was born on January 21, 1988.
John was born on December 15, 1986.
How much older is John?

POWER BUILDER B

1. 2.75 + 2.29 = _____
2. 1.65 + 4.36 = _____
3. 4.45 + 5.57 = _____
4. 2.48 + 2.48 = _____
5. 3.26 + 3.26 = _____
6. $2.85 + $1.19 = _____
7. $4.28 + $3.75 = _____
8. $8.77 + $1.77 = _____
9. $5.07 + $5.94 = _____
10. $2.68 + $4.35 = _____

11. 1.29 + 1.29 = _____
12. 5.55 + 44.48 = _____
13. 4.57 + 4.57 = _____
14. 7.79 + 7.22 = _____
15. 2.56 + 8.45 = _____
16. $9.15 + $7.88 = _____
17. $4.26 + $9.75 = _____
18. $3.76 + $3.76 = _____
19. $9.06 + $7.95 = _____
20. $3.48 + $5.48 = _____

THINK IT THROUGH

Terry was born on July 4, 1986.
Merry was born on August 3, 1987.
How much older is Terry?

When you add the same amount to each number
in a subtraction problem, the answer does not change.

Adding to both numbers **balances** the problem.

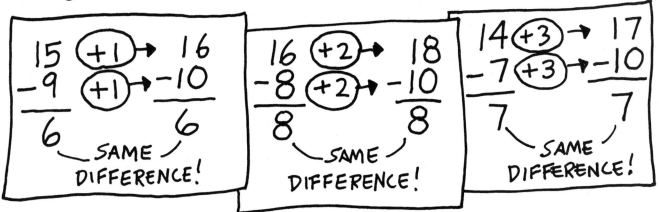

Balancing can sometimes make
subtraction easier to do in your head.

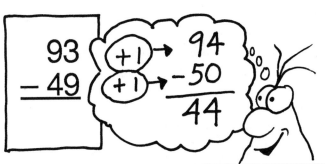
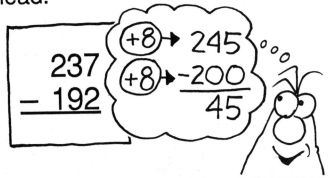

MENTAL MATH TIP ➤ Add whatever you need to change
the subtrahend (second number)
into an easily subtracted number.

TRY THESE IN YOUR HEAD.
Use balancing to make it easier.

1. 96 – 59	**4.** 132 – 88	**7.** 583 – 298
2. 65 – 19	**5.** 151 – 97	**8.** 846 – 399
3. 76 – 27	**6.** 233 – 95	**9.** 2100 – 1998
		10. 4363 – 3999

POWER BUILDER A

1. 85 − 49 = _____
2. 73 − 59 = _____
3. 84 − 37 = _____
4. 62 − 28 = _____
5. 126 − 89 = _____
6. 253 − 78 = _____
7. 461 − 95 = _____
8. 282 − 99 = _____
9. 544 − 77 = _____
10. 632 − 88 = _____

11. 469 − 198 = _____
12. 753 − 187 = _____
13. 641 − 285 = _____
14. 704 − 475 = _____
15. 333 − 189 = _____
16. 4874 − 596 = _____
17. 8343 − 997 = _____
18. 6454 − 2198 = _____
19. 7826 − 1997 = _____
20. 9544 − 7985 = _____

THINK IT THROUGH

Subtract the largest 3-digit odd number from the largest 4-digit even number.

POWER BUILDER B

1. 76 − 39 = _____
2. 84 − 48 = _____
3. 92 − 67 = _____
4. 65 − 38 = _____
5. 146 − 79 = _____
6. 273 − 85 = _____
7. 372 − 96 = _____
8. 233 − 99 = _____
9. 444 − 77 = _____
10. 745 − 78 = _____

11. 457 − 199 = _____
12. 845 − 188 = _____
13. 832 − 395 = _____
14. 803 − 565 = _____
15. 666 − 178 = _____
16. 6752 − 375 = _____
17. 9254 − 1999 = _____
18. 7243 − 4998 = _____
19. 8435 − 2997 = _____
20. 9635 − 8988 = _____

THINK IT THROUGH

Subtract the largest 4-digit odd number from the smallest 5-digit even number.

Which problem would
you rather do in your head?

$$3.42 - 1.96$$

$$3.46 - 2$$

They look different,
but they are really
the same problem.

Balance by adding 0.04 . . .

$$
\begin{array}{rcl}
3.42 & + \ 0.04 \ \rightarrow & 3.46 \\
- \ 1.96 & + \ 0.04 \ \rightarrow & - \ 2. \\
\hline
\end{array}
$$

That's how balancing can
make a problem easier.

How could you make
these problems easier
by balancing?

$$
\begin{array}{r}
7.84 \\
- \ 1.95 \\
\hline
\end{array}
$$

$$
\begin{array}{r}
1.17 \\
- \ 0.89 \\
\hline
\end{array}
$$

TRY THESE IN YOUR HEAD.
Use balancing to make them easier.

1. $4.15 - 1.9$ **4.** $8.1 - 0.7$ **7.** $3.53 - 0.88$

2. $6.4 - 3.8$ **5.** $4.23 - 1.98$ **8.** $5.75 - 0.96$

3. $9.3 - 6.9$ **6.** $7.45 - 4.98$ **9.** $8.22 - 1.94$

                                                 10. $15.362 - 4.989$

POWER BUILDER A

1. 4.7 – 2.9 = _____
2. 7.1 – 3.8 = _____
3. 9.2 – 4.7 = _____
4. 6.3 – 2.8 = _____
5. 5.14 – 0.98 = _____
6. 6.33 – 0.87 = _____
7. 8.21 – 0.95 = _____
8. 7.42 – 0.97 = _____
9. 9.32 – 2.94 = _____
10. 8.15 – 5.79 = _____

11. 6.24 – 3.86 = _____
12. 9.23 – 4.96 = _____
13. 14.52 – 3.99 = _____
14. 22.62 – 15.89 = _____
15. 36.03 – 25.95 = _____
16. 82.32 – 19.96 = _____
17. 5.276 – 1.999 = _____
18. 15.825 – 7.998 = _____
19. 23.543 – 13.985 = _____
20. 45.007 – 19.998 = _____

THINK IT THROUGH

Take the largest 3-digit decimal less than one and double it. What do you need to add to get a sum of 4?

POWER BUILDER B

1. 5.6 – 3.9 = _____
2. 8.2 – 4.7 = _____
3. 7.5 – 5.8 = _____
4. 7.2 – 3.9 = _____
5. 6.15 – 0.99 = _____
6. 7.33 – 0.88 = _____
7. 7.22 – 0.96 = _____
8. 8.31 – 0.97 = _____
9. 8.25 – 4.96 = _____
10. 9.17 – 4.88 = _____

11. 5.21 – 1.89 = _____
12. 8.34 – 2.87 = _____
13. 15.41 – 4.99 = _____
14. 21.43 – 20.99 = _____
15. 23.05 – 19.98 = _____
16. 75.34 – 29.97 = _____
17. 41.85 – 1.999 = _____
18. 12.940 – 6.998 = _____
19. 42.342 – 20.987 = _____
20. 50.002 – 30.999 = _____

THINK IT THROUGH

Take the largest 2-digit decimal less than one and triple it. What do you need to subtract to have a difference of 1?

Notice what happens when one
factor is multiplied by 10 . . .
The product is also multiplied by 10.

$$\begin{array}{r} 5 \\ \times\,3 \\ \hline 15 \end{array}$$ (x 10)→ $$\begin{array}{r} 50 \\ \times\,3 \\ \hline 150 \end{array}$$

You can use that idea to multiply numbers with trailing zeros.

For each time that a factor is multiplied by 10,
tack another trailing zero onto the product.

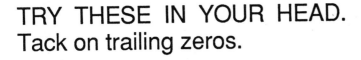

Remember these steps:

- Remove the trailing zeros.

- Multiply the remaining numbers.

- Tack on **ALL** the zeros.

60 x 300

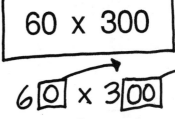

6 x 3 = 18

18 000

TRY THESE IN YOUR HEAD.
Tack on trailing zeros.

1. 4 x 20

2. 4 x 50

3. 50 x 20

4. 50 x 50

5. 300 x 9

6. 7 x 800

7. 90 x 30

8. 5 x 8000

9. 30 x 500

10. 200 x 300

POWER BUILDER A

1. 7 x 30 = _____
2. 8 x 60 = _____
3. 9 x 20 = _____
4. 5 x 40 = _____
5. 500 x 9 = _____
6. 300 x 8 = _____
7. 5 x 800 = _____
8. 30 x 200 = _____
9. 400 x 60 = _____
10. 70 x 500 = _____

11. 50 x 600 = _____
12. 300 x 50 = _____
13. 90 x 200 = _____
14. 7 x 8000 = _____
15. 50 x 6000 = _____
16. 800 x 700 = _____
17. 900 x 500 = _____
18. 7000 x 60 = _____
19. 300 x 700 = _____
20. 50 x 8000 = _____

THINK IT THROUGH

List all the different products that can be formed by multiplying any two numbers on this card.

40	30
60	20

POWER BUILDER B

1. 6 x 40 = _____
2. 7 x 50 = _____
3. 8 x 30 = _____
4. 5 x 60 = _____
5. 500 x 7 = _____
6. 300 x 6 = _____
7. 5 x 400 = _____
8. 20 x 400 = _____
9. 600 x 40 = _____
10. 500 x 90 = _____

11. 50 x 200 = _____
12. 500 x 50 = _____
13. 70 x 400 = _____
14. 3 x 600 = _____
15. 50 x 8000 = _____
16. 600 x 300 = _____
17. 800 x 500 = _____
18. 8000 x 60 = _____
19. 200 x 600 = _____
20. 50 x 4000 = _____

THINK IT THROUGH

List all the different products that can be formed by multiplying any two numbers on this card.

800	30
600	40

$$\begin{array}{r} 524 \\ \times\ \ 3 \\ \hline \end{array}$$

Multiplying in your head is easier if you break a number into parts and multiply the front-end numbers first.

- Break up 524.

- Multiply from the front to the back . . .

- Add as you go along.

$$500 + 20 + 4$$

$$\begin{array}{r} 500 \\ \times\ \ 3 \\ \hline 1500 \end{array} \quad \begin{array}{r} 20 \\ \times 3 \\ \hline 60 \end{array} \quad \begin{array}{r} 4 \\ \times 3 \\ \hline 12 \end{array}$$

$$1560 + 12$$

$$1572$$

MENTAL MATH TIP > Focus on the left (front-end) digits by covering the others.

$$\begin{array}{r} 5\ 24 \\ \times\ \ 3 \\ \hline \end{array}$$

TRY THESE IN YOUR HEAD. Multiply from the front.

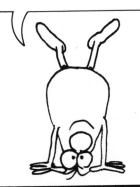

1. 4 x 55   **4.** 8 x 25   **7.** 2 x 545

2. 4 x 76   **5.** 4 x 625   **8.** 8 x 625

3. 45 x 6   **6.** 405 x 3   **9.** 450 x 5

10. 3 x 235

POWER BUILDER A

1. 6 x 28 = _____

2. 5 x 82 = _____

3. 7 x 36 = _____

4. 5 x 66 = _____

5. 4 x 84 = _____

6. 6 x 45 = _____

7. 8 x 53 = _____

8. 9 x 72 = _____

9. 4 x 126 = _____

10. 4 x 325 = _____

11. 5 x 218 = _____

12. 2 x 849 = _____

13. 6 x 55 = _____

14. 3 x 428 = _____

15. 7 x 450 = _____

16. 4 x 825 = _____

17. 5 x 315 = _____

18. 3 x 675 = _____

19. 4 x 925 = _____

20. 6 x 215 = _____

THINK IT THROUGH

Look at the number sentences in the box.
Find a pattern and use it to mentally calculate
15 x 37 and 21 x 37.

3 x 37 = 111
6 x 37 = 222
9 x 37 = 333
12 x 37 = 444

POWER BUILDER B

1. 7 x 27 = _____

2. 5 x 62 = _____

3. 8 x 46 = _____

4. 5 x 66 = _____

5. 4 x 84 = _____

6. 6 x 45 = _____

7. 8 x 53 = _____

8. 9 x 72 = _____

9. 3 x 126 = _____

10. 4 x 625 = _____

11. 5 x 219 = _____

12. 2 x 849 = _____

13. 4 x 65 = _____

14. 3 x 428 = _____

15. 7 x 450 = _____

16. 4 x 825 = _____

17. 5 x 315 = _____

18. 3 x 675 = _____

19. 8 x 525 = _____

20. 5 x 319 = _____

THINK IT THROUGH

Look at the number sentences in the box.
Find a pattern and use it to mentally calculate
28 x 15,873 and 42 x 15,873.

7 x 15,873 = 111,111
14 x 15,873 = 222,222
21 x 15,873 = 333,333

Pie _____ $1.25
Muffins (dozen) ___ $2.40
Tarts (dozen) ___ $2.15
Wheat bread (loaf) __ $.75
Nut bread (loaf) ___ $1.25
Rolls (dozen) ___ $1.20
Cake _____ $2.75

How much should I charge for 4 dozen tarts?

SchOOl BAKE SALE

Front-end multiplication is handy when you are buying or selling things.

Multiply the dollars first . . .

    then the dimes . . .

      and then the cents.

Add as you go along.

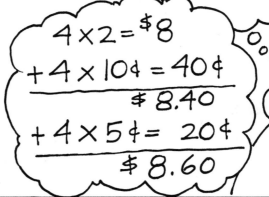

4 x $2.15

$$4 \times 2 = \$8$$
$$+ 4 \times 10¢ = 40¢$$
$$\overline{\quad\quad\quad \$8.40}$$
$$+ 4 \times 5¢ = 20¢$$
$$\overline{\quad\quad\quad \$8.60}$$

MENTAL MATH TIP ▷   **THINK** $8, $8.40, $8.60

TRY THESE IN YOUR HEAD.
Multiply from the dollars to the cents.

1. 2 pies
2. 4 dozen muffins
3. 4 loaves wheat bread
4. 3 dozen rolls
5. 5 loaves nut bread

6. 5 dozen muffins
7. 6 pies
8. 4 dozen rolls, 1 pie
9. 2 pies, 2 cakes
10. 2 dozen tarts, 2 dozen rolls

POWER BUILDER A

Calculate the total price for:

1. 2 at $1.25 each = _____

2. 4 at $2.35 each = _____

3. 3 at $4.25 each = _____

4. 5 at $0.95 each = _____

5. 7 at $0.49 each = _____

6. 3 at $3.35 each = _____

7. 4 at $7.19 each = _____

8. 5 at $3.30 each = _____

9. 6 at $4.25 each = _____

10. 2 at $7.39 each = _____

11. 2 at $10.40 each = _____

12. 5 at $21.19 each = _____

13. 3 at $29.15 each = _____

14. 2 at $49.50 each = _____

15. 4 at $25.25 each = _____

16. 3 at $33.33 each = _____

17. 2 at $0.35 and 4 at $0.45 each = _____

18. 1 at $1.79 and 2 at $2.50 each = _____

19. 3 at $4.25 and 2 at $1.50 each = _____

20. 1 at $7.77 and 2 at $3.50 each = _____

THINK IT THROUGH

The distilled water costs $0.69. The starch costs twice as much as the distilled water. The soap costs $3 more than the starch. How much does the soap cost?

POWER BUILDER B

Calculate the total price for:

1. 3 at $1.35 each = _____

2. 2 at $1.89 each = _____

3. 5 at $0.85 each = _____

4. 4 at $3.25 each = _____

5. 6 at $0.49 each = _____

6. 2 at $2.55 each = _____

7. 3 at $7.26 each = _____

8. 6 at $4.20 each = _____

9. 7 at $2.25 each = _____

10. 2 at $9.29 each = _____

11. 2 at $20.45 each = _____

12. 5 at $31.19 each = _____

13. 4 at $35.15 each = _____

14. 8 at $6.50 each = _____

15. 4 at $45.50 each = _____

16. 3 at $21.75 each = _____

17. 1 at $8.88 and 2 at $0.55 each = _____

18. 2 at $0.79 and 2 at $1.50 each = _____

19. 4 at $5.25 and 6 at $1.20 each = _____

20. 1 at $13.49 and 2 at $4.25 each = ___

THINK IT THROUGH

The filter costs $4.88. The oil costs $1.38 less than the filter. The labor costs three times the cost of the oil. How much does the labor cost?

DIVIDE IN YOUR HEAD

$$1200 \div 4$$

Numbers with trailing zeros are easy to divide in your head.

Follow these steps.

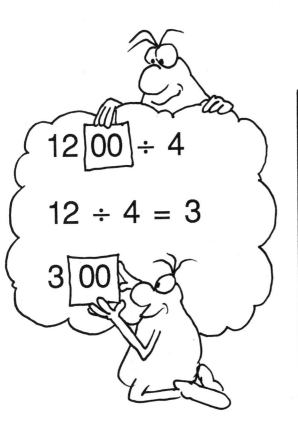

$$12\boxed{00} \div 4$$

$$12 \div 4 = 3$$

$$3\boxed{00}$$

- Remove the trailing zeros.

- Divide the remaining numbers.

- Tack the trailing zeros onto your answer.

$$\checkmark\; 4 \times 3\boxed{00} = 12\boxed{00}$$ • Check by multiplying.

TRY THESE IN YOUR HEAD.
Cut off and tack on the trailing zeros.

1. $1200 \div 2$ **4.** $7\overline{)2800}$ **7.** $9\overline{)27{,}000}$

2. $2400 \div 8$ **5.** $4\overline{)360}$ **8.** $3600 \div 6$

3. $1000 \div 5$ **6.** $12\overline{)2400}$ **9.** $3500 \div 35$

10. $15\overline{)3000}$

POWER BUILDER A

1. $2400 \div 6 =$ _____

2. $320 \div 8 =$ _____

3. $7 \overline{)420} =$ _____

4. $7 \overline{)3500} =$ _____

5. $4 \overline{)280} =$ _____

6. $7 \overline{)4900} =$ _____

7. $540 \div 6 =$ _____

8. $5600 \div 8 =$ _____

9. $2400 \div 3 =$ _____

10. $5 \overline{)3500} =$ _____

11. $1800 \div 2 =$ _____

12. $9 \overline{)18,000} =$ _____

13. $42,000 \div 6 =$ _____

14. $6 \overline{)120,000} =$ _____

15. $2500 \div 25 =$ _____

16. $48,000 \div 6 =$ _____

17. $72,000 \div 8 =$ _____

18. $7 \overline{)21,000} =$ _____

19. $5 \overline{)250,000} =$ _____

20. $3 \overline{)21,000} =$ _____

THINK IT THROUGH

How many 5-cent stamps can you buy for $25?

POWER BUILDER B

1. $3200 \div 4 =$ _____

2. $400 \div 8 =$ _____

3. $4 \overline{)280} =$ _____

4. $7 \overline{)4200} =$ _____

5. $9 \overline{)270} =$ _____

6. $8 \overline{)4800} =$ _____

7. $540 \div 6 =$ _____

8. $6300 \div 7 =$ _____

9. $2400 \div 3 =$ _____

10. $5 \overline{)2500} =$ _____

11. $1600 \div 2 =$ _____

12. $8 \overline{)16,000} =$ _____

13. $42,000 \div 6 =$ _____

14. $4 \overline{)160,000} =$ _____

15. $1500 \div 15 =$ _____

16. $36,000 \div 6 =$ _____

17. $56,000 \div 8 =$ _____

18. $7 \overline{)21,000} =$ _____

19. $5 \overline{)45,000} =$ _____

20. $3 \overline{)27,000} =$ _____

THINK IT THROUGH

How many 5-cent stamps can you buy for $100?

You can divide both numbers in a division problem by the same amount without changing the answer.

Using this idea, it's easy to simplify a problem when both numbers have trailing zeros.

SHORTCUT:

Cancel the common trailing zeros.

$8000 \div 400$

Check by multiplying.

TRY THESE IN YOUR HEAD.
Cancel the common trailing zeros.

1. $9000 \div 30$
2. $900 \div 300$
3. $9000 \div 3000$

4. $800 \div 20$
5. $1000 \div 50$
6. $2000 \div 50$

7. $5000 \div 50$
8. $3600 \div 900$
9. $10,000 \div 100$

10. $1,000,000 \div 2000$

POWER BUILDER A

1. $800 \div 40 =$ _____
2. $12,000 \div 600 =$ _____
3. $15,000 \div 30 =$ _____
4. $2400 \div 80 =$ _____
5. $60 \overline{)3600} =$ _____
6. $90 \overline{)72,000} =$ _____
7. $400 \overline{)32,000} =$ _____
8. $50 \overline{)350} =$ _____
9. $800 \overline{)4800} =$ _____
10. $4900 \div 70 =$ _____

11. $600 \overline{)1200} =$ _____
12. $50 \overline{)40,000} =$ _____
13. $72,000 \div 900 =$ _____
14. $800 \overline{)3200} =$ _____
15. $30,000 \div 60 =$ _____
16. $45,000 \div 90 =$ _____
17. $500 \overline{)20,000} =$ _____
18. $70 \overline{)4200} =$ _____
19. $81,000 \div 900 =$ _____
20. $45,000 \div 50 =$ _____

THINK IT THROUGH

The state gets a tax of 10¢ for every dollar of gasoline sold. How many dollars does the state get for gasoline sales of $400,000?

POWER BUILDER B

1. $600 \div 30 =$ _____
2. $16,000 \div 400 =$ _____
3. $18,000 \div 60 =$ _____
4. $3200 \div 80 =$ _____
5. $50 \overline{)2500} =$ _____
6. $80 \overline{)6400} =$ _____
7. $300 \overline{)27,000} =$ _____
8. $50 \overline{)450} =$ _____
9. $600 \overline{)4800} =$ _____
10. $8100 \div 90 =$ _____

11. $300 \overline{)1200} =$ _____
12. $50 \overline{)30,000} =$ _____
13. $56,000 \div 700 =$ _____
14. $400 \overline{)2800} =$ _____
15. $40,000 \div 80 =$ _____
16. $54,000 \div 90 =$ _____
17. $500 \overline{)30,000} =$ _____
18. $80 \overline{)7200} =$ _____
19. $63,000 \div 900 =$ _____
20. $35,000 \div 50 =$ _____

THINK IT THROUGH

The state gets a tax of 15¢ for every dollar of gasoline sold. How much money does the state get on gasoline sales of $600,000?

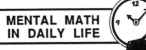

Often, when traveling by car, you may wonder how long it will take to get where you're going.

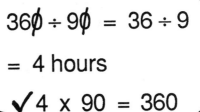

At 90 Km/h... How much longer?

CALGARY 360 km

It's easy to figure the time in your head. Just divide the distance by your speed.

Check by multiplying.

$$360 \div 90 = 36 \div 9$$
$$= 4 \text{ hours}$$
$$\checkmark 4 \times 90 = 360$$

You can use either kilometers or miles to measure distance and speed, as long as you don't mix them in the same problem.

50 60 70
SPEED - MPH

ST. LOUIS 180 miles

$$180 \div 60 = 3 \text{ hours}$$
$$\checkmark 3 \times 60 = 180$$

TRY THESE IN YOUR HEAD.
Calculate the travel time.

1. 60 mph, 480 mi
2. 50 mph, 450 mi
3. 60 mph, 180 mi
4. 60 mph, 600 mi
5. 50 mph, 550 mi

6. 90 km/h, 540 km
7. 100 km/h, 900 km
8. 90 km/h, 180 km
9. 100 km/h, 600 km
10. 80 km/h, 720 km

POWER BUILDER A

Mentally compute the time it takes to travel:

1. 240 miles at 40 mph = _____
2. 480 miles at 40 mph = _____
3. 90 miles at 45 mph = _____
4. 400 miles at 50 mph = _____
5. 220 miles at 55 mph = _____
6. 1000 miles at 50 mph = _____
7. 700 miles at 350 mph = _____
8. 900 miles at 450 mph = _____
9. 2800 miles at 400 mph = _____
10. 25,000 miles at 500 mph = _____

11. 450 km at 90 km/h = _____
12. 320 km at 80 km/h = _____
13. 350 km at 70 km/h = _____
14. 240 km at 80 km/h = _____
15. 360 km at 90 km/h = _____
16. 4000 km at 800 km/h = _____
17. 1500 km at 750 km/h = _____
18. 2700 km at 900 km/h = _____
19. 4900 km at 700 km/h = _____
20. 45,000 km at 500 km/h = _____

THINK IT THROUGH

If you have seven $50 bills, six $20 bills, five $10 bills, and four $1 bills, how much money do you have?

POWER BUILDER B

1. 300 miles at 50 mph = _____
2. 180 miles at 60 mph = _____
3. 160 miles at 40 mph = _____
4. 600 miles at 50 mph = _____
5. 240 miles at 60 mph = _____
6. 1500 miles at 50 mph = _____
7. 450 miles at 150 mph = _____
8. 1200 miles at 400 mph = _____
9. 25,000 miles at 500 mph = _____
10. 26,000 miles at 130 mph = _____

11. 360 km at 90 km/h = _____
12. 400 km at 80 km/h = _____
13. 420 km at 70 km /h = _____
14. 480 km at 80 km/h = _____
15. 540 km at 90 km/h = _____
16. 2400 km at 800 km/h = _____
17. 2100 km at 700 km/h = _____
18. 3600 km at 900 km/h = _____
19. 5600 km at 800 km/h = _____
20. 35,000 km at 700 km/h = _____

THINK IT THROUGH

If you have five $50 bills, four $20 bills, three $10 bills, two $5 bills, and one $1 bill, how much money do you have?

Items are often priced slightly less than a whole number of dollars.

To work with such prices in your head, round up to the nearest dollar.
Then add or subtract or multiply . . . and adjust your answer.

$8.99
+ $3.99

$9 + $4 = $13

But $13 is 2 cents too much, so the answer is $12.98.

$10.00
− $2.99

$10 − $3 = $7

But I subtracted one cent too many, so the answer is $7.01.

4 paperbacks @ $3.95

4 x $4 = $16,
less 4 x 5 cents = 20 cents,
or $15.80.

TRY THESE IN YOUR HEAD.
Round up, then adjust your answer.

1. $1.65 + $0.98
2. $4.99 + $3.98
3. $2.13 + $18.99
4. $5.00 − $1.99
5. $10.00 − $4.98

6. $20.00 − $5.99
7. 2 @ $1.99
8. 4 @ $2.95
9. 3 @ $24.98
10. 5 @ $99.99

POWER BUILDER A

1. $1.75 + $0.98 = _____

2. $4.99 + $3.98 = _____

3. $6.17 + $2.99 = _____

4. $9.99 + $15.99 = _____

5. $9.98 + $5.98 + $6.99 = _____

6. $10.00 − $2.99 = _____

7. $5.00 − $1.98 = _____

8. $20.00 − $12.98 = _____

9. $30.00 − $25.99 = _____

10. $30.00 − $22.98 = _____

11. 4 at $3.99 = _____

12. 7 at $2.99 = _____

13. 6 at $5.99 = _____

14. 5 at $7.98 = _____

15. 2 at $14.99 = _____

16. 5 at $19.98 = _____

17. 3 at $19.99 = _____

18. 8 at $49.98 = _____

19. 2 at $1995 = _____

20. 3 at $995 = _____

THINK IT THROUGH

The regular size box costs $1.98. The giant size box (twice as large as regular) sells for $3.79. How much do you save by buying one giant box instead of two regular?

POWER BUILDER B

1. $2.95 + $0.99 = _____

2. $3.99 + $2.98 = _____

3. $4.55 + $3.98 = _____

4. $7.99 + $17.99 = _____

5. $6.98 + $4.98 + $9.99 = _____

6. $10.00 − $3.99 = _____

7. $5.00 − $0.98 = _____

8. $20.00 − $14.98 = _____

9. $30.00 − $22.99 = _____

10. $30.00 − $21.98 = _____

11. 3 at $2.99 = _____

12. 4 at $4.98 = _____

13. 6 at $7.99 = _____

14. 2 at $14.98 = _____

15. 3 at $11.99 = _____

16. 5 at $39.98 = _____

17. 4 at $19.98 = _____

18. 5 at $29.96 = _____

19. 8 at $1995 = _____

20. 3 at $3995 = _____

THINK IT THROUGH

The regular size box costs $2.99. The giant size box (twice as large as the regular) sells for $5.47. How much do you save by buying one giant box instead of two of the regular size?

Mental Math Techniques
• USE COMPATIBLES. $4.29 + 1.75 = 4.25 + 0.04 + 1.75$
• SUBTRACT BY BALANCING. $4.76 - 1.99 = 4.77 - 2$
• TACK ON TRAILING ZEROS. $900 \times 50 = ?$
• MULTIPLY FROM THE LEFT. $127 \times 8 = ?$
• CANCEL COMMON TRAILING ZEROS. $6300 \div 90 = ?$ $60 \overline{)480}$

Do the problems below in your head. Tell which techniques you find useful for each one.

1. 500×700
2. $387 + 499$
3. $683 - 298$
4. $700 \overline{)42{,}000}$
5. 245×3
6. $3.6 - 2.99$
7. 50×8000
8. $8567 + 1999$
9. $100{,}000 \div 500$
10. 6×315

Talk about each problem below. What's an easy way to do it in your head? Tell how you would think it through.

1. $4635 + 2999$
2. $8.7 - 4.99$
3. 800×600
4. 5×226
5. $8000 \div 40$

6. $60 \overline{)5400}$
7. $375 + 296$
8. 435×2
9. 50×700
10. $654 - 198$

1. 2.75 + 1.28 = _____

2. 323 − 89 = _____

3. 4.6 − 2.9 = _____

4. 8 x 90 = _____

5. 4 x 82 = _____

6. Total cost for 2 at $0.95 each =

_____

7. 3500 ÷ 7 = _____

8. 2400 ÷ 60 = _____

9. Time to travel 480 miles at 60 mph =

_____

10. 457 + 199 = _____

11. 40 x 70 = _____

12. Total cost for 5 at $1.19 each =

_____

13. 1.49 + 2.49 = _____

14. 6 x 225 = _____

15. $500 \overline{)\ 40,000}$ = _____

16. 426 − 198 = _____

17. 825 − 399 = _____

18. $6 \overline{)\ 540}$ = _____

19. 7.3 − 4.8 = _____

20. 3.65 + 1.37 = _____

21. Time to travel 1500 km at 500 km/h =

_____

22. 45.04 − 20.95 = _____

23. Total cost for 4 at $2.49 each =

_____

24. 4 x 127 = _____

25. 2.88 + 4.15 = _____

26. 3000 x 60 = _____

27. $90 \overline{)\ 6300}$ = _____

28. Time to travel 1500 miles at 50 mph =

_____

29. 542 − 295 = _____

30. 5 x 600 = _____

31. 9543 − 2985 = _____

32. Total cost for 3 at $7.29 each =

_____

33. $6.00 − $4.98 = _____

34. Time to travel 4500 km at 90 km/h =

_____

35. 15.32 − 1.88 = _____

36. $8 \overline{)\ 7200}$ = _____

37. 8 x 725 = _____

38. 2800 ÷ 2 = _____

39. $4.98 + $2.99 = _____

40. 48,000 ÷ 800 = _____

MENTAL MATH IN JUNIOR HIGH
Copyright © 1988 by Dale Seymour Publications

Left-to-Right Multiplication

MENTALMATHLETE George Bidder, a 19th century engineer, said he learned to multiply in his head as a child while examining small objects like dried peas or marbles that he had arranged into rectangles.

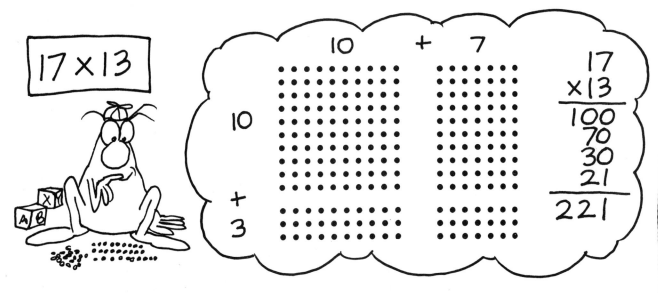

He soon realized that he didn't need objects to multiply even large numbers if he used left-to-right multiplication.

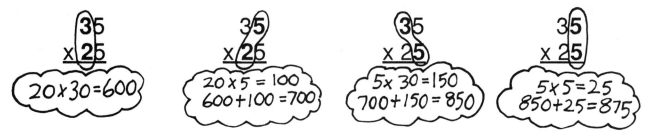

Bidder used a similar method to figure problems like 124,439,286,934 x 487,209,385,276 in his head. But he complained that such calculations gave him a headache!

YOUR TURN

See if you can use his method with these:

25 x 45   15 x 23   16 x 16

MENTAL MATH IN JUNIOR HIGH
Copyright © 1988 by Dale Seymour Publications

Left-to-Right Multiplication

To further explain this form of multiplication, prepare a transparency similar to the dot array illustrated in young George Bidder's thoughts. Cut and arrange the sections to demonstrate each step in the calculation.

Encourage the students to abbreviate the calculations whenever possible. For example, left-to-right multipliction can be varied in several ways to calculate the first exercise at the bottom of the page, 25 x 45:

$$25 \times 45 = (20 \times 45) + (5 \times 45) = 900 + 225 = 1125$$

$$\text{or} \quad 25 \times 45 = (25 \times 40) + (25 \times 5) = 1000 + 125 = 1125$$

The more able calculators in your class can be challenged to use left-to-right multiplication to multiply even larger numbers.

Usually it's difficult to add fractions in your head because there are so many steps.

$$\frac{2}{3} + \frac{4}{5}$$

Find the common denominator. Change to equivalent fractions. Add the numerators. Reduce the answer.   HELP!

But with certain special fractions, adding in your head is easy.

It's easy whenever one denominator is a multiple of the other denominator.

$$\frac{1}{2} + \frac{3}{8}$$

AHA! 8 is a multiple of 2!

Change $\frac{1}{2}$ to eighths.

$\frac{1}{2}$ = 4 eighths

4 eighths + 3 eighths = 7 eighths

$$\frac{4}{8} + \frac{3}{8} = \frac{7}{8}$$

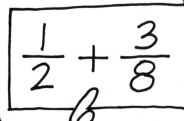

TRY THESE IN YOUR HEAD.
Which fraction will you change?

1. $\frac{1}{2} + \frac{1}{4}$

2. $\frac{1}{8} + \frac{1}{2}$

3. $\frac{1}{3} + \frac{1}{6}$

4. $\frac{1}{5} + \frac{3}{10}$

5. $\frac{1}{2} + \frac{3}{4}$

6. $1\frac{1}{2} + \frac{1}{4}$

7. $4\frac{1}{2} + \frac{1}{8}$

8. $3\frac{1}{4} + \frac{5}{8}$

9. $3\frac{3}{4} + \frac{1}{8}$

10. $1\frac{1}{10} + \frac{5}{100}$

POWER BUILDER A

1. $\frac{1}{4} + \frac{1}{2} =$ _____

2. $\frac{1}{4} + \frac{1}{8} =$ _____

3. $\frac{3}{4} + \frac{1}{4} =$ _____

4. $\frac{2}{3} + \frac{1}{6} =$ _____

5. $\frac{3}{8} + \frac{1}{2} =$ _____

6. $\frac{3}{16} + \frac{1}{2} =$ _____

7. $\frac{2}{10} + \frac{1}{2} =$ _____

8. $\frac{1}{2} + \frac{1}{6} =$ _____

9. $\frac{5}{6} + \frac{1}{3} =$ _____

10. $\frac{3}{4} + \frac{1}{2} =$ _____

11. $\frac{3}{8} + \frac{3}{4} =$ _____

12. $\frac{4}{5} + \frac{3}{10} =$ _____

13. $2\frac{1}{4} + \frac{1}{2} =$ _____

14. $3\frac{1}{8} + 1\frac{1}{4} =$ _____

15. $1\frac{1}{2} + 2\frac{1}{8} =$ _____

16. $2\frac{3}{4} + 1\frac{1}{8} =$ _____

17. $2\frac{1}{10} + 3\frac{1}{2} =$ _____

18. $3\frac{5}{8} + 1\frac{1}{4} =$ _____

19. $1\frac{3}{10} + 2\frac{3}{100} =$ _____

20. $3\frac{7}{100} + 4\frac{9}{10} =$ _____

THINK IT THROUGH

Look for a pattern:

$\frac{1}{2} = \frac{1}{4} + \frac{1}{4}$ $\qquad$ $\frac{1}{3} = \frac{1}{6} + \frac{1}{6}$ $\qquad$ $\frac{1}{5} = \frac{1}{10} + \frac{1}{10}$

Find three other equalities with the same pattern.

POWER BUILDER B

1. $\frac{1}{3} + \frac{1}{6} =$ _____

2. $\frac{1}{2} + \frac{1}{8} =$ _____

3. $\frac{1}{2} + \frac{1}{10} =$ _____

4. $\frac{3}{5} + \frac{1}{10} =$ _____

5. $\frac{1}{2} + \frac{3}{8} =$ _____

6. $\frac{1}{3} + \frac{1}{12} =$ _____

7. $\frac{1}{2} + \frac{3}{10} =$ _____

8. $\frac{1}{4} + \frac{1}{2} =$ _____

9. $\frac{1}{3} + \frac{5}{12} =$ _____

10. $\frac{5}{6} + \frac{1}{2} =$ _____

11. $\frac{1}{16} + \frac{1}{2} =$ _____

12. $\frac{2}{3} + \frac{1}{6} =$ _____

13. $2\frac{1}{3} + 1\frac{1}{12} =$ _____

14. $4\frac{1}{10} + 2\frac{1}{2} =$ _____

15. $2\frac{3}{8} + 3\frac{1}{4} =$ _____

16. $3\frac{7}{10} + 1\frac{1}{2} =$ _____

17. $1\frac{7}{12} + 2\frac{1}{2} =$ _____

18. $3\frac{3}{10} + 1\frac{2}{5} =$ _____

19. $2\frac{7}{10} + 3\frac{7}{100} =$ _____

20. $4\frac{29}{100} + 1\frac{7}{10} =$ _____

THINK IT THROUGH

Look for a pattern:

$\frac{1}{2} = \frac{1}{3} + \frac{1}{6}$ $\qquad$ $\frac{1}{3} = \frac{1}{4} + \frac{1}{12}$ $\qquad$ $\frac{1}{5} = \frac{1}{6} + \frac{1}{30}$

Find three other equalities with the same pattern.

Fractions are easy to add in your head if one denominator is a multiple of the other.

As you can probably guess, these special fractions are easy to subtract, too.

$$\frac{1}{4} + \frac{1}{8} = \frac{2}{8} + \frac{1}{8} = \frac{3}{8}$$

$$\frac{1}{5} + \frac{3}{10} = \frac{2}{10} + \frac{3}{10} = \frac{5}{10}$$

$$\frac{3}{4} - \frac{1}{8}$$

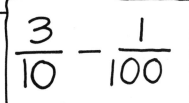

$$\frac{3}{10} - \frac{1}{100}$$

Change $\frac{3}{4}$ to 6 eighths.

6 eighths − 1 eighth is 5 eighths.

$$\frac{6}{8} - \frac{1}{8} = \frac{5}{8}$$

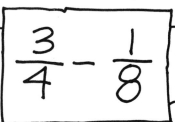

Change $\frac{3}{10}$ to 30 hundredths.

30 hundredths − 1 hundredth is 29 hundredths.

$$\frac{30}{100} - \frac{1}{100} = \frac{29}{100}$$

TRY THESE IN YOUR HEAD.
Change one of the fractions.

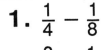

1. $\frac{1}{4} - \frac{1}{8}$

2. $\frac{3}{4} - \frac{1}{2}$

3. $\frac{2}{3} - \frac{1}{6}$

4. $\frac{7}{8} - \frac{3}{16}$

5. $\frac{2}{5} - \frac{1}{10}$

6. $\frac{5}{32} - \frac{1}{16}$

7. $\frac{45}{100} - \frac{3}{10}$

8. $\frac{3}{5} - \frac{1}{100}$

9. $\frac{4}{10} - \frac{1}{100}$

10. $\frac{9}{10} - \frac{9}{1000}$

POWER BUILDER A

1. $\frac{1}{2} - \frac{1}{8} =$ _____

2. $\frac{3}{4} - \frac{1}{2} =$ _____

3. $\frac{1}{2} - \frac{1}{6} =$ _____

4. $\frac{1}{2} - \frac{3}{10} =$ _____

5. $\frac{1}{4} - \frac{1}{8} =$ _____

6. $\frac{1}{3} - \frac{1}{6} =$ _____

7. $\frac{3}{4} - \frac{1}{8} =$ _____

8. $\frac{2}{3} - \frac{1}{6} =$ _____

9. $\frac{1}{2} - \frac{1}{10} =$ _____

10. $\frac{4}{5} - \frac{1}{10} =$ _____

11. $\frac{5}{16} - \frac{1}{4} =$ _____

12. $\frac{9}{10} - \frac{1}{5} =$ _____

13. $\frac{5}{6} - \frac{2}{3} =$ _____

14. $\frac{3}{4} - \frac{3}{8} =$ _____

15. $\frac{7}{8} - \frac{7}{16} =$ _____

16. $\frac{3}{5} - \frac{3}{10} =$ _____

17. $1\frac{2}{3} - \frac{1}{6} =$ _____

18. $1\frac{3}{4} - \frac{1}{8} =$ _____

19. $\frac{97}{100} - \frac{9}{10} =$ _____

20. $\frac{1}{10} - \frac{1}{100} =$ _____

THINK IT THROUGH

Look for a pattern:

$\frac{1}{2} - \frac{1}{3} = \frac{1}{6}$ $\frac{1}{4} - \frac{1}{5} = \frac{1}{20}$ $\frac{1}{7} - \frac{1}{8} = \frac{1}{56}$

Find three other equalities with the same pattern.

POWER BUILDER B

1. $\frac{1}{2} - \frac{1}{4} =$ _____

2. $\frac{7}{10} - \frac{1}{2} =$ _____

3. $\frac{1}{2} - \frac{1}{16} =$ _____

4. $\frac{1}{2} - \frac{3}{10} =$ _____

5. $\frac{1}{3} - \frac{1}{9} =$ _____

6. $\frac{1}{2} - \frac{1}{6} =$ _____

7. $\frac{3}{4} - \frac{3}{8} =$ _____

8. $\frac{5}{6} - \frac{2}{3} =$ _____

9. $\frac{1}{2} - \frac{1}{8} =$ _____

10. $\frac{9}{10} - \frac{1}{2} =$ _____

11. $\frac{7}{16} - \frac{1}{4} =$ _____

12. $\frac{7}{10} - \frac{1}{5} =$ _____

13. $\frac{9}{16} - \frac{1}{2} =$ _____

14. $\frac{2}{3} - \frac{2}{9} =$ _____

15. $\frac{5}{6} - \frac{7}{12} =$ _____

16. $\frac{1}{5} - \frac{1}{10} =$ _____

17. $\frac{3}{4} - \frac{3}{8} =$ _____

18. $\frac{1}{2} - \frac{1}{32} =$ _____

19. $\frac{93}{100} - \frac{7}{10} =$ _____

20. $\frac{3}{10} - \frac{3}{100} =$ _____

THINK IT THROUGH

Look for a pattern:

$\frac{1}{2} - \frac{1}{4} = \frac{1}{4}$ $\frac{1}{2} - \frac{1}{8} = \frac{3}{8}$ $\frac{1}{2} - \frac{1}{16} = \frac{7}{16}$

Find three other equalities with the same pattern.

Subtracting a part from one whole is easy to do in your head.

$$1 - \frac{1}{8}$$

$$
\begin{array}{r}
8 \text{ eighths} \\
- 1 \text{ eighth} \\
\hline
7 \text{ eighths}
\end{array}
$$

$$4 - \frac{1}{4}$$

So, to subtract a fraction from any whole number, think of it this way:

$1 - \frac{1}{4}$ is $\frac{3}{4}$...

so $4 - \frac{1}{4}$ must be $3\frac{3}{4}$.

✔ Check by adding.

$\frac{3}{4} + \frac{1}{4} = 1$

so $3\frac{3}{4} + \frac{1}{4} = 4$

TRY THESE IN YOUR HEAD.
Subtract, then check by adding.

1. $1 - \frac{1}{10}$ **4.** $4 - \frac{1}{16}$ **7.** $5 - \frac{7}{8}$

2. $5 - \frac{1}{10}$ **5.** $8 - \frac{1}{5}$ **8.** $10 - \frac{1}{10}$

3. $6 - \frac{1}{2}$ **6.** $3 - \frac{2}{3}$ **9.** $10 - \frac{1}{100}$

                              10. $10 - \frac{1}{1000}$

MENTAL MATH IN JUNIOR HIGH
Copyright © 1988 by Dale Seymour Publications

POWER BUILDER A

1. $1 - \frac{1}{3} =$ _____

2. $1 - \frac{1}{5} =$ _____

3. $1 - \frac{3}{4} =$ _____

4. $1 - \frac{2}{7} =$ _____

5. $1 - \frac{5}{9} =$ _____

6. $1 - \frac{5}{12} =$ _____

7. $3 - \frac{1}{4} =$ _____

8. $4 - \frac{1}{6} =$ _____

9. $3 - \frac{1}{5} =$ _____

10. $2 - \frac{2}{3} =$ _____

11. $7 - \frac{3}{4} =$ _____

12. $5 - \frac{4}{5} =$ _____

13. $7 - \frac{5}{9} =$ _____

14. $6 - \frac{3}{7} =$ _____

15. $9 - \frac{1}{2} =$ _____

16. $4 - \frac{5}{6} =$ _____

17. $5 - \frac{1}{10} =$ _____

18. $3 - \frac{3}{10} =$ _____

19. $3 - \frac{3}{100} =$ _____

20. $3 - \frac{3}{1000} =$ _____

THINK IT THROUGH

Name a fraction that is more than two-thirds but less than three-fourths.

POWER BUILDER B

1. $1 - \frac{1}{4} =$ _____

2. $1 - \frac{1}{6} =$ _____

3. $1 - \frac{2}{3} =$ _____

4. $1 - \frac{5}{7} =$ _____

5. $1 - \frac{4}{9} =$ _____

6. $1 - \frac{7}{12} =$ _____

7. $4 - \frac{1}{4} =$ _____

8. $2 - \frac{1}{7} =$ _____

9. $5 - \frac{1}{3} =$ _____

10. $4 - \frac{3}{4} =$ _____

11. $5 - \frac{5}{6} =$ _____

12. $2 - \frac{6}{7} =$ _____

13. $5 - \frac{5}{8} =$ _____

14. $8 - \frac{7}{9} =$ _____

15. $8 - \frac{1}{2} =$ _____

16. $5 - \frac{4}{7} =$ _____

17. $5 - \frac{1}{10} =$ _____

18. $5 - \frac{9}{10} =$ _____

19. $5 - \frac{9}{100} =$ _____

20. $5 - \frac{9}{1000} =$ _____

THINK IT THROUGH

Name a fraction that is more than three-fourths but less than five-sixths.

94

$$3 - 1\frac{2}{7}$$

Subtracting a mixed number from a whole number is easy to do in your head.

The key is to do it one step at a time.

STEP 1.

Subtract the whole number.

$$3 - 1 = 2$$

STEP 2.

Subtract the fractional part.

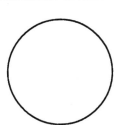 

$$2 - \frac{2}{7} = 1\frac{5}{7}$$

TRY THESE IN YOUR HEAD.
Subtract the whole, then the fraction.

1. $5 - 2\frac{1}{5}$ **4.** $9 - 8\frac{3}{5}$ **7.** $4 - 2\frac{9}{10}$

2. $4 - 1\frac{7}{8}$ **5.** $4 - 1\frac{5}{9}$ **8.** $7 - 5\frac{3}{5}$

3. $6 - 4\frac{3}{4}$ **6.** $10 - 4\frac{1}{7}$ **9.** $12 - 6\frac{3}{8}$

10. $8 - 6\frac{5}{16}$

POWER BUILDER A

1. $3 - 2\frac{1}{3} =$ _____

2. $4 - 3\frac{1}{5} =$ _____

3. $6 - 5\frac{1}{7} =$ _____

4. $3 - 2\frac{1}{2} =$ _____

5. $5 - 4\frac{1}{6} =$ _____

6. $8 - 6\frac{5}{8} =$ _____

7. $4 - 3\frac{3}{4} =$ _____

8. $8 - 7\frac{5}{9} =$ _____

9. $6 - 5\frac{3}{5} =$ _____

10. $5 - 4\frac{4}{9} =$ _____

11. $8 - 4\frac{3}{4} =$ _____

12. $5 - 2\frac{4}{5} =$ _____

13. $7 - 3\frac{5}{6} =$ _____

14. $10 - 5\frac{4}{5} =$ _____

15. $8 - 2\frac{7}{8} =$ _____

16. $5 - 2\frac{3}{4} =$ _____

17. $6 - 3\frac{4}{9} =$ _____

18. $5 - 2\frac{3}{10} =$ _____

19. $7 - 5\frac{7}{100} =$ _____

20. $8 - 3\frac{3}{100} =$ _____

THINK IT THROUGH

$\frac{1}{2} + \frac{1}{4} = \frac{3}{4}$ $\frac{1}{2} + \frac{1}{4} + \frac{1}{8} = \frac{7}{8}$

Use that pattern to calculate:

$\frac{1}{2} + \frac{1}{4} + \frac{1}{8} + \frac{1}{16} = ?$

$\frac{1}{2} + \frac{1}{4} + \frac{1}{8} + \frac{1}{16} + \frac{1}{32} = ?$

POWER BUILDER B

1. $2 - 1\frac{1}{4} =$ _____

2. $3 - 2\frac{1}{3} =$ _____

3. $5 - 4\frac{1}{6} =$ _____

4. $4 - 2\frac{1}{5} =$ _____

5. $8 - 7\frac{1}{3} =$ _____

6. $9 - 5\frac{3}{4} =$ _____

7. $7 - 6\frac{2}{5} =$ _____

8. $6 - 5\frac{4}{7} =$ _____

9. $5 - 4\frac{2}{3} =$ _____

10. $7 - 6\frac{4}{9} =$ _____

11. $6 - 2\frac{3}{4} =$ _____

12. $7 - 3\frac{2}{9} =$ _____

13. $5 - 2\frac{3}{5} =$ _____

14. $12 - 5\frac{7}{8} =$ _____

15. $6 - 3\frac{4}{7} =$ _____

16. $4 - 1\frac{2}{5} =$ _____

17. $6 - 3\frac{4}{9} =$ _____

18. $8 - 1\frac{9}{10} =$ _____

19. $9 - 4\frac{9}{100} =$ _____

20. $7 - 2\frac{11}{100} =$ _____

THINK IT THROUGH

$\frac{1}{3} + \frac{1}{9} = \frac{4}{9}$ $\frac{1}{3} + \frac{1}{9} + \frac{1}{27} = \frac{13}{27}$

Use that pattern to calculate:

$\frac{1}{3} + \frac{1}{9} + \frac{1}{27} + \frac{1}{81} = ?$

$\frac{1}{3} + \frac{1}{9} + \frac{1}{27} + \frac{1}{81} + \frac{1}{243} = ?$

In carpentry, we often work with fractions.

I have a 16-foot board.
When I cut off a $12\frac{1}{4}$-foot length, how long is the piece that's left?

You can solve this problem by breaking it into parts.
Subtract the whole number first . . .
then the fractional part.

$16 \quad - \quad 12\frac{1}{4}$

$16 - (12 + \frac{1}{4})$

$16 - 12 = 4$, minus $\frac{1}{4} = 3\frac{3}{4}$

Leftover piece is $3\frac{3}{4}$ feet.

Or, you can add on in steps.

$12\frac{1}{4} + \boxed{?} = 16$

$12\frac{1}{4} + \frac{3}{4} = 13$, plus 3 is 16

So $12\frac{1}{4} + 3\frac{3}{4} = 16$

Leftover piece is $3\frac{3}{4}$ feet.

Use whichever method seems easier to you.

TRY THESE IN YOUR HEAD.
How much is left . . .

. . . from an 8-ft board?

1. cut off $4\frac{1}{2}$ ft

2. cut off $7\frac{1}{4}$ ft

3. cut off $1\frac{1}{3}$ ft

4. cut off $3\frac{3}{4}$ ft

. . . from a 16-ft board?

5. cut off $10\frac{1}{2}$ ft

6. cut off $7\frac{3}{4}$ ft

7. cut off $3\frac{5}{12}$ ft

8. cut off $12\frac{2}{3}$ ft

POWER BUILDER A

1. $8 \text{ ft} - 5\frac{1}{2} \text{ ft} =$ _____

2. $8 \text{ ft} - 6\frac{7}{8} \text{ ft} =$ _____

3. $8 \text{ ft} - 2\frac{3}{4} \text{ ft} =$ _____

4. $8 \text{ ft} - 4\frac{2}{3} \text{ ft} =$ _____

5. $8 \text{ ft} - 6\frac{1}{3} \text{ ft} =$ _____

6. $8 \text{ ft} - 3\frac{1}{4} \text{ ft} =$ _____

7. $10 \text{ ft} - 4\frac{1}{4} \text{ ft} =$ _____

8. $10 \text{ ft} - 6\frac{2}{3} \text{ ft} =$ _____

9. $10 \text{ ft} - 5\frac{3}{4} \text{ ft} =$ _____

10. $10 \text{ ft} - 2\frac{5}{8} \text{ ft} =$ _____

11. $10 \text{ ft} - 1\frac{1}{3} \text{ ft} =$ _____

12. $10 \text{ ft} - 4\frac{7}{12} \text{ ft} =$ _____

13. $16 \text{ ft} - 5\frac{1}{4} \text{ ft} =$ _____

14. $16 \text{ ft} - 8\frac{7}{8} \text{ ft} =$ _____

15. $16 \text{ ft} - 6\frac{3}{4} \text{ ft} =$ _____

16. $16 \text{ ft} - 3\frac{2}{3} \text{ ft} =$ _____

17. $16 \text{ ft} - 9\frac{5}{12} \text{ ft} =$ _____

18. $16 \text{ ft} - 12\frac{9}{16} \text{ ft} =$ _____

19. $24 \text{ ft} - 3\frac{7}{16} \text{ ft} =$ _____

20. $24 \text{ ft} - 16\frac{7}{8} \text{ ft} =$ _____

THINK IT THROUGH

A progression is a sequence of related numbers.
Look at this progression for patterns:

$\frac{1}{3}$, 1, $\frac{5}{3}$, $2\frac{1}{3}$, 3, $3\frac{2}{3}$ ...

What is the next term?

POWER BUILDER B

1. $8 \text{ ft} - 3\frac{1}{4} \text{ ft} =$ _____

2. $8 \text{ ft} - 5\frac{3}{4} \text{ ft} =$ _____

3. $8 \text{ ft} - 1\frac{5}{8} \text{ ft} =$ _____

4. $8 \text{ ft} - 3\frac{1}{3} \text{ ft} =$ _____

5. $8 \text{ ft} - 5\frac{2}{3} \text{ ft} =$ _____

6. $8 \text{ ft} - 4\frac{7}{8} \text{ ft} =$ _____

7. $10 \text{ ft} - 3\frac{2}{3} \text{ ft} =$ _____

8. $10 \text{ ft} - 4\frac{7}{8} \text{ ft} =$ _____

9. $10 \text{ ft} - 3\frac{5}{8} \text{ ft} =$ _____

10. $10 \text{ ft} - 1\frac{1}{8} \text{ ft} =$ _____

11. $10 \text{ ft} - 2\frac{3}{4} \text{ ft} =$ _____

12. $10 \text{ ft} - 7\frac{2}{3} \text{ ft} =$ _____

13. $16 \text{ ft} - 4\frac{1}{3} \text{ ft} =$ _____

14. $16 \text{ ft} - 7\frac{7}{12} \text{ ft} =$ _____

15. $16 \text{ ft} - 8\frac{1}{4} \text{ ft} =$ _____

16. $16 \text{ ft} - 9\frac{2}{3} \text{ ft} =$ _____

17. $16 \text{ ft} - 7\frac{1}{12} \text{ ft} =$ _____

18. $16 \text{ ft} - 13\frac{1}{8} \text{ ft} =$ _____

19. $24 \text{ ft} - 5\frac{7}{16} \text{ ft} =$ _____

20. $24 \text{ ft} - 12\frac{5}{16} \text{ ft} =$ _____

THINK IT THROUGH

A progression is a sequence of related numbers.
Look at this progression for patterns:

$\frac{1}{4}$, $\frac{3}{4}$, $\frac{10}{8}$, $\frac{14}{8}$, $2\frac{1}{4}$ ...

What is the next term?

Compatible fractions are pairs of fractions that add to whole-number sums.

Recognizing compatibles can help you work with fractions in your head.

sum=5 $4\frac{7}{8}$ $\frac{1}{8}$

sum=8 $2\frac{13}{16}$ $5\frac{3}{16}$

$1\frac{3}{4}$ sum=4 $2\frac{1}{4}$

COMPATIBLES!

$$2\frac{7}{8} + 1\frac{3}{16}$$

$$4\frac{1}{3} + 2\frac{2}{3}$$

$$2\frac{3}{5} + 6\frac{2}{5}$$

$$4\frac{5}{9} + 1\frac{4}{5}$$

$$1\frac{1}{4} + 5\frac{3}{4}$$

Which of these pairs contain compatible fractions?

What are their whole-number sums?

$$1\frac{7}{8} + 1\frac{8}{7}$$

$$7\frac{4}{7} + 1\frac{3}{7}$$

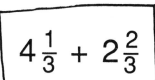

TRY THESE IN YOUR HEAD.

1. Find compatible pairs that total 1.

$\frac{3}{4}$	$\frac{1}{16}$	$\frac{1}{2}$
$\frac{1}{6}$	$\frac{2}{3}$	$\frac{15}{16}$
$\frac{4}{5}$	$\frac{5}{6}$	$\frac{1}{3}$

2. Find compatible pairs that total 10.

$2\frac{1}{4}$	$6\frac{4}{9}$	$1\frac{7}{8}$
$3\frac{3}{4}$	$7\frac{3}{4}$	$9\frac{7}{8}$
$3\frac{5}{9}$	$8\frac{1}{8}$	$2\frac{5}{9}$

POWER BUILDER A

1. $\frac{7}{8}$ + _____ = 1

2. $\frac{3}{5}$ + _____ = 1

3. _____ + $\frac{2}{3}$ = 1

4. _____ + $\frac{4}{9}$ = 1

5. _____ + $1\frac{3}{7}$ = 5

6. $2\frac{3}{5}$ + _____ = 5

7. $4\frac{2}{7}$ _____ = 8

8. $3\frac{1}{5}$ + _____ = 10

9. $7\frac{4}{5}$ + _____ = 10

10. _____ + $6\frac{7}{9}$ = 8

11. $1 - \frac{3}{5}$ = _____

12. $1 - \frac{7}{8}$ = _____

13. $1 - \frac{4}{9}$ = _____

14. $5 - 2\frac{1}{6}$ = _____

15. $5 - 4\frac{7}{8}$ = _____

16. $5 - 3\frac{3}{4}$ = _____

17. $8 - 4\frac{4}{9}$ = _____

18. $8 - 1\frac{2}{5}$ = _____

19. $10 - 2\frac{3}{7}$ = _____

20. $10 - 2\frac{8}{9}$ = _____

THINK IT THROUGH

Which two fractions in the box add to a sum less than one? Explain why.

$\frac{5}{8}$ $\frac{4}{9}$ $\frac{41}{50}$ $\frac{7}{15}$ $\frac{2}{3}$ $\frac{9}{13}$

POWER BUILDER B

1. $\frac{4}{5}$ + _____ = 1

2. $\frac{3}{8}$ + _____ = 1

3. _____ + $\frac{3}{4}$ = 1

4. _____ + $\frac{4}{9}$ = 1

5. _____ + $1\frac{4}{5}$ = 5

6. $3\frac{4}{5}$ + _____ = 5

7. $5\frac{4}{9}$ + _____ = 8

8. $2\frac{2}{5}$ + _____ = 10

9. $4\frac{5}{12}$ + _____ = 10

10. _____ + $4\frac{5}{8}$ = 8

11. $1 - \frac{7}{8}$ = _____

12. $1 - \frac{5}{8}$ = _____

13. $1 - \frac{7}{9}$ = _____

14. $5 - 4\frac{1}{5}$ = _____

15. $5 - 4\frac{7}{8}$ = _____

16. $5 - 2\frac{1}{4}$ = _____

17. $8 - 2\frac{3}{7}$ = _____

18. $8 - 1\frac{2}{5}$ = _____

19. $10 - 1\frac{4}{9}$ = _____

20. $10 - 3\frac{5}{9}$ = _____

THINK IT THROUGH

Which two fractions in the box add to a sum greater than one? Explain why.

$\frac{1}{4}$ $\frac{4}{11}$ $\frac{17}{45}$ $\frac{4}{7}$ $\frac{35}{100}$ $\frac{5}{9}$

ADD IN YOUR HEAD

$$2\frac{7}{8} + 4\frac{1}{4}$$

Ugh! That's too hard! Is there a way to make it easier?

Impossible-looking addition problems involving fractions can often be made easier.

How? By making your own compatible fractions to work with.

Like this . . .

$$2\frac{7}{8} + 4\frac{1}{4}$$

$2\frac{7}{8} + \frac{1}{8} + 4\frac{1}{8}$

COMPATIBLE!

$2\frac{7}{8} + \frac{1}{8} = 3$

$3 + 4\frac{1}{8} = 7\frac{1}{8}$

Think of $4\frac{1}{4}$ as $4\frac{1}{8} + \frac{1}{8}$.

That gives you a compatible pair.

The compatibles make a tidy sum . . . then it's easy to add the rest.

TRY THESE IN YOUR HEAD.
Try to make compatible pairs.

1. $2\frac{3}{4} + 2\frac{1}{2}$

2. $4\frac{7}{8} + 3\frac{5}{8}$

3. $3\frac{15}{16} + 4\frac{3}{16}$

4. $5\frac{31}{32} + 3\frac{17}{32}$

5. $4\frac{7}{8} + 4\frac{7}{8}$

6. $3\frac{15}{16} + 4\frac{1}{8}$

7. $9\frac{7}{8} + 3\frac{1}{4}$

8. $10\frac{1}{2} + 9\frac{5}{8}$

9. $2\frac{15}{16} + 2\frac{15}{16}$

10. $7\frac{3}{32} + 2\frac{5}{16}$

POWER BUILDER A

1. $2\frac{3}{8} + 1\frac{1}{4} =$ _____

2. $1\frac{5}{12} + 2\frac{1}{2} =$ _____

3. $3\frac{4}{9} + 1\frac{1}{3} =$ _____

4. $5\frac{1}{10} + 1\frac{1}{2} =$ _____

5. $2\frac{3}{4} + 5\frac{1}{8} =$ _____

6. $4\frac{7}{8} + 1\frac{1}{4} =$ _____

7. $8\frac{5}{6} + 2\frac{1}{3} =$ _____

8. $5\frac{1}{3} + 3\frac{7}{9} =$ _____

9. $3\frac{7}{10} + 3\frac{1}{2} =$ _____

10. $5\frac{3}{4} + 2\frac{1}{2} =$ _____

11. $4\frac{7}{8} + 3\frac{3}{4} =$ _____

12. $5\frac{7}{10} + 1\frac{1}{2} =$ _____

13. $1\frac{5}{6} + 2\frac{1}{2} =$ _____

14. $3\frac{1}{4} + 5\frac{7}{8} =$ _____

15. $4\frac{9}{10} + 2\frac{1}{5} =$ _____

16. $5\frac{11}{12} + 4\frac{1}{4} =$ _____

17. $3\frac{1}{8} + 2\frac{15}{16} =$ _____

18. $1\frac{17}{20} + 2\frac{1}{2} =$ _____

19. $5\frac{13}{16} + 1\frac{1}{4} =$ _____

20. $3\frac{1}{3} + 7\frac{11}{12} =$ _____

THINK IT THROUGH

Mentally calculate the following sum.
Look for a shortcut.

$2\frac{1}{2} + 4\frac{7}{16} + 2\frac{2}{3} + 2\frac{1}{2} + \frac{9}{16} + 1\frac{1}{3}$

POWER BUILDER B

1. $1\frac{1}{4} + 2\frac{5}{8} =$ _____

2. $3\frac{1}{12} + 2\frac{1}{2} =$ _____

3. $4\frac{5}{9} + 2\frac{1}{3} =$ _____

4. $7\frac{3}{10} + 1\frac{1}{2} =$ _____

5. $3\frac{1}{4} + 4\frac{3}{8} =$ _____

6. $5\frac{3}{4} + 2\frac{1}{2} =$ _____

7. $4\frac{1}{3} + 3\frac{5}{6} =$ _____

8. $3\frac{8}{9} + 2\frac{1}{3} =$ _____

9. $4\frac{9}{10} + 2\frac{1}{2} =$ _____

10. $4\frac{1}{2} + 1\frac{7}{8} =$ _____

11. $2\frac{5}{6} + 3\frac{1}{3} =$ _____

12. $2\frac{9}{10} + 3\frac{1}{2} =$ _____

13. $4\frac{1}{2} + 2\frac{5}{6} =$ _____

14. $2\frac{1}{2} + 6\frac{7}{8} =$ _____

15. $1\frac{1}{5} + 2\frac{9}{10} =$ _____

16. $2\frac{11}{12} + 3\frac{1}{3} =$ _____

17. $5\frac{3}{8} + 4\frac{13}{16} =$ _____

18. $6\frac{15}{16} + 1\frac{1}{2} =$ _____

19. $4\frac{13}{16} + 2\frac{1}{2} =$ _____

20. $1\frac{1}{4} + 5\frac{11}{12} =$ _____

THINK IT THROUGH

Mentally calculate the following.
Look for a shortcut.

$1\frac{3}{8} + 1\frac{2}{3} - \frac{3}{8} - 1\frac{3}{4} + 1\frac{1}{3} + 2\frac{3}{4}$

Balancing can make it easier to subtract
whole numbers in your head.

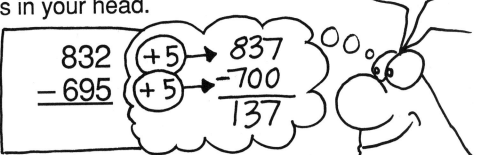

$$\begin{array}{r} 832 \\ -695 \end{array} \quad \begin{array}{c} \boxed{+5} \\ \boxed{+5} \end{array} \rightarrow \begin{array}{r} 837 \\ -700 \\ \hline 137 \end{array}$$

The same idea can also make subtracting fractions easier.

Add something to change
the subtrahend (second number)
into a whole number.
Then add the same to
the first number.

$$\begin{array}{r} 5\frac{1}{4} \\ -3\frac{7}{8} \\ \hline \end{array}$$

THINK . . .

Adding $\frac{1}{8}$ would make
a tidy subtrahend.

$$5\frac{2}{8} \quad \boxed{+\frac{1}{8}} \rightarrow 5\frac{3}{8}$$
$$-3\frac{7}{8} \quad \boxed{+\frac{1}{8}} \rightarrow -4$$
$$\hline \qquad\qquad\qquad 1\frac{3}{8}$$

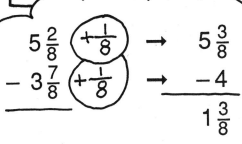

TRY THESE IN YOUR HEAD.
Subtract by balancing.

1. $5 - 2\frac{4}{5}$ **4.** $7\frac{1}{8} - 1\frac{5}{8}$ **7.** $9\frac{3}{8} - 2\frac{7}{8}$

2. $10 - 4\frac{15}{16}$ **5.** $5\frac{1}{3} - \frac{2}{3}$ **8.** $4\frac{3}{16} - 1\frac{15}{16}$

3. $6\frac{1}{4} - 2\frac{1}{2}$ **6.** $3\frac{3}{5} - \frac{4}{5}$ **9.** $5\frac{3}{10} - 3\frac{9}{10}$

                                                        10. $10\frac{5}{16} - 4\frac{11}{16}$

POWER BUILDER A

1. $4 - 1\frac{3}{5} =$ _____

2. $7 - 2\frac{3}{4} =$ _____

3. $9 - 3\frac{4}{7} =$ _____

4. $5 - 1\frac{5}{9} =$ _____

5. $4\frac{3}{8} - \frac{7}{8} =$ _____

6. $5\frac{1}{6} - \frac{5}{6} =$ _____

7. $2\frac{2}{7} - \frac{5}{7} =$ _____

8. $6\frac{3}{10} - \frac{7}{10} =$ _____

9. $3\frac{1}{8} - 1\frac{5}{8} =$ _____

10. $4\frac{2}{5} - 2\frac{4}{5} =$ _____

11. $5\frac{2}{9} - 3\frac{7}{9} =$ _____

12. $7\frac{1}{10} - 3\frac{3}{10} =$ _____

13. $5\frac{1}{4} - 2\frac{1}{2} =$ _____

14. $7\frac{1}{5} - 2\frac{7}{10} =$ _____

15. $7\frac{1}{6} - 2\frac{2}{3} =$ _____

16. $4\frac{1}{2} - 1\frac{5}{6} =$ _____

17. $9\frac{1}{4} - 2\frac{7}{8} =$ _____

18. $5\frac{5}{12} - 1\frac{2}{3} =$ _____

19. $3\frac{2}{3} - 1\frac{5}{6} =$ _____

20. $5\frac{3}{8} - 2\frac{3}{4} =$ _____

THINK IT THROUGH

Paul threw the shot put $43\frac{3}{4}$ ft. Eric threw it $29\frac{7}{8}$ ft. How much further did Paul throw it than Eric?

POWER BUILDER B

1. $3 - 1\frac{2}{3} =$ _____

2. $4 - 2\frac{5}{7} =$ _____

3. $6 - 3\frac{7}{9} =$ _____

4. $7 - 4\frac{3}{4} =$ _____

5. $5\frac{1}{3} - \frac{2}{3} =$ _____

6. $4\frac{3}{7} - \frac{4}{7} =$ _____

7. $2\frac{1}{6} - \frac{5}{6} =$ _____

8. $5\frac{1}{10} - \frac{9}{10} =$ _____

9. $8\frac{1}{6} - 2\frac{5}{6} =$ _____

10. $3\frac{2}{5} - 1\frac{3}{5} =$ _____

11. $4\frac{2}{9} - 1\frac{8}{9} =$ _____

12. $6\frac{1}{12} - 2\frac{5}{12} =$ _____

13. $3\frac{1}{4} - 1\frac{3}{4} =$ _____

14. $5\frac{1}{3} - 1\frac{5}{6} =$ _____

15. $7\frac{1}{6} - 2\frac{1}{2} =$ _____

16. $3\frac{1}{2} - 1\frac{7}{8} =$ _____

17. $6\frac{1}{5} - 1\frac{9}{10} =$ _____

18. $5\frac{5}{12} - 1\frac{2}{3} =$ _____

19. $4\frac{3}{4} - 1\frac{7}{8} =$ _____

20. $3\frac{3}{10} - 1\frac{3}{5} =$ _____

THINK IT THROUGH

Jean's long jump was $17\frac{1}{4}$ ft. Molly's jump was $15\frac{3}{4}$ ft. How much further did Jean jump than Molly?

These numbers are compatible. Can you tell why?

$\frac{2}{3}$ of 12

With compatibles, it's easy to find the fractional part in your head.

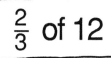

Think of the unit fraction first, and divide . . .

Then multiply to adjust your answer.

$\frac{1}{3}$ of 12 = 12 ÷ 3 = 4

$\frac{2}{3}$ of 12 = 2 × ($\frac{1}{3}$ of 12)

          = 2 × 4 = 8

Now try this one.

$\frac{3}{4}$ × 28

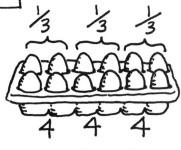

$\frac{1}{4}$ × 28 = 28 ÷ 4 = 7

$\frac{3}{4}$ × 28 = 3 × ($\frac{1}{4}$ × 28)

          = 3 × 7 = 21

TRY THESE IN YOUR HEAD.
Divide, then multiply.

1. $\frac{1}{8}$ of 32

2. $\frac{3}{8}$ of 32

3. $\frac{5}{8}$ of 32

4. $\frac{3}{4}$ of 12

5. $\frac{17}{36}$ of 360

6. 54 × $\frac{5}{9}$

7. $\frac{5}{8}$ × 48

8. 50 × $\frac{3}{10}$

9. $\frac{3}{8}$ × 72

10. $\frac{4}{3}$ × 12

POWER BUILDER A

1. $\frac{1}{4}$ of 12 = _____
2. $\frac{1}{5}$ of 35 = _____
3. $\frac{1}{8}$ of 40 = _____
4. $\frac{1}{3}$ of 45 = _____
5. $\frac{1}{7}$ of 28 = _____
6. $\frac{3}{7}$ of 28 = _____
7. $\frac{1}{5}$ of 45 = _____
8. $\frac{2}{5}$ of 45 = _____
9. $\frac{1}{10}$ of 70 = _____
10. $\frac{3}{10}$ of 70 = _____

11. $\frac{4}{5}$ of 20 = _____
12. $\frac{3}{7}$ of 42 = _____
13. $\frac{3}{4}$ of 100 = _____
14. $\frac{2}{3}$ of 90 = _____
15. $\frac{3}{5}$ of 100 = _____
16. $\frac{5}{8}$ of 40 = _____
17. $\frac{2}{3}$ of 600 = _____
18. $\frac{3}{4}$ of 200 = _____
19. $\frac{4}{5}$ of 200 = _____
20. $\frac{2}{3}$ of 450 = _____

THINK IT THROUGH

Two-thirds of the number is 240.
What is the number?

POWER BUILDER B

1. $\frac{1}{3}$ of 15 = _____
2. $\frac{1}{5}$ of 25 = _____
3. $\frac{1}{4}$ of 40 = _____
4. $\frac{1}{8}$ of 48 = _____
5. $\frac{1}{7}$ of 35 = _____
6. $\frac{2}{7}$ of 35 = _____
7. $\frac{1}{3}$ of 90 = _____
8. $\frac{2}{3}$ of 90 = _____
9. $\frac{1}{10}$ of 60 = _____
10. $\frac{3}{10}$ of 60 = _____

11. $\frac{3}{4}$ of 20 = _____
12. $\frac{2}{7}$ of 28 = _____
13. $\frac{4}{5}$ of 100 = _____
14. $\frac{3}{4}$ of 80 = _____
15. $\frac{2}{5}$ of 100 = _____
16. $\frac{3}{8}$ of 80 = _____
17. $\frac{2}{3}$ of 300 = _____
18. $\frac{3}{4}$ of 100 = _____
19. $\frac{4}{5}$ of 200 = _____
20. $\frac{2}{3}$ of 900 = _____

THINK IT THROUGH

Three-fourths of the number is 1200.
What is the number?

106

To save money when we shop, we need to compare prices. Here's one way to do this:

Find a way to compare equal amounts. That way you learn just how much you can save with the better buy.

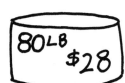

$2 \times$ 5 LB $=$ 10 LB

$2 \times \$2.15 = \$4.30$

I can save 20 cents if I buy the 10-lb size!

5 LB $2.15   10 LB $4.10

Sometimes you will need to use fractions to make equal amounts.

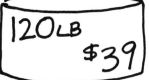

80 LB $28   120 LB $39

$\frac{3}{2} \times$ 80 LB $=$ 120 LB

$\frac{3}{2} \times \$28 = 3 \times \frac{1}{2}$ of $\$28 = 3 \times 14 = \$42$

Savings of $3 if I buy the 120-lb barrel!

TRY THESE IN YOUR HEAD.
Find the better buy and the savings.

| 69¢ 8 oz | $1.75 250 mL | $1.20 6 LB | $45 5 kg |
| $2.40 32 oz | $5 750 mL | $1.89 9 LB | $85 10 kg |

POWER BUILDER A

Determine the better buy. Circle it.

1. 3 ft for $1.50   or   6 ft for $2.75
2. 5 lb for $1.60   or   10 lb for $3.40
3. 6 for $1.40   or   12 for $2.50
4. 4 m for $11.25   or   12 m for $34.00
5. 2 mL for $29   or   12 mL for $170
6. 5 kg for $3.98   or   10 kg for $7.60
7. 8 ft for $3.60   or   16 ft for $7.50
8. 6 yd for $24.98   or   12 yd for $48.75
9. 12 for $1.89   or   24 for $3.75
10. 15 yd for $550   or   30 yd for $1075

11. 3 ft for $1.50   or   9 ft for $5.00
12. 4 lb for $1.60   or   6 lb for $2.50
13. 5 for $1.39   or   15 for $4.00
14. 15 m for $25   or   10 m for $18
15. 5 oz for $9.75   or   10 oz for $19.75
16. 5 kg for $1.89   or   10 kg for $3.60
17. 12 ft for $3.60   or   16 ft for $5
18. 8 yd for $24   or   12 yd for $35
19. 20 for $1.98   or   25 for $2.50
20. 15 yd for $350   or   30 yd for $690

THINK IT THROUGH

If a basketball player scores 18 free throws for every 24 attempts, how many does she score in 48 attempts? in 72 attempts? in 60 attempts?

POWER BUILDER B

Determine the better buy. Circle it.

1. 5 ft for $1.79   or   2 ft for 80¢
2. 4 lb for $1.80   or   6 lb for $2.90
3. 24 for $10   or   36 for $14.25
4. 15 m for $25   or   5 m for $8
5. 5 oz for $9.75   or   10 oz for $19.75
6. 100 kg for $250   or   50 kg for $136
7. 16 ft for $12   or   24 ft for $17.50
8. 6 for $40   or   15 for $104
9. 10 for $30   or   25 for $81
10. 12 yd for $300   or   18 yd for $550

11. 6 ft for $1.80   or   2 ft for 55¢
12. 18 lb for $3.25   or   9 lb for $1.75
13. 24 for $10   or   12 for $5.25
14. 5 m for $35   or   15 m for $104
15. 100 kg for $500   or   150 kg for $700
16. 4 L for $9   or   6 L for $13
17. 16 ft for $3.60   or   32 ft for $7.00
18. 3 bags for $12   or   5 bags for $21
19. 10 for $29.99   or   15 for $49.99
20. 15 yd for $750   or   20 yd for $950

THINK IT THROUGH

If Raoul has 24 hits for every 36 times at bat, how many hits can we expect from him in 72 times at bat? in 90 times at bat? in 108 times at bat?

Mental Math Techniques

- **CHANGE SPECIAL FRACTIONS TO ADD OR SUBTRACT.**

  $\frac{1}{2} + \frac{1}{4} = ?$ $\frac{7}{8} - \frac{1}{2} = ?$

- **SUBTRACT FRACTIONS FROM WHOLE NUMBERS.**

  $3 - \frac{1}{4} = ?$ $3 - 1\frac{3}{4} = ?$

- **USE COMPATIBLE FRACTIONS.**

  $4\frac{1}{2} + 2\frac{1}{2} = ?$

- **BALANCE TO SUBTRACT FRACTIONS.**

  $5\frac{1}{2} - 3\frac{7}{8} = ?$ (add $\frac{1}{8}$ to balance)

- **DIVIDE, THEN MULTIPLY, TO FIND FRACTIONAL PARTS.**

  $\frac{2}{3}$ of $12 = ?$ $\frac{3}{4} \times 24 = ?$

Do the problems below in your head. Tell which techniques you find useful for each one.

1. $8 - \frac{7}{8}$

2. $12 - 1\frac{3}{4}$

3. $4\frac{1}{4} - 1\frac{7}{8}$

4. $\frac{2}{3}$ of 18

5. $\frac{1}{2} + \frac{3}{4}$

6. $\frac{1}{2} + \frac{3}{4} - \frac{1}{8}$

7. $2\frac{1}{2} + 1\frac{1}{2} + 1\frac{3}{4}$

8. $5\frac{1}{16} - 2\frac{15}{16}$

9. $18 - 4\frac{1}{2}$

10. $\frac{3}{8} \times 48$

Talk about each problem below. What's an easy way to do it in your head? Tell how you would think it through.

1. $3\frac{1}{4} + 4\frac{3}{4}$

2. $11\frac{3}{8} - 3\frac{7}{8}$

3. $4\frac{1}{8} + 5\frac{7}{8}$

4. $\frac{1}{4} \times 48$

5. $20 - 4\frac{9}{10}$

6. $1\frac{7}{8} - \frac{1}{4}$

7. $12 - 5\frac{3}{8}$

8. $\frac{5}{6}$ of 24

9. $4\frac{3}{4} + 2\frac{1}{4} + 3\frac{5}{16}$

10. $\frac{1}{2} + \frac{1}{4} + \frac{1}{8}$

1. $\frac{1}{2} - \frac{1}{10} =$ _____

2. $12 - 2\frac{9}{10} =$ _____

3. $6 - 4\frac{7}{8} =$ _____

4. $\frac{1}{2} + \frac{1}{3} =$ _____

5. $1\frac{1}{4} + 2\frac{3}{8} =$ _____

6. $\frac{1}{7}$ of $35 =$ _____

7. 8 ft $- 4\frac{1}{3}$ ft $=$ _____

8. $4 - \frac{4}{5} =$ _____

9. Which is the better buy:
   4 for $3.49 or 8 for $6.89?

   _____

10. $8 - 4\frac{5}{9} =$ _____

11. $\frac{1}{2} + \frac{1}{8} =$ _____

12. $1 - \frac{5}{9} =$ _____

13. 16 ft $- 2\frac{3}{4}$ ft $=$ _____

14. $6\frac{11}{12} + 1\frac{1}{2} =$ _____

15. Which is the better buy:
    5 for $0.39 or 10 for $0.85?

    _____

16. $\frac{3}{4} - \frac{1}{8} =$ _____

17. $6 - 1\frac{3}{5} =$ _____

18. $\frac{3}{10}$ of $90 =$ _____

19. $2\frac{1}{2} + \frac{3}{4} =$ _____

20. $4\frac{1}{8} - 1\frac{7}{8} =$ _____

21. 24 ft $- 16\frac{2}{3}$ ft $=$ _____

22. Which is the better buy:
    6 for $1.20 or 9 for $1.67?

    _____

23. $5\frac{1}{4} - 2\frac{1}{2} =$ _____

24. $\frac{7}{10} - \frac{1}{5} =$ _____

25. $5 - 2\frac{1}{6} =$ _____

26. $4\frac{1}{2} - 1\frac{7}{12} =$ _____

27. $\frac{3}{10} + \frac{1}{5} =$ _____

28. $7 - 3\frac{2}{5} =$ _____

29. $6\frac{3}{10} - 1\frac{7}{10} =$ _____

30. $\frac{2}{3} - \frac{1}{2} =$ _____

31. $1 - \frac{3}{8} =$ _____

32. $3 - \frac{2}{3} =$ _____

33. $4 - 1\frac{2}{3} =$ _____

34. 10 ft $- 4\frac{3}{8}$ ft $=$ _____

35. $4 - 2\frac{4}{7} =$ _____

36. $2\frac{5}{6} + 4\frac{1}{3} =$ _____

37. $4\frac{1}{8} - 1\frac{5}{8} =$ _____

38. $\frac{2}{5}$ of 15 _____

39. Which is the better buy:
    8 for $4.00 or 12 for $6.99?

    _____

40. $\frac{5}{8}$ of $40 =$ _____

Squaring Numbers

$$2^2 = 3 \times 1 + 1$$
$$3^2 = 4 \times 2 + 1$$
$$4^2 = 5 \times 3 + 1$$
$$5^2 = 6 \times 4 + 1$$
$$6^2 =$$
$$7^2 =$$
$$8^2 =$$
$$9^2 =$$
$$10^2 =$$

Here is a number pattern based on the squares of numbers.

Can you complete the pattern?

MENTALMATHLETES use this pattern to square numbers that are close to a multiple of 10.

 19^2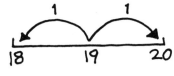

$$20 \times 18 = 360$$
$$360 + 1 = 361$$
$$19^2 = 361$$

 21^2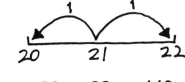

$$20 \times 22 = 440$$
$$440 + 1 = 441$$
$$21^2 = 441$$

YOUR TURN

Use this idea to square the following numbers:

29   31   39   41

How could you modify this rule to square numbers like 18, 22, 28, 32, and so on?

Expert mental calculators have rules for even larger numbers. Here's how MENTALMATHLETE Arthur Benjamin squared 4273:

$$4273^2 = (4273 + 273) \times (4273 - 273) + 273^2$$
$$= 4546 \times 4000 + 273^2$$
$$= 18,184,000 + 74,529$$
$$= 18,258,529$$

Squaring Numbers

The number pattern illustrated on this page (top right) is obvious and few students will find it difficult to complete the unfinished calculations in this table. However, most students will need some help to see how they can use this pattern to calculate squares.

The pattern can be modified for squaring numbers that end in 8 or 2, such as 18, 22, 28, 32, and so on. For such numbers, we can move 2 in either direction on the number line, multiply, and then add 4 (the square of 2) instead of 1 (the square of 1). That is:

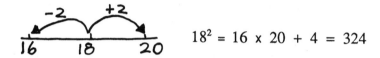

$$18^2 = 16 \times 20 + 4 = 324$$

Challenge students to develop a similar pattern for squaring numbers that end in 7 or 3 (17, 23, 27, 33, and so on). Demonstrate that even larger numbers such as 98 and 197 can be readily squared by following patterns like these. That is:

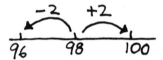

$$98^2 = 96 \times 100 + 4 = 9604$$

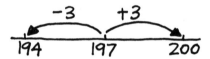

$$197^2 = 194 \times 200 + 9 = 38,800 + 9 = 38,809$$

When we multiply a mixed number on paper, we change it to an improper fraction.

$8 \times 4\frac{3}{4}$

$\frac{8}{1} \times \frac{19}{4}$

THAT'S TOO HARD TO DO IN MY HEAD!

Here's a better way to multiply in your head:

Break the mixed number into parts.

Multiplying by parts makes the calculation much easier.

$$8$$
$$4 \quad\boxed{4 \times 8 = 32}$$
$$+$$
$$\frac{3}{4} \quad \boxed{\frac{3}{4} \text{ of } 8 = 6}$$

$$8 \times 4\tfrac{3}{4} = 32 + 6 = 38$$

Sometimes subtraction works.   **THINK . . .**

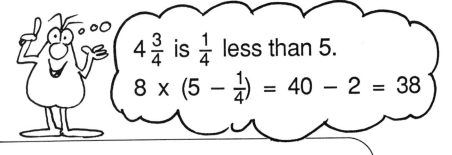

$4\frac{3}{4}$ is $\frac{1}{4}$ less than 5.

$8 \times (5 - \frac{1}{4}) = 40 - 2 = 38$

Choose whichever is easier for you.

TRY THESE IN YOUR HEAD.
Break mixed numbers into parts.

1. $4 \times 2\frac{1}{2}$ **4.** $8 \times 2\frac{1}{4}$ **7.** $5\frac{3}{4} \times 8$

2. $6 \times 3\frac{1}{2}$ **5.** $8 \times 1\frac{7}{8}$ **8.** $16 \times 2\frac{3}{8}$

3. $12 \times 4\frac{1}{2}$ **6.** $16 \times 2\frac{7}{8}$ **9.** $100 \times 1\frac{9}{10}$

10. $64 \times 1\frac{1}{4}$

POWER BUILDER A

1. $3 \times 5\frac{1}{5} =$ _____

2. $5 \times 2\frac{1}{6} =$ _____

3. $2 \times 1\frac{2}{7} =$ _____

4. $4 \times 3\frac{2}{9} =$ _____

5. $4 \times 3\frac{1}{2} =$ _____

6. $2 \times 4\frac{1}{2} =$ _____

7. $3\frac{1}{4} \times 4 =$ _____

8. $2\frac{1}{4} \times 8 =$ _____

9. $1\frac{1}{3} \times 6 =$ _____

10. $2\frac{1}{3} \times 3 =$ _____

11. $3 \times 2\frac{1}{2} =$ _____

12. $9 \times 3\frac{2}{3} =$ _____

13. $6 \times 4\frac{2}{3} =$ _____

14. $12 \times 2\frac{3}{4} =$ _____

15. $5 \times 2\frac{3}{5} =$ _____

16. $8 \times 1\frac{3}{4} =$ _____

17. $24 \times 2\frac{1}{3} =$ _____

18. $16 \times 1\frac{5}{8} =$ _____

19. $100 \times 7\frac{7}{10} =$ _____

20. $2\frac{1}{8} \times 64 =$ _____

THINK IT THROUGH

If a 6-foot vertical rod casts a shadow 15 feet long,
how high is a flagpole that casts a shadow 60 feet long?
75 feet long?

POWER BUILDER B

1. $4 \times 2\frac{1}{5} =$ _____

2. $3 \times 3\frac{1}{6} =$ _____

3. $3 \times 2\frac{2}{9} =$ _____

4. $3 \times 2\frac{2}{7} =$ _____

5. $3 \times 2\frac{5}{6} =$ _____

6. $3\frac{1}{4} \times 8 =$ _____

7. $3\frac{1}{6} \times 6 =$ _____

8. $2\frac{1}{4} \times 8 =$ _____

9. $1\frac{1}{3} \times 6 =$ _____

10. $3\frac{1}{5} \times 5 =$ _____

11. $5 \times 2\frac{1}{2} =$ _____

12. $9 \times 4\frac{2}{3} =$ _____

13. $8 \times 3\frac{3}{4} =$ _____

14. $15 \times 2\frac{2}{3} =$ _____

15. $15 \times 4\frac{3}{5} =$ _____

16. $16 \times 1\frac{3}{4} =$ _____

17. $24 \times 3\frac{1}{8} =$ _____

18. $9 \times 2\frac{2}{3} =$ _____

19. $100 \times 5\frac{3}{10} =$ _____

20. $3\frac{1}{9} \times 90 =$ _____

THINK IT THROUGH

A good mixture for concrete is 1 part cement, $2\frac{1}{4}$ parts sand,
3 parts gravel, and 5 gallons of water. If you start with 9 parts
sand, how much of the other ingredients do you need?

MENTAL MATH
IN DAILY LIFE

Mental math is a handy tool in the kitchen. Often we want to change a recipe to make more or less. For example . . .

DATE BREAD (1 loaf)	
Dates, cut up	$1\frac{1}{4}$ cups
Boiling water	$\frac{3}{4}$ cup
Baking soda	1 tsp
Eggs	1
Brown sugar	$\frac{3}{4}$ cup
Salt	$\frac{3}{4}$ tsp
Vanilla	1 tsp
Flour	$1\frac{3}{4}$ cups
Baking powder	1 tsp
Chopped nuts	$\frac{1}{2}$ cup
Melted butter	$\frac{3}{8}$ cup

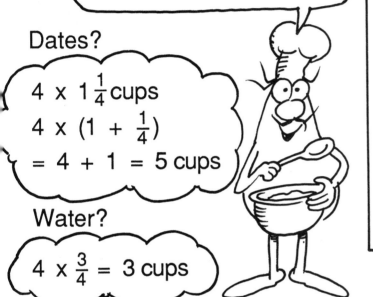

To make 4 loaves, how much of each ingredient do I need?

Dates?

$4 \times 1\frac{1}{4}$ cups

$4 \times (1 + \frac{1}{4})$

$= 4 + 1 = 5$ cups

Water?

$4 \times \frac{3}{4} = 3$ cups

For mixed numbers, try multiplying in parts.

TRY THESE IN YOUR HEAD.

How much would you need of each ingredient?

	DATES	WATER	SODA	EGGS	SUGAR	SALT	VANILLA	FLOUR	B. POWDER	NUTS	BUTTER
4 loaves											
8 loaves											
16 loaves											

POWER BUILDER A

Vegetable Stir Fry (serves 3 people)
$\frac{3}{4}$ pounds of fresh shrimp
$\frac{1}{4}$ cup sliced carrots
$\frac{2}{3}$ cup chopped broccoli
$1\frac{1}{2}$ T of finely diced onion
$1\frac{1}{4}$ cups sliced squash
$\frac{1}{2}$ cup mushrooms
$2\frac{1}{3}$ tsp soy sauce
1 T cornstarch
$\frac{1}{8}$ tsp garlic powder
$2\frac{1}{2}$ T oil

Double the recipe.

1. _____
2. _____
3. _____
4. _____
5. _____
6. _____
7. _____
8. _____
9. _____
10. _____

About how much for 12 people?

11. _____
12. _____
13. _____
14. _____
15. _____
16. _____
17. _____
18. _____
19. _____
20. _____

THINK IT THROUGH

Which is more: triple two-thirds or double three-fourths?

POWER BUILDER B

Trail Mix
$\frac{1}{2}$ cup shredded coconut
$\frac{2}{3}$ cup sunflower seeds
$1\frac{1}{4}$ cups raisins
$\frac{2}{3}$ cup pecans
$\frac{1}{3}$ cup chopped walnuts
$\frac{1}{2}$ cup peanut butter
$\frac{3}{4}$ cup honey
$2\frac{1}{3}$ cups oats
$1\frac{1}{2}$ tsp vanilla
$1\frac{1}{4}$ tsp cinnamon

Double the recipe.

1. _____
2. _____
3. _____
4. _____
5. _____
6. _____
7. _____
8. _____
9. _____
10. _____

Triple the recipe.

11. _____
12. _____
13. _____
14. _____
15. _____
16. _____
17. _____
18. _____
19. _____
20. _____

THINK IT THROUGH

Which is more: triple two-fifths or double three-eighths?

DID YOU KNOW...

You can take half of one factor and double the other factor without changing the product!

$$
\begin{array}{c}
4 \\
\times\ 5 \\
\hline
20
\end{array}
\quad
\begin{array}{c}
\text{HALF} \rightarrow \\
\text{DOUBLE} \rightarrow
\end{array}
\quad
\begin{array}{c}
2 \\
\times\ 10 \\
\hline
20
\end{array}
$$

$$
\begin{array}{c}
8 \\
\times\ 5 \\
\hline
40
\end{array}
\quad
\begin{array}{c}
\text{HALF} \rightarrow \\
\text{DOUBLE} \rightarrow
\end{array}
\quad
\begin{array}{c}
4 \\
\times\ 10 \\
\hline
40
\end{array}
$$

Halving and doubling is a good mental math trick.

It can make some mental calculations easier.

HALF of 8, DOUBLE 15

4 x 30

120

8 x 15

POOF!

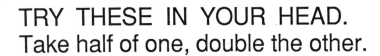

TRY THESE IN YOUR HEAD.
Take half of one, double the other.

1. 15 x 4   **4.** 13 x 8   **7.** 35 x 12

2. 6 x 15   **5.** 16 x 25   **8.** 8 x 250

3. 4 x 35   **6.** 8 x 18   **9.** 12 x 225

                              10. 15 x 32

POWER BUILDER A

Halve one and double the other.

1. 4 x 45 = _____
2. 4 x 65 = _____
3. 8 x 27 = _____
4. 8 x 127 = _____
5. 74 x 4 = _____
6. 122 x 8 = _____
7. 45 x 16 = _____
8. 85 x 16 = _____
9. 16 x 16 = _____
10. 16 x 64 = _____

11. 6 x 35 = _____
12. 6 x 45 = _____
13. 14 x 45 = _____
14. 55 x 14 = _____
15. 8 x 350 = _____
16. 4500 x 8 = _____
17. 12 x 45 = _____
18. 350 x 18 = _____
19. 12 x 550 = _____
20. 250 x 16 = _____

THINK IT THROUGH

Suppose you double one penny 10 times.
How many dollars will you have?

POWER BUILDER B

Halve one and double the other.

1. 4 x 55 = _____
2. 4 x 85 = _____
3. 8 x 26 = _____
4. 8 x 125 = _____
5. 64 x 4 = _____
6. 112 x 8 = _____
7. 51 x 16 = _____
8. 95 x 16 = _____
9. 14 x 16 = _____
10. 16 x 54 = _____

11. 6 x 55 = _____
12. 6 x 65 = _____
13. 14 x 55 = _____
14. 65 x 14 = _____
15. 8 x 275 = _____
16. 3500 x 8 = _____
17. 12 x 35 = _____
18. 450 x 18 = _____
19. 12 x 450 = _____
20. 350 x 16 = _____

THINK IT THROUGH

A 512-cm board is cut in two equal pieces. One of
these pieces is cut in half again. How many cuts
(always halving) must be made to get a 1-cm piece?

To multiply decimals in your head, try **HALVING** and **DOUBLING** to make an easier problem.

8 x 1.5

HALF of 8, **DOUBLE** 1.5

4 x 3

12

Sometimes it helps to halve and double more than once.

88 x 0.125

HALF		DOUBLE
88	x	0.125
44	x	0.25
22	x	0.50
11	x	1

TRY THESE IN YOUR HEAD.
Halve one, double the other.

1. 6 x 3.5   **4.** 18 x 4.5   **7.** 24 x 0.25

2. 24 x 1.5   **5.** 20 x 6.5   **8.** 32 x 1.25

3. 42 x 2.5   **6.** 420 x 1.5   **9.** 48 x 0.125

10. 72 x 1.125

POWER BUILDER A

Halve one and double the other.

1. 4 x 4.5 = _____
2. 6 x 2.5 = _____
3. 4 x 5.3 = _____
4. 6 x 3.1 = _____
5. 8 x 1.6 = _____
6. 2.2 x 8 = _____
7. 5.5 x 8 = _____
8. 16 x 1.5 = _____
9. 6 x 6.5 = _____
10. 9.3 x 6 = _____

11. 4 x 0.125 = _____
12. 16 x 1.25 = _____
13. 8 x 0.42 = _____
14. 32 x 2.25 = _____
15. 24 x 1.125 = _____
16. 48 x 0.125 = _____
17. 16 x 1.75 = _____
18. 8 x 3.25 = _____
19. 16 x 4.25 = _____
20. 0.75 x 16 = _____

THINK IT THROUGH

Given that 35 x 35 = 1225, what is 35 x 37?
3.5 x 3.5?   17.5 x 70?

POWER BUILDER B

Halve one and double the other.

1. 4 x 6.5 = _____
2. 4 x 8.2 = _____
3. 6 x 3.5 = _____
4. 6 x 8.5 = _____
5. 8 x 3.6 = _____
6. 2.4 x 8 = _____
7. 8.5 x 8 = _____
8. 16 x 2.5 = _____
9. 6 x 5.5 = _____
10. 8.3 x 6 = _____

11. 4 x 0.225 = _____
12. 8 x 2.25 = _____
13. 16 x 2.25 = _____
14. 32 x 0.125 = _____
15. 16 x 4.125 = _____
16. 24 x 0.125 = _____
17. 1.75 x 12 = _____
18. 32 x 3.25 = _____
19. 24 x 2.25 = _____
20. 1.5 x 24 = _____

THINK IT THROUGH

Given that 25 x 25 = 625, what is 25 x 27?
2.5 x 2.5?   12.5 x 50?

Sometimes thinking of money can help you multiply in your head.

16 x 5

16 nickels . . . I'll think of dimes.
16 nickels equals $\frac{1}{2}$ of 16 dimes or 8 dimes.

16 x 5 = 80

16 x 25

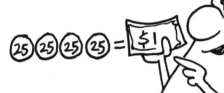

16 quarters . . . I'll think of dollars.
16 quarters equals $\frac{1}{4}$ of 16 dollars or 4 dollars.

16 x 25 = 400

16 x 50

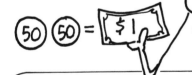

16 half dollars . . . I'll think of dollars.
16 half dollars equals $\frac{1}{2}$ of 16 dollars or 8 dollars.

16 x 50 = 800

TRY THESE IN YOUR HEAD.
Think money!

1. 12 x 5
2. 5 x 18
3. 12 x 25

4. 14 x 50
5. 64 x 50
6. 32 x 25

7. 48 x 25
8. 500 x 18
9. 50 x 38
10. 250 x 12

POWER BUILDER A

1. 12 x 5 = _____

2. 26 x 5 = _____

3. 16 x 50 = _____

4. 5 x 88 = _____

5. 12 x 50 = _____

6. 5 x 48 = _____

7. 64 x 50 = _____

8. 25 x 32 = _____

9. 5 x 66 = _____

10. 36 x 5 = _____

11. 26 x 50 = _____

12. 50 x 36 = _____

13. 25 x 64 = _____

14. 56 x 5 = _____

15. 54 x 50 = _____

16. 25 x 320 = _____

17. 50 x 210 = _____

18. 25 x 88 = _____

19. 25 x 240 = _____

20. 50 x 124 = _____

THINK IT THROUGH

A ream of paper usually contains 500 sheets. How many sheets are in 12 reams? 24 reams? 33 reams?

POWER BUILDER B

1. 18 x 5 = _____

2. 5 x 14 = _____

3. 16 x 50 = _____

4. 48 x 25 = _____

5. 5 x 44 = _____

6. 28 x 50 = _____

7. 5 x 64 = _____

8. 50 x 48 = _____

9. 36 x 25 = _____

10. 5 x 32 = _____

11. 22 x 50 = _____

12. 25 x 44 = _____

13. 50 x 120 = _____

14. 56 x 5 = _____

15. 54 x 50 = _____

16. 25 x 280 = _____

17. 50 x 140 = _____

18. 25 x 124 = _____

19. 25 x 220 = _____

20. 5 x 6666 = _____

THINK IT THROUGH

Using 25 x 28 = 700, calculate the following:

75 x 28   25 x 14   2.5 x 28   0.25 x 29

How would you do this in your head? Multiplying the numbers in order, step by step, is NOT the answer.

$$25 \times 5 \times 9 \times 2 \times 4$$

$25 \times 5 = 125,\ 125 \times 9 = \ldots$
TOO HARD!

To make multiplication easier, search for compatible factors.

Then rearrange the factors to simplify your figuring.

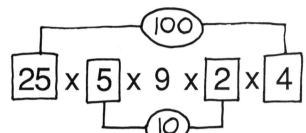

$$25 \times 5 \times 9 \times 2 \times 4$$
with 100 grouping 25 and 5, and 10 grouping 2 and 4...

$9 \times 100 \times 10$

$9 \times 1000 = 9000$

TRY THESE IN YOUR HEAD.
Search for compatible factors.

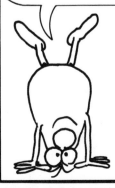

1. $2 \times 8 \times 5$
2. $2 \times 7 \times 15$
3. $4 \times 11 \times 50$
4. $4 \times 13 \times 25$
5. $6 \times 9 \times 500$

6. $2 \times 19 \times 5$
7. $25 \times 5 \times 4 \times 2$
8. $2 \times 13 \times 5 \times 5 \times 2$
9. $4 \times 7 \times 3 \times 250$
10. $15 \times 3 \times 2 \times 2 \times 15$

POWER BUILDER A

1. 5 x 7 x 2 = _____

2. 2 x 13 x 5 = _____

3. 2 x 6 x 15 = _____

4. 15 x 4 x 5 = _____

5. 20 x 7 x 5 = _____

6. 2 x 7 x 5 x 6 = _____

7. 15 x 7 x 2 x 3 = _____

8. 6 x 4 x 5 x 25 = _____

9. 11 x 4 x 2 x 25 = _____

10. 25 x 5 x 4 x 8 = _____

11. 15 x 3 x 4 x 2 = _____

12. 4 x 4 x 15 x 5 = _____

13. 5 x 5 x 6 x 2 x 2 = _____

14. 5 x 7 x 5 x 4 = _____

15. 9 x 3 x 4 x 5 = _____

16. 13 x 2 x 3 x 5 = _____

17. 5 x 7 x 7 x 2 = _____

18. 5 x 5 x 8 x 2 x 4 = _____

19. 11 x 2 x 6 x 25 = _____

20. 9 x 8 x 50 x 2 = _____

THINK IT THROUGH

The dimensions of a large tank are 25 m by 25 m by 8 m. What is the volume of water it can hold?

POWER BUILDER B

1. 4 x 6 x 25 = _____

2. 2 x 29 x 5 = _____

3. 7 x 15 x 2 = _____

4. 4 x 15 x 5 = _____

5. 5 x 3 x 12 = _____

6. 6 x 4 x 5 x 2 x 5 = _____

7. 11 x 5 x 2 x 6 = _____

8. 3 x 4 x 25 x 13 = _____

9. 12 x 3 x 4 x 25 = _____

10. 4 x 13 x 25 x 2 = _____

11. 2 x 3 x 5 x 13 = _____

12. 9 x 8 x 5 x 2 = _____

13. 5 x 3 x 9 x 2 = _____

14. 7 x 5 x 3 x 4 = _____

15. 15 x 4 x 5 x 5 = _____

16. 11 x 5 x 5 x 8 = _____

17. 7 x 5 x 20 x 8 = _____

18. 25 x 9 x 5 x 4 = _____

19. 50 x 3 x 8 x 3 = _____

20. 125 x 11 x 2 x 4 = _____

THINK IT THROUGH

Fifteen workers each worked 40 hours a week for 5 weeks at a rate of $8.00 an hour. Calculate the cost of the payroll.

To simplify this multiplication, rearrange one or both of the numbers.

The trick is to look for pairs of factors that are compatible.

Then complete the multiplication in steps.

28 x 25

Let's see . . .
4 x 25 = 100 . . .
And 4 is a factor of 28!

28 x 25

7 x 4 x 25

7 x 100

700

Can you find another pair of compatible factors to check your calculation?

TRY THESE IN YOUR HEAD.
Make your own compatible factors.

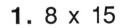

1. 8 x 15   **4.** 12 x 25   **7.** 15 x 36

2. 4 x 45   **5.** 18 x 15   **8.** 36 x 25

3. 15 x 14   **6.** 28 x 50   **9.** 32 x 500

                                         10. 12 x 150

POWER BUILDER A

1. 35 x 4 = _____

2. 4 x 45 = _____

3. 15 x 14 = _____

4. 24 x 15 = _____

5. 15 x 18 = _____

6. 12 x 25 = _____

7. 5 x 24 = _____

8. 18 x 50 = _____

9. 25 x 16 = _____

10. 5 x 32 = _____

11. 22 x 15 = _____

12. 25 x 18 = _____

13. 45 x 16 = _____

14. 15 x 36 = _____

15. 35 x 12 = _____

16. 60 x 25 = _____

17. 55 x 40 = _____

18. 45 x 80 = _____

19. 25 x 180 = _____

20. 450 x 8 = _____

THINK IT THROUGH

Rearrange the factors in these problems and calculate the products mentally:

1.5 x 8   25 x 1.2   2.5 x 48

POWER BUILDER B

1. 6 x 25 = _____

2. 35 x 6 = _____

3. 55 x 4 = _____

4. 6 x 45 = _____

5. 45 x 8 = _____

6. 6 x 55 = _____

7. 35 x 8 = _____

8. 8 x 25 = _____

9. 15 x 22 = _____

10. 25 x 14 = _____

11. 25 x 18 = _____

12. 25 x 28 = _____

13. 45 x 12 = _____

14. 15 x 26 = _____

15. 35 x 14 = _____

16. 40 x 35 = _____

17. 50 x 24 = _____

18. 250 x 16 = _____

19. 40 x 450 = _____

20. 15 x 180 = _____

THINK IT THROUGH

The dimensions of a box are 15 by 10 by 24. If one dimension is doubled, what is the new volume? What happens to the volume if one dimension is halved and another doubled? What if all the dimensions are doubled?

$\boxed{0.234 \times 10}$

Watch what happens when we multiply a decimal number by 10.

The decimal point appears to slide **one** place to the right!

Think of it as $\frac{234}{1000} \times 10$

$= \frac{2340}{1000} = 2\frac{340}{1000} = 2\frac{34}{100} = 2.34$

Or . . . $0.234 \times 10 =$

$0.234 \times 10 = 2.34$

$\boxed{0.234 \times 100}$

$0.234 \times 10 = 2.34$

$2.34 \times 10 = 23.4$

That is...

$0.234 \times 100 = 23.4$

Multiplying by 100 is like multiplying by 10 twice. So . . . the decimal point slides **two** places to the right.

$0.234 \times 1000 = 234.0$

As you can probably guess, when we multiply by 1000, the decimal point slides **three** places to the right.

TRY THESE IN YOUR HEAD.
Slide the decimal point to the right.

1. 1.56×10 **4.** 15.3×10 **7.** 11.6×100

2. 0.38×100 **5.** 1.62×100 **8.** 1.2×1000

3. 0.999×1000 **6.** 0.856×10 **9.** 2.45×1000

10. 1.1111×100

POWER BUILDER A

1. 1.5 x 10 = _____
2. 100 x 2.3 = _____
3. 1000 x 3.5 = _____
4. 10 x 0.46 = _____
5. 100 x 0.53 = _____
6. 1000 x 0.49 = _____
7. 10 x 16.5 = _____
8. 1.89 x 100 = _____
9. 1000 x 1.25 = _____
10. 10 x 11.23 = _____

11. 15.56 x 100 = _____
12. 14.78 x 1000 = _____
13. 10 x 48.175 = _____
14. 59.625 x 100 = _____
15. 1000 x 12.345 = _____
16. 10 x 18.2356 = _____
17. 7.8926 x 100 = _____
18. 15.555 x 1000 = _____
19. 0.00123 x 100 = _____
20. 0.00035 x 1000 = _____

THINK IT THROUGH

Complete the following number statement:
0.123456789 x ? = 123456789

POWER BUILDER B

1. 1.4 x 10 = _____
2. 100 x 3.2 = _____
3. 1000 x 8.5 = _____
4. 10 x 0.64 = _____
5. 100 x 0.11 = _____
6. 1000 x 0.99 = _____
7. 10 x 55.5 = _____
8. 9.81 x 100 = _____
9. 1000 x 5.25 = _____
10. 10 x 10.03 = _____

11. 25.50 x 100 = _____
12. 24.78 x 1000 = _____
13. 10 x 84.175 = _____
14. 99.999 x 100 = _____
15. 1000 x 54.321 = _____
16. 10 x 11.1111 = _____
17. 1.8926 x 100 = _____
18. 10.005 x 1000 = _____
19. 0.00321 x 100 = _____
20. 0.35035 x 1000 = _____

THINK IT THROUGH

A human hair is approximately 0.005 mm
in diameter. How many hairs placed side by side
would be needed to reach 1 mm? 1 cm? 1 m?

When we divide a number by 10, the decimal point slides **one** place to the left.

$$123 \div 10 = \frac{123}{10}$$
$$= 12\frac{3}{10} = 12.3$$

Or . . . $123.0 \div 10 =$

$123.0 \div 10 = 12.3$

Dividing by 100 is like dividing by 10 twice. So . . . the decimal point slides **two** places to the left.

$123.0 \div 100 = 1.23$

Similarly, when we divide by 1000, the decimal point slides **three** places to the left.

$123.0 \div 1000 = 0.123$

Make up similar rules for multiplying by . . .

$\frac{1}{10}$, $\frac{1}{100}$, and $\frac{1}{1000}$

or 0.1, 0.01, and 0.001

$\frac{1}{10}$ of 23.6

15.36×0.01

TRY THESE IN YOUR HEAD.
Slide the decimal point to the left.

1. $2.54 \div 10$ **4.** $116.43 \div 1000$ **7.** 0.01×360

2. $2.54 \div 100$ **5.** $0.025 \div 10$ **8.** 5280×0.001

3. $180 \div 100$ **6.** $\frac{1}{10}$ of 18   **9.** $\frac{1}{100}$ of 120

10. 0.001×1.23

POWER BUILDER A

1. 55 ÷ 10 = _____

2. 86 ÷ 100 = _____

3. 99 ÷ 1000 = _____

4. 0.1 x 4.35 = _____

5. 1.49 x 0.01 = _____

6. 0.001 x 456.7 = _____

7. $\frac{1}{10}$ x 45.3 = _____

8. 123 x $\frac{1}{100}$ = _____

9. 1456 x $\frac{1}{1000}$ = _____

10. 0.001 x 2111 = _____

11. 1856 ÷ 10 = _____

12. 5555 ÷ 100 = _____

13. 111 ÷ 1000 = _____

14. 0.1 x 0.123 = _____

15. 0.01 x 0.01 = _____

16. 0.008 x 0.1 = _____

17. 0.099 x 0.001 = _____

18. 1234 x 0.001 = _____

19. 0.001 x 0.01 = _____

20. 0.01 x 1.23 x 0.1 = _____

THINK IT THROUGH

An attometer is a millionth of a millionth of a millionth of a meter. If you wrote it as a decimal number, how many zeroes would follow the decimal point?

POWER BUILDER B

1. 44 ÷ 10 = _____

2. 88 ÷ 100 = _____

3. 69 ÷ 1000 = _____

4. 0.1 x 1.35 = _____

5. 4.44 x 0.01 = _____

6. 0.001 x 765.4 = _____

7. $\frac{1}{10}$ x 10.3 = _____

8. 333 x $\frac{1}{100}$ = _____

9. 2457 x $\frac{1}{1000}$ = _____

10. 0.001 x 2222 = _____

11. 8856 ÷ 10 = _____

12. 1111 ÷ 100 = _____

13. 222 ÷ 1000 = _____

14. 0.1 x 0.1414 = _____

15. 0.01 x 0.1 = _____

16. 0.002 x 0.1 = _____

17. 0.999 x 0.001 = _____

18. 4234 x 0.001 = _____

19. 0.001 x 0.001 = _____

20. 0.01 x 4.23 x 0.1 = _____

THINK IT THROUGH

The human brain has 10,000,000,000 nerve cells or neurons. It loses about 1000 cells every day after the age of 18. How many days would it take to lose all the brain cells? About how many years?

METRIC UNITS OF LENGTH

When you are working with metric lengths, you need to know how to change a measurement from one unit to another.

Fortunately, this figuring is easy to do in your head.

240 cm = ? m

100 cm = 1 m

so 240 cm = (240 ÷ 100) m

240.0 ÷ 100 = 2.4 m

480 cm = ? mm

1 cm = 10 mm

so 480 cm = (480 x 10) mm

480.0 x 10 = 4800 mm

MENTAL MATH TIP

Changing to a larger unit gives you fewer units.

Changing to a smaller unit gives you more units.

TRY THESE IN YOUR HEAD.

Change to mm . . .
1. 3 m
2. 3.5 m
3. 0.5 m
4. 1.75 m
5. 15.55 m

Change to m . . .
6. 3550 mm
7. 25,115 mm
8. 180 cm
9. 4700 cm
10. 1855 mm

POWER BUILDER A

Change to meters:

1. 105 cm = _____

2. 185 cm = _____

3. 1234 cm = _____

4. 500 cm = _____

5. 75 cm = _____

6. 1500 mm = _____

7. 2500 mm = _____

8. 750 mm = _____

9. 40,000 mm = _____

10. 10 mm = _____

Change to millimeters:

11. 2.5 m = _____

12. 4.8 m = _____

13. 0.5 m = _____

14. 0.25 m = _____

15. 0.005 m = _____

16. 180 cm = _____

17. 5 cm = _____

18. 0.5 cm = _____

19. 0.01 cm = _____

20. 250 cm = _____

THINK IT THROUGH

A dollar bill is about 15 cm long. If one million dollars were laid end to end, for how many kilometers would the line of bills stretch?

POWER BUILDER B

Change to meters:

1. 205 cm = _____

2. 355 cm = _____

3. 4321 cm = _____

4. 900 cm = _____

5. 55 cm = _____

6. 4500 mm = _____

7. 7500 mm = _____

8. 500 mm = _____

9. 50,000 mm = _____

10. 1 mm = _____

Change to millimeters:

11. 5.5 m = _____

12. 8.8 m = _____

13. 0.75 m = _____

14. 0.45 m = _____

15. 0.001 m = _____

16. 150 cm = _____

17. 50 cm = _____

18. 0.05 cm = _____

19. 0.355 cm = _____

20. 1.25 cm = _____

THINK IT THROUGH

The U.S. national debt is over one trillion dollars ($1,000,000,000,000.00). If one trillion dollar bills, each about 15 cm long, were laid end to end, for how many kilometers would they reach?

Mental Math Techniques
• **BREAK MIXED NUMBERS INTO PARTS.** $4 \times 2\frac{1}{2} = ?$
• **HALVE ONE, DOUBLE THE OTHER.** $8 \times 15 = ?$ $12 \times 1.5 = ?$
• **THINK MONEY.** $16 \times 25 = ?$ $18 \times 50 = ?$
• **USE COMPATIBLE FACTORS.** $25 \times 7 \times 4 = ?$ $8 \times 15 = 120$, so $24 \times 15 = ?$
• **SLIDE THE DECIMAL POINT.** $0.152 \times 100 = ?$ $2.13 \div 100 = ?$

Do the problems below in your head. Tell which techniques you find useful for each one.

1. 8×25
2. $6 \times 2\frac{1}{3}$
3. 16×15
4. 15×12
5. 0.369×1000
6. $12.56 \div 1000$
7. $25 \times 13 \times 2 \times 2$
8. 25×32
9. 50×64
10. 16×35

Talk about each problem below. What's an easy way to do it in your head? Tell how you would think it through.

1. 12.3×100
2. 5×48
3. 500×45
4. $14 \times 25 \times 8$
5. 35×18
6. $8 \times 5\frac{1}{2}$
7. $100.01 \div 10$
8. 25×64
9. $0.356 \div 100$
10. 250×12

1. Double $2\frac{2}{3}$ = _____

2. 100 x 3.4 = _____

3. 6 x 2 x 50 = _____

4. 8 x 6.5 = _____

5. 50 x 36 = _____

6. Change to meters:

    105 cm = _____ m

7. 1000 x 5.021 = _____

8. 6 x $3\frac{1}{3}$ = _____

9. 4 x 85 = _____

10. Triple $\frac{1}{2}$ = _____

11. 7 x 6 x 25 x 4 = _____

12. 53.4 ÷ 100 = _____

13. 8 x 450 = _____

14. 5 x 66 = _____

15. Change to meters:

    246.3 mm = _____ m

16. 22 x 35 = _____

17. 8 x $4\frac{1}{4}$ = _____

18. 5 x 18 x 20 = _____

19. 16 x 1.75 = _____

20. 10 x 0.46 = _____

21. 12 x 25 = _____

22. $1\frac{3}{4}$ x 12 = _____

23. Change to meters:

    4256.1 cm = _____ m

24. 14 x 35 = _____

25. 25 x 4.40 = _____

26. 100 x 0.0415 = _____

27. 4 x 3 x 9 x 25 = _____

28. Double $\frac{3}{4}$ = _____

29. Change to meters:

    40,000 mm = _____ m

30. 15 x 18 = _____

31. 15 x $2\frac{2}{3}$ = _____

32. $1.25 x 16 = _____

33. 0.01 x 5.27 = _____

34. 50 x 12.80 = _____

35. Triple $1\frac{1}{3}$ = _____

36. 125.6 x 0.001 = _____

37. 16 x 42 = _____

38. 45 x 12 = _____

39. 0.1 x 42.73 = _____

40. 8 x 0.45 = _____

Cube Roots

Shakuntala Devi, a woman from India, found the 23rd root of a 201-digit number in 50 seconds. That's a feat beyond most MENTALMATHLETES. But . . .

Expert mental calculators find it **easy** to calculate cube roots in their heads. That's because there is a helpful pattern.

Use a calculator to finish this table. What pattern do you see?

A MENTALMATHLETE can do some quick estimating, look at the ending digits of a number, and figure the cube root.

CUBE ROOT	CUBE	CUBE ROOT	CUBE
0	0	10	1000
1	1	11	1331
2	8	12	1728
3	27	13	2197
4	64	14	
5	125	15	
6	216	16	
7	343	17	
8	512	18	
9	729	19	

FIND THE
CUBE ROOT OF
1728

Must be between 10 and 20 because $10^3 = 1000$ and $20^3 = 8000$.

The last digit is 8 . . . so the cube root must be 12.

YOUR TURN

Use this method to calculate the cube roots of the following numbers. Check your answers with a calculator.

3375	5832	6859	15,625
21,952	68,921	571,787	166,375

MENTAL MATH IN JUNIOR HIGH
Copyright © 1988 by Dale Seymour Publications

Cube Roots

This strategy not only gives students a better understanding of cubes and cube roots, it offers a chance for some valuable practice in estimating. After students have completed the cube root and cube table (using calculators), help them make the following generalizations:

1. If the ending digit of a perfect cube is either 0, 1, 4, 5, 6, or 9, then the cube root has the same ending digit. For example, the cube root of the perfect cube 24,389 must end in 9.

2. If the ending digit of a perfect cube is either 2, 3, 7, or 8, then the cube root ends in the tens complement (8 + 2 = 10; 7 + 3 = 10). For example, the cube root of the perfect cube 54,872 must end in 8.

Emphasize that these patterns apply only to the cube roots of perfect cubes. That is, the cube root of 135 will not end in 5 because 135 is not a perfect cube.

Challenge students to construct a table showing the ending digits of squares and square roots and to develop a similar rule for determining the square roots of perfect squares.

Working with dozens, or with feet and inches, we often have to figure with the number 12.

Let's face it . . .12 is simply not as easy to work with as 10.

But there's a trick that makes multiplying and dividing by 12 easier.

Here's the key . . .

$12 = 3 \times 2 \times 2$

To multiply by 12 . . . **TRIPLE, DOUBLE,** and **DOUBLE** again.

| 16 feet = ? inches |

- **TRIPLE** 16 → 48
- **DOUBLE** 48 → 96
- **DOUBLE** 96 → 192

16 feet = 192 inches

To divide by 12 . . . take $\frac{1}{3}, \frac{1}{2}$, and $\frac{1}{2}$ again.

| 180 muffins = ? dozen |

- $\frac{1}{3}$ of 180 → 60
- $\frac{1}{2}$ of 60 → 30
- $\frac{1}{2}$ of 30 → 15

180 muffins = 15 dozen

TRY THESE IN YOUR HEAD.
Use the factors of 12.

Change to feet.

1. 72 inches
2. 96 inches
3. 108 inches
4. 144 inches
5. 264 inches

Change to units.

6. 7 dozen
7. 11 dozen
8. 13 dozen
9. 15 dozen
10. 25 dozen

POWER BUILDER A

Change to single units or inches:

1. 5 dozen buns = _____

2. 8 feet = _____

3. 9 dozen cookies = _____

4. 12 feet = _____

5. 11 dozen chocolates = _____

6. 16 feet = _____

7. 25 dozen bottles = _____

8. 15 feet = _____

9. 14 feet = _____

10. 22 dozen eggs = _____

Change to dozens or feet:

11. 96 inches = _____

12. 60 inches = _____

13. 120 bottles = _____

14. 180 inches = _____

15. 156 washers = _____

16. 720 inches = _____

17. 240 eggs = _____

18. 192 inches = _____

19. 300 inches = _____

20. 720 buns = _____

THINK IT THROUGH

If a gross is 12 dozen, how many pencils
are in 5 gross? $2\frac{1}{2}$ gross? 7.5 gross?

POWER BUILDER B

Change to single units or inches:

1. 4 feet = _____

2. 12 feet = _____

3. 6 dozen rolls = _____

4. 5 dozen doughnuts = _____

5. 25 feet = _____

6. 13 dozen eggs = _____

7. 16 feet = _____

8. 17 dozen bottles = _____

9. 24 dozen pens = _____

10. 18 feet = _____

Change to dozens or feet:

11. 240 nails = _____

12. 720 inches = _____

13. 108 inches = _____

14. 168 muffins = _____

15. 288 cookies = _____

16. 360 inches = _____

17. 480 eggs = _____

18. 192 cupcakes = _____

19. 312 inches = _____

20. 1440 inches = _____

THINK IT THROUGH

Use the fact that 24 = 2 x 2 x 2 x 3 to make up rules
for converting days to hours and hours to days. Use
your rules to calculate:

168 hours = ? days   15 days = ? hours

DIVIDE IN YOUR HEAD

515 ÷ 5

For mental division, try breaking up the dividend into parts.

$5 \overline{)5 \vert 15}$

$\dfrac{100+3}{5 \overline{)500+15}}$

$100+3=103$

$\checkmark 5 \times 103 = 500+15 = 515$

- BREAK UP 515 into 500 and 15.

- DIVIDE both parts by 5.

- ADD the answers together.

- CHECK by multiplying.

Thinking about place value can help you eliminate silly mistakes.

What mistake has been made here? What should the answer be?

$\dfrac{14}{4 \overline{)416}}$ $4 \div 4 = 1$
$16 \div 4 = 4$

TRY THESE IN YOUR HEAD.
Break up the dividend.

1. 440 ÷ 2	**4.** 436 ÷ 4	**7.** $5 \overline{)5005}$
2. 636 ÷ 3	**5.** 1248 ÷ 4	**8.** $12 \overline{)2436}$
3. 648 ÷ 6	**6.** 1208 ÷ 2	**9.** $7 \overline{)5649}$
		10. $4 \overline{)1616}$

POWER BUILDER A

1. $69 \div 3 =$ _____
2. $77 \div 7 =$ _____
3. $168 \div 8 =$ _____
4. $146 \div 2 =$ _____
5. $147 \div 7 =$ _____
6. $303 \div 3 =$ _____
7. $105 \div 5 =$ _____
8. $126 \div 6 =$ _____
9. $714 \div 7 =$ _____
10. $333 \div 3 =$ _____

11. $404 \div 4 =$ _____
12. $515 \div 5 =$ _____
13. $639 \div 3 =$ _____
14. $648 \div 6 =$ _____
15. $816 \div 8 =$ _____
16. $918 \div 9 =$ _____
17. $5005 \div 5 =$ _____
18. $8008 \div 4 =$ _____
19. $2424 \div 6 =$ _____
20. $3636 \div 4 =$ _____

THINK IT THROUGH

Using the fact $4096 \div 2 = 2048$, calculate the following problems mentally:

$4096 \div 4$ $4096 \div 8$ $4096 \div 16$

POWER BUILDER B

1. $99 \div 3 =$ _____
2. $88 \div 8 =$ _____
3. $168 \div 4 =$ _____
4. $846 \div 2 =$ _____
5. $217 \div 7 =$ _____
6. $306 \div 6 =$ _____
7. $205 \div 5 =$ _____
8. $126 \div 3 =$ _____
9. $814 \div 2 =$ _____
10. $999 \div 3 =$ _____

11. $808 \div 4 =$ _____
12. $618 \div 6 =$ _____
13. $939 \div 3 =$ _____
14. $486 \div 6 =$ _____
15. $1818 \div 9 =$ _____
16. $918 \div 3 =$ _____
17. $4004 \div 2 =$ _____
18. $8048 \div 4 =$ _____
19. $3636 \div 6 =$ _____
20. $3648 \div 4 =$ _____

THINK IT THROUGH

Using the fact $256 \div 8 = 32$, calculate the following problems mentally:

$264 \div 8$ $256 \div 4$ $8256 \div 8$ $1056 \div 8$

140

$$128 \div 8$$

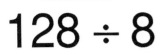

$$128 = 80 + 48$$

8 divides 80, and
8 divides 48 . . .

$$8 \overline{)\begin{array}{c} 10 + 6 = 16 \\ 80 + 48 \end{array}}$$

✓ 8 x 16 = 80 + 48 = 128

You can make some division problems easier by rearranging the dividend.

The trick is to look for numbers compatible with the divisor—in this example, numbers that can be divided by 8.

Then divide by parts, and add the answers.

Check by multiplying.

$$152 \div 8$$

Sometimes you can use subtraction to make compatibles.

$$152 = 160 - 8$$

$$8 \overline{)\begin{array}{c} 20 - 1 = 19 \\ 160 - 8 \end{array}}$$

✓ 8 x 19 = 80 + 72 = 152

TRY THESE IN YOUR HEAD.
Make compatibles.
Check by multiplying.

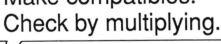

1. 56 ÷ 4	**4.** 52 ÷ 2	**7.** 135 ÷ 3
2. 76 ÷ 4	**5.** 84 ÷ 6	**8.** 114 ÷ 6
3. 96 ÷ 8	**6.** 84 ÷ 7	**9.** 256 ÷ 4
		10. 232 ÷ 8

POWER BUILDER A

1. $42 \div 3 =$ _____

2. $76 \div 2 =$ _____

3. $96 \div 8 =$ _____

4. $54 \div 2 =$ _____

5. $70 \div 5 =$ _____

6. $58 \div 2 =$ _____

7. $72 \div 3 =$ _____

8. $98 \div 7 =$ _____

9. $78 \div 6 =$ _____

10. $80 \div 5 =$ _____

11. $144 \div 6 =$ _____

12. $135 \div 3 =$ _____

13. $154 \div 7 =$ _____

14. $198 \div 9 =$ _____

15. $156 \div 6 =$ _____

16. $256 \div 8 =$ _____

17. $225 \div 9 =$ _____

18. $465 \div 5 =$ _____

19. $325 \div 5 =$ _____

20. $512 \div 8 =$ _____

THINK IT THROUGH

What number divided by 2, then by 3, then by 5, and finally by 7 equals 10?

POWER BUILDER B

1. $56 \div 4 =$ _____

2. $98 \div 2 =$ _____

3. $78 \div 3 =$ _____

4. $96 \div 4 =$ _____

5. $52 \div 4 =$ _____

6. $81 \div 3 =$ _____

7. $60 \div 5 =$ _____

8. $91 \div 7 =$ _____

9. $84 \div 6 =$ _____

10. $90 \div 5 =$ _____

11. $144 \div 4 =$ _____

12. $126 \div 7 =$ _____

13. $165 \div 3 =$ _____

14. $180 \div 4 =$ _____

15. $252 \div 6 =$ _____

16. $192 \div 8 =$ _____

17. $207 \div 9 =$ _____

18. $156 \div 4 =$ _____

19. $360 \div 8 =$ _____

20. $162 \div 3 =$ _____

THINK IT THROUGH

What number divided in half 5 times equals 100?

When you multiply the numbers in a division problem by the same number, the answer does not change.

Multiplying this way **balances** the problem.

Sometimes this balancing trick makes the division easier to do.

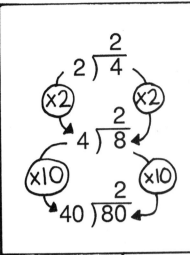

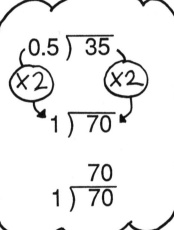

$$40 \div 5 = 8$$

MENTAL MATH TIP

Use balancing to change the **DIVISOR** to a nice whole number.

TRY THESE IN YOUR HEAD.
Balance before dividing.

1. $3 \div 0.5$ **4.** $18 \div 25$ **7.** $0.5 \overline{)2.7}$

2. $3 \div 0.2$ **5.** $1500 \div 250$ **8.** $26 \div 6\frac{1}{2}$

3. $0.25 \overline{)4}$ **6.** $2\frac{1}{2} \div \frac{1}{8}$ **9.** $8 \div 0.5$

10. $50 \overline{)180}$

POWER BUILDER A

1. $1 \div \frac{1}{2} =$ _____

2. $2 \div \frac{1}{2} =$ _____

3. $3 \div \frac{1}{2} =$ _____

4. $0.25 \overline{)\, 4} =$ _____

5. $0.1 \overline{)\, 15} =$ _____

6. $12 \div 25 =$ _____

7. $36 \div 50 =$ _____

8. $450 \div 200 =$ _____

9. $25 \overline{)\, 700} =$ _____

10. $50 \overline{)\, 1600} =$ _____

11. $250 \overline{)\, 1600} =$ _____

12. $180 \div 500 =$ _____

13. $150 \div 250 =$ _____

14. $1.5 \div 0.5 =$ _____

15. $2\frac{1}{4} \div \frac{1}{4} =$ _____

16. $10 \div \frac{1}{5} =$ _____

17. $\frac{1}{2} \div \frac{1}{3} =$ _____

18. $0.1 \overline{)\, 2.35} =$ _____

19. $4.8 \div 0.5 =$ _____

20. $5.5 \div 0.25 =$ _____

THINK IT THROUGH

If 0.25 liters of cooking oil costs $1.50, what would it cost to buy 4 liters?

POWER BUILDER B

1. $2 \div \frac{1}{4} =$ _____

2. $3 \div \frac{1}{4} =$ _____

3. $5 \div \frac{1}{2} =$ _____

4. $0.25 \overline{)\, 10} =$ _____

5. $0.1 \overline{)\, 25} =$ _____

6. $13 \div 25 =$ _____

7. $28 \div 50 =$ _____

8. $450 \div 500 =$ _____

9. $25 \overline{)\, 900} =$ _____

10. $50 \overline{)\, 1800} =$ _____

11. $500 \overline{)\, 1600} =$ _____

12. $180 \div 25 =$ _____

13. $7500 \div 250 =$ _____

14. $4.5 \div 0.5 =$ _____

15. $3\frac{1}{4} \div \frac{1}{4} =$ _____

16. $4 \div \frac{1}{16} =$ _____

17. $\frac{1}{3} \div \frac{1}{2} =$ _____

18. $0.1 \overline{)\, 5.35} =$ _____

19. $6.4 \div 0.5 =$ _____

20. $3.5 \div 0.25 =$ _____

THINK IT THROUGH

Using the fact 4 x 775 = 3100, calculate the following:

775 ÷ 25   77.5 ÷ 2.5   7.75 ÷ 2.5

 Often we need to change percents to decimals or decimals to percents.

To change a percent to a decimal . . .

- Think of it as a fraction with a denominator of 100.

- Divide by 100, sliding the decimal point two places to the left.

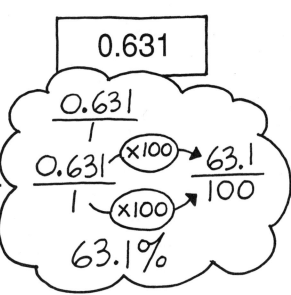

12.5%

$$12.5\% = \frac{12.5}{100}$$

$$12.5 \div 100 = 0.125$$

To change a decimal to a percent . . .

- Think of it as a ratio.

- Multiply each term by 100 to get a fraction with a denominator of 100.

- Express it as a percent.

0.631

$$\frac{0.631}{1}$$

$$\frac{0.631}{1} \xrightarrow{\times 100} \frac{63.1}{100}$$

63.1%

TRY THESE IN YOUR HEAD.

Change to a percent.
1. 0.53
2. 0.10
3. 0.36
4. 1.5
5. 0.025

Change to a decimal.
6. 65%
7. 20%
8. 27.5%
9. 165%
10. 3.3%

POWER BUILDER A

Change to a percent:

1. 0.01 = _____

2. 0.08 = _____

3. 0.11 = _____

4. 0.18 = _____

5. 0.29 = _____

6. 0.7 = _____

7. 0.9 = _____

8. 0.123 = _____

9. 0.009 = _____

10. 1.4 = _____

Change to a decimal:

11. 10% = _____

12. 3% = _____

13. 25% = _____

14. 38% = _____

15. 99% = _____

16. 50% = _____

17. 66.6% = _____

18. 0.1% = _____

19. 1.125% = _____

20. 114% = _____

THINK IT THROUGH

Which is larger: $\frac{1}{10}$ of 1%, or 1% of $\frac{1}{10}$?

POWER BUILDER B

Change to a percent:

1. 0.05 = _____

2. 0.09 = _____

3. 0.22 = _____

4. 0.81 = _____

5. 0.99 = _____

6. 0.6 = _____

7. 0.7 = _____

8. 0.5555 = _____

9. 0.0099 = _____

10. 5.5 = _____

Change to a decimal:

11. 20% = _____

12. 1% = _____

13. 35% = _____

14. 83% = _____

15. 91% = _____

16. 40% = _____

17. 99.99% = _____

18. 0.3% = _____

19. 2.125% = _____

20. 200% = _____

THINK IT THROUGH

Advertisements claim that a popular brand of soap is $99\frac{99}{100}$% pure. What percent and fraction of the soap is "impure"?

PRICES SLASHED! SAVE from 10% to 50% ON ALL MERCHANDISE

A Sale! A Sale!

If you learn by heart the few equivalents in this table, figuring with percents will be much easier.

PERCENT	50%	$33\frac{1}{3}$%	10%	1%
BASIC UNIT FRACTION	$\frac{1}{2}$	$\frac{1}{3}$	$\frac{1}{10}$	$\frac{1}{100}$

$14.50

SALE 10% OFF

How much do you save?

10% of $14.50

$\frac{1}{10}$ of $14.50 = $1.45

I save $1.45!

$8.50

SAVE 50%

How much do you save?

50% of $8.50

$\frac{1}{2}$ of $8.50 = $4.25

I save $4.25!

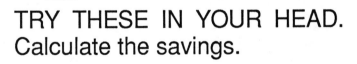

TRY THESE IN YOUR HEAD.
Calculate the savings.

1. 10% of $36.00

2. 1% of $1800.00

3. 50% of $80.00

4. $33\frac{1}{3}$% of $90.00

5. 10% of $36.50

6. 1% of $20.00

7. 50% of $1.80

8. $33\frac{1}{3}$% of $15.60

9. 10% of $21.87

10. 50% of $14.89

POWER BUILDER A

Change to a percent:

1. $\frac{1}{3}$ = _____

2. $\frac{1}{2}$ = _____

3. $\frac{1}{10}$ = _____

4. $\frac{1}{100}$ = _____

5. $1\frac{1}{3}$ = _____

6. $1\frac{1}{10}$ = _____

7. $2\frac{1}{100}$ = _____

8. $\frac{4}{3}$ = _____

9. $\frac{5}{2}$ = _____

10. $5\frac{1}{10}$ = _____

Calculate the amount:

11. $\frac{1}{10}$ of $40 = _____

12. $\frac{1}{2}$ of $50 = _____

13. 10% of $80 = _____

14. 50% of $90 = _____

15. 110% of $80 = _____

16. 150% of $90 = _____

17. $33\frac{1}{3}$% of $120 = _____

18. 1% of $350 = _____

19. 101% of $350 = _____

20. $233\frac{1}{3}$% of $150 = _____

THINK IT THROUGH

Use the fact that $\frac{1}{2}$ = 50% to determine the equivalent percentages of these fractions:

$\frac{1}{4}, \frac{1}{8}, \frac{3}{8}, \frac{1}{16}$

POWER BUILDER B

Change to a percent:

1. $\frac{1}{2}$ = _____

2. $\frac{1}{3}$ = _____

3. $\frac{1}{100}$ = _____

4. $\frac{1}{10}$ = _____

5. $1\frac{1}{2}$ = _____

6. $2\frac{1}{10}$ = _____

7. $4\frac{1}{100}$ = _____

8. $\frac{7}{3}$ = _____

9. $\frac{9}{2}$ = _____

10. $\frac{601}{100}$ = _____

Calculate the amount:

11. $\frac{1}{10}$ of $50 = _____

12. $\frac{1}{2}$ of $60 = _____

13. 10% of $180 = _____

14. 50% of $70 = _____

15. 110% of $180 = _____

16. 150% of $70 = _____

17. $33\frac{1}{3}$% of $270 = _____

18. 1% of $1050 = _____

19. 101% of $1050 = _____

20. $433\frac{1}{3}$% of $150 = _____

THINK IT THROUGH

If the value of the dollar increases by 10% in one year and another 10% in the next year, what is the total percentage increase?

$$\frac{1}{3} = 33\frac{1}{3}\%$$
$$\frac{1}{10} = 10\%$$
$$\frac{1}{100} = 1\%$$
$$\frac{1}{2} = 50\%$$

If you remember the percentage equivalents for the basic unit fractions, you can reason out other equivalents (and later learn them by heart).

Express $\frac{2}{3}$ as a percent.

$$\frac{2}{3} = 2 \times \frac{1}{3} = 2 \times 33\frac{1}{3}\% = 66\frac{2}{3}\%$$

Express $\frac{3}{10}$ as a percent.

$$\frac{3}{10} = 3 \times \frac{1}{10} = 3 \times 10\% = 30\%$$

You can also do this reasoning in reverse.

Express 20% as a fraction.

$$20\% = 2 \times 10\% = 2 \times \frac{1}{10} = \frac{2}{10} = \frac{1}{5}$$

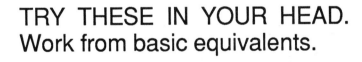

TRY THESE IN YOUR HEAD.
Work from basic equivalents.

Express as a percent.

1. $\frac{7}{10}$ **3.** $\frac{4}{3}$

2. $\frac{9}{100}$ **4.** $\frac{3}{2}$

5. $\frac{45}{100}$

Express as a fraction in lowest terms.

6. 3%   **8.** 40%

7. 70%   **9.** $66\frac{2}{3}\%$

10. 190%

POWER BUILDER A

Calculate the amount:

1. 10% of $25.00 = _____
2. 20% of $25.00 = _____
3. 30% of $25.00 = _____
4. 40% of $25.00 = _____
5. 1% of $80.00 = _____
6. 2% of $80.00 = _____
7. 3% of $80.00 = _____
8. 4% of $80.00 = _____
9. $33\frac{1}{3}$% of $15.00 = _____
10. $66\frac{2}{3}$% of $15.00 = _____

11. $133\frac{1}{3}$% of $15.00 = _____
12. 30% of $40.00 = _____
13. 10% of $19.00 = _____
14. 20% of $19.00 = _____
15. 2% of $650.00 = _____
16. 3% of $2500.00 = _____
17. $33\frac{1}{3}$% of $45.36 = _____
18. $66\frac{2}{3}$% of $45.36 = _____
19. 2% of $450.00 = _____
20. 101% of $72.00 = _____

THINK IT THROUGH

Form a message using the first few letters of these words:
20% of INDIA, 50% of LOVESEAT, 30% of MENDACIOUS,
60% of TALON, $33\frac{1}{3}$% of MATHEMATICAL.
What's the message?

POWER BUILDER B

Calculate the amount:

1. 10% of $45.00 = _____
2. 20% of $45.00 = _____
3. 30% of $45.00 = _____
4. 40% of $45.00 = _____
5. 1% of $1200.00 = _____
6. 2% of $1200.00 = _____
7. 3% of $1200.00 = _____
8. 4% of $1200.00 = _____
9. $33\frac{1}{3}$% of $45.00 = _____
10. $66\frac{2}{3}$% of $45.00 = _____

11. $133\frac{1}{3}$% of $45.00 = _____
12. 30% of $50.00 = _____
13. 10% of $69.00 = _____
14. 20% of $69.00 = _____
15. 2% of $750.00 = _____
16. 3% of $1500.00 = _____
17. $33\frac{1}{3}$% of $15.48 = _____
18. $66\frac{2}{3}$% of $15.48 = _____
19. 2% of $1.50 = _____
20. 110% of $52.00 = _____

THINK IT THROUGH

Form a message using the first few letters of these words:
60% of FIGHT, 20% of UNITE, 50% of RINGSIDE, $33\frac{1}{3}$% of ISLAND,
50% of FUNNEL. What's the message?

You can use the percentage equivalents for the basic unit fractions to work out more difficult equivalents.

PERCENT	50%	$33\frac{1}{3}\%$	10%	1%
BASIC UNIT FRACTION	$\frac{1}{2}$	$\frac{1}{3}$	$\frac{1}{10}$	$\frac{1}{100}$

FOR EXAMPLE . . .

Express $\frac{1}{4}$ and $\frac{1}{8}$ as percents.

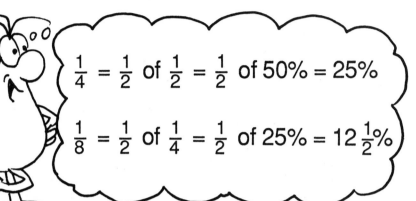

$$\frac{1}{4} = \frac{1}{2} \text{ of } \frac{1}{2} = \frac{1}{2} \text{ of } 50\% = 25\%$$

$$\frac{1}{8} = \frac{1}{2} \text{ of } \frac{1}{4} = \frac{1}{2} \text{ of } 25\% = 12\frac{1}{2}\%$$

Sometimes you can reason out equivalents in more than one way.

Express $\frac{3}{8}$ as a percent.

$$\frac{3}{8} = 3 \times \frac{1}{8} = 3 \times 12\frac{1}{2}\%$$

$$3 \times 12\frac{1}{2}\% = (36 + 1\frac{1}{2})\,\% = 37\frac{1}{2}\%$$

$$\frac{3}{8} = \frac{1}{4} + \frac{1}{8} = 25\% + 12\frac{1}{2}\%$$

$$25\% + 12\frac{1}{2}\% = 37\frac{1}{2}\%$$

TRY THESE IN YOUR HEAD.
Start with basic equivalents.

Express as a percent.

1. $\frac{3}{4}$ 3. $\frac{5}{8}$

2. $\frac{1}{20}$ 4. $\frac{1}{200}$

5. $\frac{1}{16}$

Express as a fraction in lowest terms.

6. 25%   8. 5%

7. 75%   9. $112\frac{1}{2}\%$

10. 2.5%

MENTAL MATH IN JUNIOR HIGH
Copyright © 1988 by Dale Seymour Publications

POWER BUILDER A

Change to a percent:

1. $\frac{1}{3}$ = _____

2. $\frac{1}{2}$ = _____

3. $\frac{1}{4}$ = _____

4. $\frac{1}{8}$ = _____

5. $\frac{3}{8}$ = _____

6. $\frac{5}{8}$ = _____

7. $\frac{7}{8}$ = _____

8. $1\frac{1}{8}$ = _____

9. $\frac{1}{5}$ = _____

10. $\frac{3}{5}$ = _____

Calculate the amount:

11. 25% of $40 = _____

12. 12.5% of $40.00 = _____

13. 37.5% of $40.00 = _____

14. 75% of $40.00 = _____

15. 112.5% of $40.00 = _____

16. 50% of $70.00 = _____

17. 25% of $70.00 = _____

18. 10% of $80.00 = _____

19. 5% of $80.00 = _____

20. 2.5% of $80.00 = _____

THINK IT THROUGH

Which is the better buy on a $200 bike:
(a) reduced by 20%, or
(b) reduced by 10% and then by another 10%?

POWER BUILDER B

Change to a percent:

1. $\frac{1}{3}$ = _____

2. $\frac{2}{3}$ = _____

3. $\frac{1}{4}$ = _____

4. $\frac{1}{8}$ = _____

5. $\frac{1}{16}$ = _____

6. $\frac{3}{16}$ = _____

7. $\frac{3}{8}$ = _____

8. $\frac{3}{4}$ = _____

9. $\frac{7}{8}$ = _____

10. $\frac{5}{8}$ = _____

Calculate the amount:

11. 25% of $480 = _____

12. 12.5% of $480 = _____

13. 37.5% of $480 = _____

14. 75% of $480 = _____

15. 112.5% of $480 = _____

16. 50% of $45.00 = _____

17. 25% of $45.00 = _____

18. 10% of $18.40 = _____

19. 5% of $18.40 = _____

20. 3% of $80.00 = _____

THINK IT THROUGH

Which is the best buy on a $20 shirt:
(a) marked down $5;
(b) reduced 15%; or
(c) reduced 15% and then another 10%?

Given an uncommon percent, see if it's close to a percent that you **know** how to work with.

Then try to add or subtract from this known percent.

90% of 150 = ?

$$100\% \text{ of } 150 = 150$$
$$- \ 10\% \text{ of } 150 = - \ 15$$
$$90\% \text{ of } 150 = 135$$

125% of 240 = ?

$$100\% \text{ of } 240 = 240$$
$$+ \ 25\% \text{ of } 240 = + \ 60$$
$$125\% \text{ of } 240 = 300$$

45% of 40 = ?

$$50\% \text{ of } 40 = 20$$
$$- \tfrac{1}{2}(10)\% \text{ of } 40 = - \ 2$$
$$45\% \text{ of } 40 = 18$$

TRY THESE IN YOUR HEAD.
Work from a known percent.

1. 80% of 150   **4.** 75% of 480   **7.** 175% of 400

2. 110% of 50   **5.** 45% of 140   **8.** 15% of 50

3. 90% of 250   **6.** 110% of 45   **9.** $112\tfrac{1}{2}$% of 800

10. 95% of 50

POWER BUILDER A

Calculate the amount:

1. 100% of $60 = _____
2. 10% of $60 = _____
3. 110% of $60 = _____
4. 90% of $60 = _____
5. 95% of $60 = _____
6. 50% of $140 = _____
7. 40% of $140 = _____
8. 45% of $140 = _____
9. 10% of $65 = _____
10. 5% of $65 = _____

11. 10% of $75 = _____
12. 20% of $75 = _____
13. 15% of $75 = _____
14. 25% of $75 = _____
15. 200% of $250 = _____
16. 250% of $250 = _____
17. 5% of $80 = _____
18. 2.5% of $80 = _____
19. 1.25% of $80 = _____
20. 0.5% of $200 = _____

THINK IT THROUGH

My phone number has 7 digits, is an even number, has only two different digits, and these alternate. The sum of the digits is 11. What is my phone number?

POWER BUILDER B

Calculate the amount:

1. 100% of $1800 = _____
2. 10% of $1800 = _____
3. 110% of $1800 = _____
4. 90% of $1800 = _____
5. 95% of $1800 = _____
6. 50% of $4.80 = _____
7. 10% of $4.80 = _____
8. 5% of $4.80 = _____
9. 55% of $4.80 = _____
10. 45% of $4.80 = _____

11. 75% of $400 = _____
12. 80% of $400 = _____
13. 1% of $800 = _____
14. 0.25% of $800 = _____
15. 10% of $64.80 = _____
16. 5% of $64.80 = _____
17. 15% of $64.80 = _____
18. 25% of $64.80 = _____
19. 2.5% of $64.80 = _____
20. 1.25% of $64.80 = _____

THINK IT THROUGH

My phone number has 7 digits, is an odd number, has only two different digits, and these alternate. The sum of the digits is 18. What is my phone number?

When you need to figure
a percent in your head,
look for a way to use
a fraction equivalent.

What's the tax?

How much tip?

How much
interest
do I earn?

What's the
discount price?

What would the tax be?
10% would be easy to figure. . .

10% of $480 = $\frac{1}{10}$ of $480 = $48

And 5% is half of 10% . . .

$\frac{1}{2}$ of $48 = $24

So 5% of $480 is $24 tax.

If I want to leave
a 15% tip, how much
would that be?

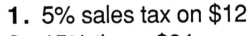

HINT:
Think of
10% + 5%.

TRY THESE IN YOUR HEAD.
Think of fraction equivalents.

1. 5% sales tax on $12
2. 15% tip on $24
3. $12\frac{1}{2}$% interest on $400
4. 25% savings on $30
5. $12\frac{1}{2}$% savings on $40

6. 75% profit on $480
7. 125% increase on $30
8. $2\frac{1}{2}$% increase on $60
9. 2% increase on $50
10. 15% tip on $36

POWER BUILDER A

Calculate the amount:

1. 5% tax on $60 = _____
2. 15% tip on $30 = _____
3. 10% interest on $145 = _____
4. 50% profit on $5000 = _____
5. 25% profit on $250 = _____
6. 20% loss on $140 = _____
7. 12.5% discount on $888 = _____
8. $33\frac{1}{3}$% profit on $4800 = _____
9. $66\frac{2}{3}$% commission on $3600 =

   _____
10. 8% royalty on $500 = _____

11. 15% duty on $45 = _____
12. 2% tax on $350 = _____
13. 10% discount on $36.99 = _____
14. 25% profit on $600 stock = _____
15. 15% tip on $25 = _____
16. 110% profit on $4000 = _____
17. 150% profit on $50,000 property =

   _____
18. 37.5% royalty on $8000 = _____
19. 4% tax on $55 = _____
20. 35% duty on $500 = _____

THINK IT THROUGH

The price of a $100 coat is increased by 10%,
then later reduced by 10%. What is the sale
price of the coat?

POWER BUILDER B

Calculate the amount:

1. 2% tax on $60 = _____
2. 5% tip on $40 = _____
3. 10% interest on $245 = _____
4. 50% profit on $2500 = _____
5. 25% profit on $2500 = _____
6. 20% loss on $180 = _____
7. 12.5% discount on $1600 = _____
8. $33\frac{1}{3}$% profit on $4500 = _____
9. $66\frac{2}{3}$% commission on $2100 =

   _____
10. 6% royalty on $500 _____

11. 15% duty on $300 = _____
12. 3% tax on $350 = _____
13. 10% discount on $48 = _____
14. 95% profit on $600 stock = _____
15. 15% tip on $50 = _____
16. 105% profit on $4000 = _____
17. 40% profit on $75,000 property =

   _____
18. 37.5% royalty on $4800 = _____
19. 5% tax on $55 = _____
20. 2.5% tax on $800 = _____

THINK IT THROUGH

If, as is happening in some countries, prices
increase 50% each year, what will be the
price of a $100 coat in 3 years?

Mental Math Techniques
• **USE FACTORS OF 12 (3 x 2 x 2).** $8 \times 12 = ?$ $60 \div 12 = ?$
• **BREAK UP THE DIVIDEND.** $515 \div 5 = (500 + 15) \div 5 = ?$
• **MAKE COMPATIBLES TO DIVIDE.** $128 \div 8 = (80 + 48) \div 8 = ?$
• **BALANCE BEFORE DIVIDING.** $16 \div 0.25 = ?$
• **USE FRACTIONAL EQUIVALENTS OF PERCENTS.** 10% of $17.50 = ?$ $\frac{1}{4} = 25\%$, so $\frac{3}{4} = ?\%$
• **USE SIMPLE PERCENTS TO FIGURE HARDER ONES.** 10% of $15 = $1.50, so 5% of $15 = ?$

Do the problems below in your head. Tell which techniques you find useful for each one.

1. 10% of $135
2. 5% of $135
3. 15% of $135
4. 95% of $135
5. 12×14
6. $636 \div 6$
7. $20 \div 0.25$
8. $25 \div \frac{1}{5}$
9. $\frac{1}{4} = ?\%$
10. $\frac{3}{8} = ?\%$

Talk about each problem below. What's an easy way to do it in your head? Tell how you would think it through.

1. $144 \div 12$
2. $4848 \div 8$
3. $85 \div 5$
4. 75% of $120
5. $\frac{2}{3} = ?\%$
6. 15% of $24
7. $15 \div 0.25$
8. 110% of $50
9. 45% of $50
10. $33\frac{1}{3}\%$ of $24.36

1. $72 \div 6 =$ _____

2. 10% of $60 = _____

3. $250 \overline{) 1200} =$ _____

4. $0.43 =$ _____ %

5. 30% of $55 = _____

6. $636 \div 6 =$ _____

7. 8 dozen eggs = _____ eggs

8. $\frac{1}{8} =$ _____ %

9. 3% of $45.00 = _____

10. $9009 \div 3 =$ _____

11. $0.9 =$ _____ %

12. 3% of $1500 = _____

13. $2 \div 0.25 =$ _____

14. 25% of $84 = _____

15. $848 \div 4 =$ _____

16. 13 feet = _____ inches

17. 99% of $200 = _____

18. 50% of $260 = _____

19. $3.2 \div 0.5 =$ _____

20. $1.3 =$ _____ %

21. 12.5% of $56 = _____

22. $315 \div 5 =$ _____

23. $4242 \div 7 =$ _____

24. 1% of $39 = _____

25. 15% of $12 = _____

26. 112.5% of $16 = _____

27. $66\frac{2}{3}$% of $600 = _____

28. $288 \div 9 =$ _____

29. 720 inches = _____ feet

30. 101% of $85 = _____

31. $\frac{3}{16} =$ _____ %

32. $33\frac{1}{3}$ of $75 = _____

33. $1\frac{1}{3} \div \frac{1}{3} =$ _____

34. $84 \div 7 =$ _____

35. 20% of $50 = _____

36. 110% profit on $54 = _____

37. $0.025 =$ _____ %

38. 72 rolls = _____ dozen rolls

39. 9% loss on $700 = _____

40. 250% of $18 = _____

MENTAL MATH IN JUNIOR HIGH

CUMULATIVE TESTS
and
ANSWER KEYS
for Power Builder Sets and Tests

1. $544 + 27 =$ _____

2. $3.7 + 0.4 + 2.5 =$ _____

3. $80 \times 700 =$ _____

4. $837 - 224 =$ _____

5. $15,000 \div 300 =$ _____

6. $348 + 455 =$ _____

7. $10 - 8.42 =$ _____

8. $5 - 2\frac{1}{3} =$ _____

9. The difference in time from
1:25 P.M. to 7:15 P.M. =

_____

10. $433 - 297 =$ _____

11. $8 \times 325 =$ _____

12. $5.2 - 1.8 =$ _____

13. $\frac{1}{2} + \frac{3}{8} =$ _____

14. $6 \times \$1.49 =$ _____

15. $5600 \div 8 =$ _____

16. $3 - \frac{4}{9} =$ _____

17. $16 \text{ ft} - 4\frac{5}{12} \text{ ft} =$ _____

18. $500 - 184 =$ _____

19. $5477 + 1999 =$ _____

20. $400 \overline{)\,28,000} =$ _____

21. 10% of $\$85 =$ _____

22. $\frac{1}{2} - \frac{1}{10} =$ _____

23. $\$50 - \$20.64 =$ _____

24. $1000 \times 0.416 =$ _____

25. $6 \times 2\frac{2}{3} =$ _____

26. Which is the better buy:
6 for $0.37 or 12 for $0.70?

_____

27. $650 + 270 =$ _____

28. Double $2\frac{3}{4} =$ _____

29. $16 \times 50 =$ _____

30. $8.00 - 1.85 =$ _____

31. $3\frac{1}{2} + 2\frac{5}{8} =$ _____

32. $16 \times 2.25 =$ _____

33. 12.5% of $\$32 =$ _____

34. $5 - 2\frac{5}{6} =$ _____

35. $4.77 + 2.26 =$ _____

36. $50 \times \$14 =$ _____

37. $66\frac{2}{3}\%$ of $\$120 =$ _____

38. $108 \div 9 =$ _____

39. $5 \times 19 \times 4 \times 5 =$ _____

40. $6 \div \frac{1}{3} =$ _____

41. $54.16 \times 0.1 =$ _____

42. Change to meters:

5126 cm = _____

43. $4 - 2\frac{1}{2} =$ _____

44. $35 \times 14 =$ _____

45. 24 feet = _____ inches

46. 105% of $\$70 =$ _____

47. $2424 \div 4 =$ _____

48. $1.1 =$ _____ %

49. $\frac{5}{8}$ of $40 =$ _____

50. 15% tip on $\$30 =$ _____

1. 154 + 28 = _____

2. 2.6 + 0.7 + 1.5 = _____

3. 30 x 900 = _____

4. 569 − 143 = _____

5. 64,000 ÷ 800 = _____

6. 255 + 647 = _____

7. 10 − 6.57 = _____

8. $7 - 2\frac{5}{8}$ = _____

9. The difference in time from
    12:20 P.M. to 6:15 P.M. =

    _____

10. 544 − 399 = _____

11. 6 x 4.5 = _____

12. 6.3 − 2.9 = _____

13. $\frac{1}{2} + \frac{1}{5}$ = _____

14. 3 x $4.26 = _____

15. 4200 ÷ 6 = _____

16. $5 - \frac{2}{3}$ = _____

17. $12 \text{ ft} - 3\frac{5}{8} \text{ ft}$ = _____

18. 700 − 250 = _____

19. 6457 + 2999 = _____

20. $90 \overline{)\,36{,}000}$ = _____

21. 150% of $80 = _____

22. $\frac{1}{2} - \frac{1}{8}$ = _____

23. $20 − $10.36 = _____

24. 100 x 0.417 = _____

25. $8 \times 4\frac{3}{4}$ = _____

26. Which is the better buy:
    4 for $0.69 or 8 for $1.50?

    _____

27. 350 + 190 = _____

28. Double $1\frac{2}{3}$ = _____

29. 16 x 150 = _____

30. 6.00 − 2.85 = _____

31. $4\frac{1}{2} + 1\frac{5}{6}$ = _____

32. 32 x 1.25 = _____

33. 5% of $16.80 = _____

34. $7 - 3\frac{7}{8}$ = _____

35. 1.75 + 2.77 = _____

36. 50 x $24 = _____

37. 3% of $60 = _____

38. 85 ÷ 5 = _____

39. 5 x 17 x 5 x 4 = _____

40. $5 \div \frac{1}{2}$ = _____

41. 41.72 x 0.01 = _____

42. Change to centimeters:

    415.6 mm = _____ cm

43. $7 - 2\frac{1}{2}$ = _____

44. 35 x 16 = _____

45. 20 dozen eggs = _____ eggs

46. 90% of $340 = _____

47. 4242 ÷ 6 = _____

48. 0.1 = _____ %

49. $\frac{3}{5}$ of 40 = _____

50. 9% tax on $35 = _____

Answer Key for Power Builders

LESSON 1

Power Builder A **1.** 84 **2.** 82 **3.** 83 **4.** 82 **5.** 103
6. 303 **7.** 475 **8.** 773 **9.** 863 **10.** 873 **11.** 7.5
12. 5.3 **13.** 8.2 **14.** 13.0 **15.** 9.2 **16.** 19.3 **17.** 29.5
18. 49.6 **19.** 49.0 **20.** 58.7
Think It Through: 10 + 31 + 28 + 21 = 90, 91 in leap year

Power Builder B **1.** 74 **2.** 72 **3.** 85 **4.** 82 **5.** 83
6. 492 **7.** 667 **8.** 572 **9.** 681 **10.** 794 **11.** 9.1
12. 7.3 **13.** 8.3 **14.** 8.2 **15.** 9.2 **16.** 19.5 **17.** 48.0
18. 59.1 **19.** 46.1 **20.** 78.0
Think It Through: 9 + 31 + 31 + 21 = 92

LESSON 2

Power Builder A **1.** 73 **2.** 82 **3.** 94 **4.** 93 **5.** 90
6. 52 **7.** 89 **8.** 75 **9.** 82 **10.** 94 **11.** 630 **12.** 810
13. 907 **14.** 627 **15.** 826 **16.** 401 **17.** 700 **18.** 902
19. 9125 **20.** 4700
Think It Through: 2, 3, 4, 5, 6

Power Builder B **1.** 81 **2.** 82 **3.** 96 **4.** 93 **5.** 90
6. 65 **7.** 55 **8.** 90 **9.** 100 **10.** 98 **11.** 830 **12.** 910
13. 907 **14.** 619 **15.** 926 **16.** 601 **17.** 600 **18.** 801
19. 8000 **20.** 5600
Think It Through: 40, 40, 20, and 10

LESSON 3

Power Builder A **1.** 4.2 **2.** 16.6 **3.** 7.0 **4.** 8.3
5. 9.2 **6.** 4.7 **7.** 8.9 **8.** 0.76 **9.** 0.96 **10.** 0.88
11. $0.90 **12.** $0.70 **13.** $3.90 **14.** $7.00 **15.** $4.00
16. $6.75 **17.** $7.35 **18.** $6.30 **19.** $8.55 **20.** $7.70
Think It Through: 7625

Power Builder B **1.** 5.1 **2.** 18.2 **3.** 5.6 **4.** 8.2
5. 9.0 **6.** 5.9 **7.** 9.0 **8.** 0.88 **9.** 0.85 **10.** 1.42
11. $0.60 **12.** $1.00 **13.** $3.80 **14.** $6.00 **15.** $4.20
16. $8.25 **17.** $5.65 **18.** $5.90 **19.** $8.25 **20.** $6.95
Think It Through: 2875

LESSON 4

Power Builder A **1.** 112 **2.** 326 **3.** 212 **4.** 405
5. 351 **6.** 4115 **7.** 1100 **8.** 6433 **9.** 3513
10. 13,323 **11.** 3.72 **12.** 2.02 **13.** 6.03 **14.** 4.11
15. 2.50 **16.** 10.12 **17.** 11.11 **18.** 21.22 **19.** 40.03
20. 50.55
Think It Through: 8 and 10

Power Builder B **1.** 135 **2.** 338 **3.** 622 **4.** 605
5. 651 **6.** 4334 **7.** 2300 **8.** 5121 **9.** 3211
10. 32,341 **11.** 4.21 **12.** 2.02 **13.** 2.02 **14.** 1.03
15. 3.21 **16.** 10.03 **17.** 10.12 **18.** 15.22 **19.** 10.01
20. 54.27
Think It Through: 10 and 12

LESSON 5

Power Builder A **1.** 18 **2.** 36 **3.** 29 **4.** 21 **5.** 48
6. 54 **7.** 5.4 **8.** 6.3 **9.** 2.8 **10.** 1.2 **11.** 275
12. 309 **13.** 525 **14.** 290 **15.** 545 **16.** 175 **17.** 3.80
18. 3.99 **19.** $16.25 **20.** $1.37
Think It Through: 75

Power Builder B **1.** 18 **2.** 27 **3.** 29 **4.** 32 **5.** 47
6. 31 **7.** 5.5 **8.** 4.9 **9.** 4.9 **10.** 2.3 **11.** 250
12. 209 **13.** 299 **14.** 350 **15.** 350 **16.** 265 **17.** 4.80
18. 5.99 **19.** $7.75 **20.** $13.45
Think It Through: 38

LESSON 6

Power Builder A **1.** 55 **2.** 27 **3.** 81 **4.** 42 **5.** 63
6. 650 **7.** 725 **8.** 365 **9.** 124 **10.** 556 **11.** 275
12. 61 **13.** 156 **14.** 301 **15.** 364 **16.** 225 **17.** 157
18. 267 **19.** 155 **20.** 215
Think It Through: 9435 mm, 9.435 m

Power Builder B **1.** 45 **2.** 24 **3.** 71 **4.** 57 **5.** 32
6. 750 **7.** 625 **8.** 555 **9.** 241 **10.** 334 **11.** 125
12. 151 **13.** 467 **14.** 201 **15.** 166 **16.** 325 **17.** 166
18. 156 **19.** 165 **20.** 642
Think It Through: 7500 m, or 7.5 km

LESSON 7

Power Builder A **1.** 104 **2.** 102 **3.** 103 **4.** 103
5. 101 **6.** 201 **7.** 402 **8.** 503 **9.** 502 **10.** 603
11. 1003 **12.** 1001 **13.** 911 **14.** 1001 **15.** 901
16. 1003 **17.** 1003 **18.** 3001 **19.** 601 **20.** 1002
Think It Through: 1002; 1000; 10.00

Power Builder B **1.** 101 **2.** 102 **3.** 101 **4.** 102
5. 103 **6.** 201 **7.** 402 **8.** 302 **9.** 501 **10.** 404
11. 1004 **12.** 1002 **13.** 1002 **14.** 1001 **15.** 1003
16. 901 **17.** 702 **18.** 4801 **19.** 801 **20.** 1003
Think It Through: 2010; 2000; 20.00

LESSON 8

Power Builder A **1.** $0.48 **2.** $0.31 **3.** 0.64
4. 0.12 **5.** 0.59 **6.** $7.55 **7.** $5.49 **8.** 0.62 **9.** 6.31
10. 4.26 **11.** $0.05 **12.** $1.31 **13.** 3.37 **14.** 3.3
15. 1.8 **16.** 5.6 **17.** 2.36 **18.** 9.26 **19.** 0.655
20. 0.255
Think It Through: 11

Power Builder B **1.** $0.36 **2.** $0.27 **3.** $0.56
4. 0.23 **5.** 0.61 **6.** $6.65 **7.** $3.48 **8.** 1.72 **9.** 5.41
10. 3.32 **11.** $1.28 **12.** $1.43 **13.** 3.41 **14.** 2.4
15. 2.7 **16.** 4.5 **17.** 1.62 **18.** 9.26 **19.** 0.875
20. 0.915
Think It Through: $1.75 (5 quarters and 5 dimes)

LESSON 9

Power Builder A **1.** 1 hr 40 min **2.** 3 hr 10 min **3.** 7 hr 15 min **4.** 3 hr 20 min **5.** 6 hr 15 min **6.** 5 hr 10 min **7.** 4 hr 10 min **8.** 7 hr 50 min **9.** 6 hr 30 min **10.** 3 hr 10 min **11.** 2 hr 35 min **12.** 5 hr 15 min **13.** 5 hr 55 min **14.** 45 min **15.** 5 hr 45 min **16.** 55 min **17.** 2 hr 55 min **18.** 11 hr **19.** 2 hr 50 min **20.** 6 hr 40 min
Think It Through: 12:02 P.M.

Power Builder B **1.** 3 hr 40 min **2.** 6 hr 10 min **3.** 4 hr 20 min **4.** 3 hr 20 min **5.** 7 hr 20 min **6.** 4 hr 20 min **7.** 5 hr 10 min **8.** 7 hr 40 min **9.** 6 hr 20 min **10.** 6 hr 20 min **11.** 1 hr 40 min **12.** 2 hr 25 min **13.** 3 hr 55 min **14.** 2 hr 55 min **15.** 6 hr 55 min **16.** 1 hr 50 min **17.** 3 hr 45 min **18.** 50 min **19.** 3 hr 55 min **20.** 11 hr 5 min
Think It Through: 2:04 P.M.

LESSON 10

Power Builder A **1.** $6.25 **2.** $8.13 **3.** $2.55 **4.** $5.02 **5.** $9.22 **6.** $5.65 **7.** $10.25 **8.** $7.66 **9.** $17.31 **10.** $0.57 **11.** $2.54 **12.** $2.74 **13.** $3.16 **14.** $7.05 **15.** $4.19 **16.** $5.56 **17.** $6.51 **18.** $2.23 **19.** $45.14 **20.** $26.35
Think It Through: nine coins: one 50¢, one 25¢, one 10¢, two 5¢ , and four 1¢

Power Builder B **1.** $5.72 **2.** $7.07 **3.** $3.45 **4.** $4.96 **5.** $9.11 **6.** $10.15 **7.** $5.45 **8.** $7.53 **9.** $16.41 **10.** $0.63 **11.** $1.93 **12.** $3.21 **13.** $2.82 **14.** $8.14 **15.** $4.19 **16.** $6.67 **17.** $5.56 **18.** $63.34 **19.** $48.52 **20.** $10.31
Think It Through: eight coins: one 25¢, one 10¢, two 5¢, and four 1¢

LESSON 11

Power Builder A **1.** 5.03 **2.** 4.02 **3.** 6.01 **4.** 8.98 **5.** 3.54 **6.** $6.04 **7.** $7.04 **8.** $4.51 **9.** $8.01 **10.** $6.03 **11.** 4.55 **12.** 7.02 **13.** 7.12 **14.** 4.55 **15.** 6.02 **16.** $4.01 **17.** $19.02 **18.** $6.54 **19.** $26.02 **20.** $13.96
Think It Through: 402 days

Power Builder B **1.** 5.04 **2.** 6.01 **3.** 10.02 **4.** 4.96 **5.** 6.52 **6.** $4.04 **7.** $8.03 **8.** $10.54 **9.** $11.01 **10.** $7.03 **11.** 2.58 **12.** 50.03 **13.** 9.14 **14.** 15.01 **15.** 11.01 **16.** $17.03 **17.** $14.01 **18.** $7.52 **19.** $17.01 **20.** $8.96
Think It Through: 395 days

LESSON 12

Power Builder A **1.** 36 **2.** 14 **3.** 47 **4.** 34 **5.** 37 **6.** 175 **7.** 366 **8.** 183 **9.** 467 **10.** 544 **11.** 271 **12.** 566 **13.** 356 **14.** 229 **15.** 144 **16.** 4278 **17.** 7346 **18.** 4256 **19.** 5829 **20.** 1559
Think It Through: 8999

Power Builder B **1.** 37 **2.** 36 **3.** 25 **4.** 27 **5.** 67 **6.** 188 **7.** 276 **8.** 134 **9.** 367 **10.** 667 **11.** 258 **12.** 657 **13.** 437 **14.** 238 **15.** 488 **16.** 6377 **17.** 7255 **18.** 2245 **19.** 5438 **20.** 647
Think It Through: 1

LESSON 13

Power Builder A **1.** 1.8 **2.** 3.3 **3.** 4.5 **4.** 3.5 **5.** 4.16 **6.** 5.46 **7.** 7.26 **8.** 6.45 **9.** 6.38 **10.** 2.36 **11.** 2.38 **12.** 4.27 **13.** 10.53 **14.** 6.73 **15.** 10.08 **16.** 62.36 **17.** 3.277 **18.** 7.827 **19.** 9.558 **20.** 25.009
Think It Through: 2.002

Power Builder B **1.** 1.7 **2.** 3.5 **3.** 1.7 **4.** 3.3 **5.** 5.16 **6.** 6.45 **7.** 6.26 **8.** 7.34 **9.** 3.29 **10.** 4.29 **11.** 3.32 **12.** 5.47 **13.** 10.42 **14.** 0.44 **15.** 3.07 **16.** 45.37 **17.** 39.851 **18.** 5.942 **19.** 21.355 **20.** 19.003
Think It Through: 1.97

LESSON 14

Power Builder A **1.** 210 **2.** 480 **3.** 180 **4.** 200 **5.** 4500 **6.** 2400 **7.** 4000 **8.** 6000 **9.** 24,000 **10.** 35,000 **11.** 30,000 **12.** 15,000 **13.** 18,000 **14.** 56,000 **15.** 300,000 **16.** 560,000 **17.** 450,000 **18.** 420,000 **19.** 210,000 **20.** 400,000
Think It Through: Five products: 600, 800, 1200, 1800, 2400

Power Builder B **1.** 240 **2.** 350 **3.** 240 **4.** 300 **5.** 3500 **6.** 1800 **7.** 2000 **8.** 8000 **9.** 24,000 **10.** 45,000 **11.** 10,000 **12.** 25,000 **13.** 28,000 **14.** 1800 **15.** 400,000 **16.** 180,000 **17.** 400,000 **18.** 480,000 **19.** 120,000 **20.** 200,000
Think It Through: five products: 1200; 18,000; 24,000; 32,000; 480,000

LESSON 15

Power Builder A **1.** 168 **2.** 410 **3.** 252 **4.** 330 **5.** 336 **6.** 270 **7.** 424 **8.** 648 **9.** 504 **10.** 1300 **11.** 1090 **12.** 1698 **13.** 330 **14.** 1284 **15.** 3150 **16.** 3300 **17.** 1575 **18.** 2025 **19.** 3700 **20.** 1290
Think It Through: 555; 777

Power Builder B   **1.** 189   **2.** 310   **3.** 368   **4.** 330
5. 336   **6.** 270   **7.** 424   **8.** 648   **9.** 378   **10.** 2500
11. 1095   **12.** 1698   **13.** 260   **14.** 1284   **15.** 3150
16. 3300   **17.** 1575   **18.** 2025   **19.** 4200   **20.** 1595
Think It Through: 444,444; 666,666

LESSON 16

Power Builder A   **1.** $2.50   **2.** $9.40   **3.** $12.75
4. $4.75   **5.** $3.43   **6.** $10.05   **7.** $28.76   **8.** $16.50
9. $25.50   **10.** $14.78   **11.** $20.80   **12.** $105.95
13. $87.45   **14.** $99.00   **15.** $101.00   **16.** $99.99
17. $2.50   **18.** $6.79   **19.** $15.75   **20.** $14.77
Think It Through: $4.38

Power Builder B   **1.** $4.05   **2.** $3.78   **3.** $4.25
4. $13.00   **5.** $2.94   **6.** $5.10   **7.** $21.78   **8.** $25.20
9. $15.75   **10.** $18.58   **11.** $40.90   **12.** $155.95
13. $140.60   **14.** $52.00   **15.** $182.00   **16.** $65.25
17. $9.98   **18.** $4.58   **19.** $28.20   **20.** $21.99
Think It Through: $10.50

LESSON 17

Power Builder A   **1.** 400   **2.** 40   **3.** 60   **4.** 500   **5.** 70
6. 700   **7.** 90   **8.** 700   **9.** 800   **10.** 700   **11.** 900
12. 2000   **13.** 7000   **14.** 20,000   **15.** 100   **16.** 8000
17. 9000   **18.** 3000   **19.** 50,000   **20.** 7000
Think It Through: 500

Power Builder B   **1.** 800   **2.** 50   **3.** 70   **4.** 600   **5.** 30
6. 600   **7.** 90   **8.** 900   **9.** 800   **10.** 500   **11.** 800
12. 2000   **13.** 7000   **14.** 40,000   **15.** 100   **16.** 6000
17. 7000   **18.** 3000   **19.** 9000   **20.** 9000
Think It Through: 2000

LESSON 18

Power Builder A   **1.** 20   **2.** 20   **3.** 500   **4.** 30   **5.** 60
6. 800   **7.** 80   **8.** 7   **9.** 6   **10.** 70   **11.** 2   **12.** 800
13. 80   **14.** 4   **15.** 500   **16.** 500   **17.** 40   **18.** 60
19. 90   **20.** 900
Think It Through: $40,000

Power Builder B   **1.** 20   **2.** 40   **3.** 300   **4.** 40   **5.** 50
6. 80   **7.** 90   **8.** 9   **9.** 8   **10.** 90   **11.** 4   **12.** 600
13. 80   **14.** 7   **15.** 500   **16.** 600   **17.** 60   **18.** 90
19. 70   **20.** 700
Think It Through: $90,000

LESSON 19

Power Builder A   **1.** 6 hr   **2.** 12 hr   **3.** 2 hr   **4.** 8 hr
5. 4 hr   **6.** 20 hr   **7.** 2 hr   **8.** 2 hr   **9.** 7 hr   **10.** 50 hr
11. 5 hr   **12.** 4 hr   **13.** 5 hr   **14.** 3 hr   **15.** 4 hr
16. 5 hr   **17.** 2 hr   **18.** 3 hr   **19.** 7 hr   **20.** 90 hr
Think It Through: $524

Power Builder B   **1.** 6 hr   **2.** 3 hr   **3.** 4 hr   **4.** 12 hr
5. 4 hr   **6.** 30 hr   **7.** 3 hr   **8.** 3 hr   **9.** 50 hr   **10.** 200 hr
11. 4 hr   **12.** 5 hr   **13.** 6 hr   **14.** 6 hr   **15.** 6 hr
16. 3 hr   **17.** 3 hr   **18.** 4 hr   **19.** 7 hr   **20.** 50 hr
Think It Through: $371

LESSON 20

Power Builder A   **1.** $2.73   **2.** $8.97   **3.** $9.16
4. $25.98   **5.** $22.95   **6.** $7.01   **7.** $3.02   **8.** $7.02
9. $4.01   **10.** $7.02   **11.** $15.96   **12.** $20.93
13. $35.94   **14.** $39.90   **15.** $29.98   **16.** $99.90
17. $59.97   **18.** $399.84   **19.** $3990   **20.** $2985
Think It Through: $0.17

Power Builder B   **1.** $3.94   **2.** $6.97   **3.** $8.53
4. $25.98   **5.** $21.95   **6.** $6.01   **7.** $4.02   **8.** $5.02
9. $7.01   **10.** $8.02   **11.** $8.97   **12.** $19.92
13. $47.94   **14.** $29.96   **15.** $35.97   **16.** $199.90
17. $79.92   **18.** $149.80   **19.** $15,960   **20.** $11,985
Think It Through: $0.51

LESSON 21

Power Builder A   **1.** $\frac{3}{4}$ **2.** $\frac{3}{8}$ **3.** 1   **4.** $\frac{5}{6}$ **5.** $\frac{7}{8}$ **6.** $\frac{11}{16}$
7. $\frac{7}{10}$ **8.** $\frac{4}{6}$ or $\frac{2}{3}$ **9.** $\frac{7}{6}$ or $1\frac{1}{6}$ **10.** $\frac{5}{4}$ or $1\frac{1}{4}$
11. $\frac{9}{8}$ or $1\frac{1}{8}$ **12.** $\frac{11}{10}$ or $1\frac{1}{10}$ **13.** $2\frac{3}{4}$ **14.** $4\frac{3}{8}$
15. $3\frac{5}{8}$ **16.** $3\frac{7}{8}$ **17.** $5\frac{6}{10}$ or $5\frac{3}{5}$ **18.** $4\frac{7}{8}$ **19.** $3\frac{33}{100}$
20. $7\frac{97}{100}$
Think It Through: Answers will vary; pattern:
$$\frac{1}{n} = \frac{1}{2n} + \frac{1}{2n}$$

Power Builder B   **1.** $\frac{3}{6}$ or $\frac{1}{2}$ **2.** $\frac{5}{8}$ **3.** $\frac{6}{10}$ or $\frac{3}{5}$ **4.** $\frac{7}{10}$
5. $\frac{7}{8}$ **6.** $\frac{5}{12}$ **7.** $\frac{8}{10}$ or $\frac{4}{5}$ **8.** $\frac{3}{4}$ **9.** $\frac{9}{12}$ or $\frac{3}{4}$
10. $\frac{8}{6}$ or $1\frac{1}{3}$ **11.** $\frac{9}{16}$ **12.** $\frac{5}{6}$ **13.** $3\frac{5}{12}$
14. $6\frac{6}{10}$ or $6\frac{3}{5}$ **15.** $5\frac{5}{8}$ **16.** $4\frac{12}{10}$ or $5\frac{1}{5}$
17. $3\frac{13}{12}$ or $4\frac{1}{12}$ **18.** $4\frac{7}{10}$ **19.** $5\frac{77}{100}$ **20.** $5\frac{99}{100}$
Think It Through: Answers will vary; pattern:
$$\frac{1}{n} = \frac{1}{n+1} + \frac{1}{n(n+1)}$$

LESSON 22

Power Builder A 1. $\frac{3}{8}$ 2. $\frac{1}{4}$ 3. $\frac{2}{6}$ or $\frac{1}{3}$ 4. $\frac{2}{10}$ or $\frac{1}{5}$
5. $\frac{1}{8}$ 6. $\frac{1}{6}$ 7. $\frac{5}{8}$ 8. $\frac{3}{6}$ or $\frac{1}{2}$ 9. $\frac{4}{10}$ or $\frac{2}{5}$ 10. $\frac{7}{10}$ 11. $\frac{1}{16}$
12. $\frac{7}{10}$ 13. $\frac{1}{6}$ 14. $\frac{3}{8}$ 15. $\frac{7}{16}$ 16. $\frac{3}{10}$ 17. $1\frac{3}{6}$ or $1\frac{1}{2}$
18. $1\frac{5}{8}$ 19. $\frac{7}{100}$ 20. $\frac{9}{100}$

Think It Through: Answers will vary; pattern:
$\frac{1}{n} - \frac{1}{n+1} = \frac{1}{n(n+1)}$

Power Builder B 1. $\frac{1}{4}$ 2. $\frac{2}{10}$ or $\frac{1}{5}$ 3. $\frac{7}{16}$ 4. $\frac{2}{10}$ or $\frac{1}{5}$
5. $\frac{2}{9}$ 6. $\frac{2}{6}$ or $\frac{1}{3}$ 7. $\frac{3}{8}$ 8. $\frac{1}{6}$ 9. $\frac{3}{8}$ 10. $\frac{4}{10}$ or $\frac{2}{5}$ 11. $\frac{3}{16}$
12. $\frac{5}{10}$ or $\frac{1}{2}$ 13. $\frac{1}{16}$ 14. $\frac{4}{9}$ 15. $\frac{3}{12}$ or $\frac{1}{4}$ 16. $\frac{1}{10}$ 17. $\frac{3}{8}$
18. $\frac{15}{32}$ 19. $\frac{23}{100}$ 20. $\frac{27}{100}$

Think It Through: Answers will vary; pattern: the numerator in the difference equals half of the larger denominator minus 1, while the denominator equals the larger denominator

LESSON 23

Power Builder A 1. $\frac{2}{3}$ 2. $\frac{4}{5}$ 3. $\frac{1}{4}$ 4. $\frac{5}{7}$ 5. $\frac{4}{9}$ 6. $\frac{7}{12}$
7. $2\frac{3}{4}$ 8. $3\frac{5}{6}$ 9. $2\frac{4}{5}$ 10. $1\frac{1}{3}$ 11. $6\frac{1}{4}$ 12. $4\frac{1}{5}$
13. $6\frac{4}{9}$ 14. $5\frac{4}{7}$ 15. $8\frac{1}{2}$ 16. $3\frac{1}{6}$ 17. $4\frac{9}{10}$ 18. $2\frac{7}{10}$
19. $2\frac{97}{100}$ 20. $2\frac{997}{1000}$

Think It Through: Answers will vary.

Power Builder B 1. $\frac{3}{4}$ 2. $\frac{5}{6}$ 3. $\frac{1}{3}$ 4. $\frac{2}{7}$ 5. $\frac{5}{9}$ 6. $\frac{5}{12}$
7. $3\frac{3}{4}$ 8. $1\frac{6}{7}$ 9. $4\frac{2}{3}$ 10. $3\frac{1}{4}$ 11. $4\frac{1}{6}$ 12. $1\frac{1}{7}$
13. $4\frac{3}{8}$ 14. $7\frac{2}{9}$ 15. $7\frac{1}{2}$ 16. $4\frac{3}{7}$ 17. $4\frac{9}{10}$ 18. $4\frac{1}{10}$
19. $4\frac{91}{100}$ 20. $4\frac{991}{1000}$

Think It Through: Answers will vary.

LESSON 24

Power Builder A 1. $\frac{2}{3}$ 2. $\frac{4}{5}$ 3. $\frac{6}{7}$ 4. $\frac{1}{2}$ 5. $\frac{5}{6}$ 6. $1\frac{3}{8}$
7. $\frac{1}{4}$ 8. $\frac{4}{9}$ 9. $\frac{2}{5}$ 10. $\frac{5}{9}$ 11. $3\frac{1}{4}$ 12. $2\frac{1}{5}$ 13. $3\frac{1}{6}$
14. $4\frac{1}{5}$ 15. $5\frac{1}{8}$ 16. $2\frac{1}{4}$ 17. $2\frac{5}{9}$ 18. $2\frac{7}{10}$ 19. $1\frac{93}{100}$
20. $4\frac{97}{100}$

Think It Through: $\frac{15}{16}$; $\frac{31}{32}$; pattern: numerator is the largest denominator minus 1, while the denominator equals the largest denominator

Power Builder B

Power Builder B 1. $\frac{3}{4}$ 2. $\frac{2}{3}$ 3. $\frac{5}{6}$ 4. $1\frac{4}{5}$ 5. $\frac{2}{3}$
6. $3\frac{1}{4}$ 7. $\frac{3}{5}$ 8. $\frac{3}{7}$ 9. $\frac{1}{3}$ 10. $\frac{5}{9}$ 11. $3\frac{1}{4}$ 12. $3\frac{7}{9}$
13. $2\frac{2}{5}$ 14. $6\frac{1}{8}$ 15. $2\frac{3}{7}$ 16. $2\frac{3}{5}$ 17. $2\frac{5}{9}$ 18. $6\frac{1}{10}$
19. $4\frac{91}{100}$ 20. $4\frac{89}{100}$

Think It Through: $\frac{40}{81}$; $\frac{121}{243}$; pattern: numerator is found by dividing by 2 the largest denominator minus 1, while the denominator equals the largest denominator

LESSON 25

Power Builder A 1. $2\frac{1}{2}$ ft 2. $1\frac{1}{8}$ ft 3. $5\frac{1}{4}$ ft
4. $3\frac{1}{3}$ ft 5. $1\frac{2}{3}$ ft 6. $4\frac{3}{4}$ ft 7. $5\frac{3}{4}$ ft 8. $3\frac{1}{3}$ ft
9. $4\frac{1}{4}$ ft 10. $7\frac{3}{8}$ ft 11. $8\frac{2}{3}$ ft 12. $5\frac{5}{12}$ ft
13. $10\frac{3}{4}$ ft 14. $7\frac{1}{8}$ ft 15. $9\frac{1}{4}$ ft 16. $12\frac{1}{3}$ ft
17. $6\frac{7}{12}$ ft 18. $3\frac{7}{16}$ ft 19. $20\frac{9}{16}$ ft 20. $7\frac{1}{8}$ ft

Think It Through: $4\frac{1}{3}$; adding $\frac{2}{3}$ to each term

Power Builder B 1. $4\frac{3}{4}$ ft 2. $2\frac{1}{4}$ ft 3. $6\frac{3}{8}$ ft
4. $4\frac{2}{3}$ ft 5. $2\frac{1}{3}$ ft 6. $3\frac{1}{8}$ ft 7. $6\frac{1}{3}$ ft 8. $5\frac{1}{8}$ ft
9. $6\frac{3}{8}$ ft 10. $8\frac{7}{8}$ ft 11. $7\frac{1}{4}$ ft 12. $2\frac{1}{3}$ ft
13. $11\frac{2}{3}$ ft 14. $8\frac{5}{12}$ ft 15. $7\frac{3}{4}$ ft 16. $6\frac{1}{3}$ ft
17. $8\frac{11}{12}$ ft 18. $2\frac{7}{8}$ ft 19. $18\frac{9}{16}$ ft 20. $11\frac{11}{16}$ ft

Think It Through: $2\frac{3}{4}$; pattern: add $\frac{1}{2}$ to each number

LESSON 26

Power Builder A 1. $\frac{1}{8}$ 2. $\frac{2}{5}$ 3. $\frac{1}{3}$ 4. $\frac{5}{9}$ 5. $3\frac{4}{7}$
6. $2\frac{2}{5}$ 7. $3\frac{5}{7}$ 8. $6\frac{4}{5}$ 9. $2\frac{1}{5}$ 10. $1\frac{2}{9}$ 11. $\frac{2}{5}$ 12. $\frac{1}{8}$
13. $\frac{5}{9}$ 14. $2\frac{5}{6}$ 15. $\frac{1}{8}$ 16. $1\frac{1}{4}$ 17. $3\frac{5}{9}$ 18. $6\frac{3}{5}$
19. $7\frac{4}{7}$ 20. $7\frac{1}{9}$

Think It Through: $\frac{4}{9}$ and $\frac{7}{15}$; both are less than $\frac{1}{2}$, so the sum is less than 1

Power Builder B 1. $\frac{1}{5}$ 2. $\frac{5}{8}$ 3. $\frac{1}{4}$ 4. $\frac{5}{9}$ 5. $3\frac{1}{5}$
6. $1\frac{1}{5}$ 7. $2\frac{5}{9}$ 8. $7\frac{3}{5}$ 9. $5\frac{7}{12}$ 10. $3\frac{3}{8}$ 11. $\frac{1}{8}$ 12. $\frac{3}{8}$
13. $\frac{2}{9}$ 14. $\frac{4}{5}$ 15. $\frac{1}{8}$ 16. $2\frac{3}{4}$ 17. $5\frac{4}{7}$ 18. $6\frac{3}{5}$
19. $8\frac{5}{9}$ 20. $6\frac{4}{9}$

Think It Through: $\frac{4}{7}$ and $\frac{5}{9}$; both are greater than $\frac{1}{2}$, so the sum is larger than 1

LESSON 27

Power Builder A   1. $3\frac{5}{8}$ 2. $3\frac{11}{12}$ 3. $4\frac{7}{9}$
4. $6\frac{6}{10}$ or $6\frac{3}{5}$ 5. $7\frac{7}{8}$ 6. $6\frac{1}{8}$ 7. $11\frac{1}{6}$ 8. $9\frac{1}{9}$
9. $7\frac{2}{10}$ or $7\frac{1}{5}$ 10. $8\frac{1}{4}$ 11. $8\frac{5}{8}$ 12. $7\frac{2}{10}$ or $7\frac{1}{5}$
13. $4\frac{2}{6}$ or $4\frac{1}{3}$ 14. $9\frac{1}{8}$ 15. $7\frac{1}{10}$ 16. $10\frac{2}{12}$ or $10\frac{1}{6}$
17. $6\frac{1}{16}$ 18. $4\frac{7}{20}$ 19. $7\frac{1}{16}$ 20. $11\frac{3}{12}$ or $11\frac{1}{4}$
Think It Through: 14

Power Builder B   1. $3\frac{7}{8}$ 2. $5\frac{7}{12}$ 3. $6\frac{8}{9}$
4. $8\frac{8}{10}$ or $8\frac{4}{5}$ 5. $7\frac{5}{8}$ 6. $8\frac{1}{4}$ 7. $8\frac{1}{8}$ 8. $6\frac{2}{9}$
9. $7\frac{4}{10}$ or $7\frac{2}{5}$ 10. $6\frac{3}{8}$ 11. $6\frac{1}{6}$ 12. $6\frac{4}{10}$ or $6\frac{2}{5}$
13. $7\frac{2}{6}$ or $7\frac{1}{3}$ 14. $9\frac{3}{8}$ 15. $4\frac{1}{10}$ 16. $6\frac{3}{12}$ or $6\frac{1}{4}$
17. $10\frac{3}{16}$ 18. $8\frac{7}{16}$ 19. $7\frac{5}{16}$ 20. $7\frac{2}{12}$ or $7\frac{1}{6}$
Think It Through: 5

LESSON 28

Power Builder A   1. $2\frac{2}{5}$ 2. $4\frac{1}{4}$ 3. $5\frac{3}{7}$ 4. $3\frac{4}{9}$
5. $3\frac{1}{2}$ 6. $4\frac{1}{3}$ 7. $1\frac{4}{7}$ 8. $5\frac{6}{10}$ or $5\frac{3}{5}$ 9. $1\frac{1}{2}$ 10. $1\frac{3}{5}$
11. $1\frac{4}{9}$ 12. $3\frac{8}{10}$ or $3\frac{4}{5}$ 13. $2\frac{3}{4}$ 14. $4\frac{5}{10}$ or $4\frac{1}{2}$
15. $4\frac{3}{6}$ or $4\frac{1}{2}$ 16. $2\frac{4}{6}$ or $2\frac{2}{3}$ 17. $3\frac{9}{12}$ or $3\frac{3}{4}$
18. $3\frac{9}{12}$ or $3\frac{3}{4}$ 19. $1\frac{5}{6}$ 20. $2\frac{5}{8}$
Think It Through: $13\frac{7}{8}$ ft

Power Builder B   1. $1\frac{1}{3}$ 2. $1\frac{2}{7}$ 3. $2\frac{2}{9}$ 4. $2\frac{1}{4}$
5. $4\frac{2}{3}$ 6. $3\frac{6}{7}$ 7. $1\frac{2}{6}$ or $1\frac{1}{3}$ 8. $4\frac{2}{10}$ or $4\frac{1}{5}$
9. $5\frac{2}{6}$ or $5\frac{1}{3}$ 10. $1\frac{4}{5}$ 11. $2\frac{3}{9}$ or $2\frac{1}{3}$
12. $3\frac{8}{12}$ or $3\frac{2}{3}$ 13. $1\frac{1}{2}$ 14. $3\frac{3}{6}$ or $3\frac{1}{2}$
15. $4\frac{4}{6}$ or $4\frac{2}{3}$ 16. $1\frac{5}{8}$ 17. $4\frac{3}{10}$ 18. $3\frac{9}{12}$ or $3\frac{3}{4}$
19. $2\frac{7}{8}$ 20. $1\frac{7}{10}$

Think It Through: $1\frac{1}{2}$ ft

LESSON 29

Power Builder A   1. 3   2. 7   3. 5   4. 15   5. 4   6. 12
7. 9   8. 18   9. 7   10. 21   11. 16   12. 18   13. 75
14. 60   15. 60   16. 25   17. 400   18. 150   19. 160
20. 300
Think It Through: 360

Power Builder B   1. 5   2. 5   3. 10   4. 6   5. 5   6. 10
7. 30   8. 60   9. 6   10. 18   11. 15   12. 8   13. 80
14. 60   15. 40   16. 30   17. 200   18. 75   19. 160
20. 600
Think It Through: 1600

LESSON 30

Power Builder A   1. 6 ft for $2.75   2. 5 lb for $1.60
3. 12 for $2.50   4. 4 m for $11.25   5. 12 mL for $170
6. 10 kg for $7.60   7. 8 ft for $3.60
8. 12 yd for $48.75   9. 24 for $3.75
10. 30 yd for $1075   11. 3 ft for $1.50
12. 4 lb for $1.60   13. 15 for $4.00   14. 15 m for $25
15. 5 oz for $9.75   16. 10 kg for $3.60
17. 12 ft for $3.60   18. 12 yd for $35   19. 20 for $1.98
20. 30 yd for $690
Think It Through: 36, 54, 45

Power Builder B   1. 5 ft for $1.79   2. 4 lb for $1.80
3. 36 for $14.25   4. 5 m for $8   5. 5 oz for $9.75
6. 100 kg for $250   7. 24 ft for $17.50   8. 6 for $40
9. 10 for $30   10. 12 yd for $300   11. 2 ft for 55¢
12. 18 lb for $3.25   13. 24 for $10   14. 15 m for $104
15. 150 kg for $700   16. 6 L for $13
17. 32 ft for $7.00   18. 3 bags for $12
19. 10 for $29.99   20. 20 yd for $950
Think It Through: 48, 60, 72

LESSON 31

Power Builder A   1. $15\frac{3}{5}$ 2. $10\frac{5}{6}$ 3. $2\frac{4}{7}$ 4. $12\frac{8}{9}$
5. 14   6. 9   7. 13   8. 18   9. 8   10. 7   11. $7\frac{1}{2}$ 12. 33
13. 28   14. 33   15. 13   16. 14   17. 56   18. 26
19. 770   20. 136
Think It Through: 24 feet; 30 feet

Power Builder B   1. $8\frac{4}{5}$ 2. $9\frac{1}{2}$ 3. $6\frac{2}{3}$ 4. $6\frac{6}{7}$
5. $8\frac{1}{2}$ 6. 26   7. 19   8. 18   9. 8   10. 16   11. $12\frac{1}{2}$
12. 42   13. 30   14. 40   15. 69   16. 28   17. 75
18. 24   19. 530   20. 280
Think It Through: 4 parts cement, 12 parts gravel,
20 gallons water

LESSON 32

Power Builder A   1. $1\frac{1}{2}$ lbs shrimp   2. $\frac{1}{2}$ cup carrots
3. $1\frac{1}{3}$ cups broccoli   4. 3 T onion   5. $2\frac{1}{2}$ cups squash
6. 1 cup mushrooms
7. $4\frac{2}{3}$ tsp soy sauce (1 T + $1\frac{2}{3}$ tsp)   8. 2 T cornstarch
9. $\frac{1}{4}$ tsp garlic powder   10. 5 T oil   11. 3 lbs shrimp
12. 1 cup carrots   13. $2\frac{2}{3}$ cups broccoli   14. 6 T onion
15. 5 cups squash   16. 2 cups mushrooms
17. $9\frac{1}{3}$ tsp soy sauce (3 T + $\frac{1}{3}$ tsp)   18. 4 T cornstarch
19. $\frac{1}{2}$ tsp garlic powder   20. 10 T oil
Think It Through: triple two-thirds

Power Builder B **1.** 1 cup coconut

2. $1\frac{1}{3}$ cups sunflower seeds **3.** $2\frac{1}{2}$ cups raisins

4. $1\frac{1}{3}$ cups pecans **5.** $\frac{2}{3}$ cup walnuts

6. 1 cup peanut butter **7.** $1\frac{1}{2}$ cups honey

8. $4\frac{2}{3}$ cups oats **9.** 3 tsp vanilla

10. $2\frac{1}{2}$ tsp cinnamon **11.** $1\frac{1}{2}$ cups coconut

12. 2 cups sunflower seeds **13.** $3\frac{3}{4}$ cups raisins

14. 2 cups pecans **15.** 1 cup walnuts

16. $1\frac{1}{2}$ cups peanut butter **17.** $2\frac{1}{4}$ cups honey

18. 7 cups oats **19.** $4\frac{1}{2}$ tsp vanilla ($1\,T + 1\frac{1}{2}$ tsp)

20. $3\frac{3}{4}$ tsp cinnamon ($1\,T + \frac{3}{4}$ tsp)

Think It Through: triple two-fifths

LESSON 33

Power Builder A **1.** 180 **2.** 260 **3.** 216 **4.** 1016
5. 296 **6.** 976 **7.** 720 **8.** 1360 **9.** 256 **10.** 1024
11. 210 **12.** 270 **13.** 630 **14.** 770 **15.** 2800
16. 36,000 **17.** 540 **18.** 6300 **19.** 6600 **20.** 4000
Think It Through: $10.24

Power Builder B **1.** 220 **2.** 340 **3.** 208 **4.** 1000
5. 256 **6.** 896 **7.** 816 **8.** 1520 **9.** 224 **10.** 864
11. 330 **12.** 390 **13.** 770 **14.** 910 **15.** 2200
16. 28,000 **17.** 420 **18.** 8100 **19.** 5400 **20.** 5600
Think It Through: 9 cuts

LESSON 34

Power Builder A **1.** 18 **2.** 15 **3.** 21.2 **4.** 18.6
5. 12.8 **6.** 17.6 **7.** 44 **8.** 24 **9.** 39 **10.** 55.8
11. 0.5 **12.** 20 **13.** 3.36 **14.** 72 **15.** 27 **16.** 6
17. 28 **18.** 26 **19.** 68 **20.** 12
Think It Through: 1295; 12.25; 1225

Power Builder B **1.** 26 **2.** 32.8 **3.** 21 **4.** 51
5. 28.8 **6.** 19.2 **7.** 68 **8.** 40 **9.** 33 **10.** 49.8
11. 0.9 **12.** 18 **13.** 36 **14.** 4 **15.** 66 **16.** 3
17. 21 **18.** 104 **19.** 54 **20.** 36
Think It Through: 675; 6.25; 625

LESSON 35

Power Builder A **1.** 60 **2.** 130 **3.** 800 **4.** 440
5. 600 **6.** 240 **7.** 3200 **8.** 800 **9.** 330 **10.** 180
11. 1300 **12.** 1800 **13.** 1600 **14.** 280 **15.** 2700
16. 8000 **17.** 10,500 **18.** 2200 **19.** 6000 **20.** 6200
Think It Through: 6,000; 12,000; 16,500

Power Builder B **1.** 90 **2.** 70 **3.** 800 **4.** 1200
5. 220 **6.** 1400 **7.** 320 **8.** 2400 **9.** 900 **10.** 160
11. 1100 **12.** 1100 **13.** 6000 **14.** 280 **15.** 2700
16. 7000 **17.** 7000 **18.** 3100 **19.** 5500 **20.** 33,330
Think It Through: 2100; 350; 70; 7.25

LESSON 36

Power Builder A **1.** 70 **2.** 130 **3.** 180 **4.** 300
5. 700 **6.** 420 **7.** 630 **8.** 3000 **9.** 2200 **10.** 4000
11. 360 **12.** 1200 **13.** 600 **14.** 700 **15.** 540
16. 390 **17.** 490 **18.** 1600 **19.** 3300 **20.** 7200
Think It Through: 5000 cubic meters

Power Builder B **1.** 600 **2.** 290 **3.** 210 **4.** 300
5. 180 **6.** 1200 **7.** 660 **8.** 3900 **9.** 3600 **10.** 2600
11. 390 **12.** 720 **13.** 270 **14.** 420 **15.** 1500
16. 2200 **17.** 5600 **18.** 4500 **19.** 3600 **20.** 11,000
Think It Through: $24,000.00

LESSON 37

Power Builder A **1.** 140 **2.** 180 **3.** 210 **4.** 360
5. 270 **6.** 300 **7.** 120 **8.** 900 **9.** 400 **10.** 160
11. 330 **12.** 450 **13.** 720 **14.** 540 **15.** 420
16. 1500 **17.** 2200 **18.** 3600 **19.** 4500 **20.** 3600
Think It Through: 12; 30; 120

Power Builder B **1.** 150 **2.** 210 **3.** 220 **4.** 270
5. 360 **6.** 330 **7.** 280 **8.** 200 **9.** 330 **10.** 350
11. 450 **12.** 700 **13.** 540 **14.** 390 **15.** 490
16. 1400 **17.** 1200 **18.** 4000 **19.** 18,000 **20.** 2700
Think It Through: 7200 cubic units; no change in
volume; volume increases by 8 times

LESSON 38

Power Builder A **1.** 15 **2.** 230 **3.** 3500 **4.** 4.6
5. 53 **6.** 490 **7.** 165 **8.** 189 **9.** 1250 **10.** 112.3
11. 1556 **12.** 14,780 **13.** 481.75 **14.** 5962.5
15. 12,345 **16.** 182.356 **17.** 789.26 **18.** 15,555
19. 0.123 **20.** 0.35
Think It Through: 1,000,000,000

Power Builder B **1.** 14 **2.** 320 **3.** 8500 **4.** 6.4
5. 11 **6.** 990 **7.** 555 **8.** 981 **9.** 5250 **10.** 100.3
11. 2550 **12.** 24,780 **13.** 841.75 **14.** 9999.9
15. 54,321 **16.** 111.111 **17.** 189.26 **18.** 10,005
19. 0.321 **20.** 350.35
Think It Through: 200; 2,000; 200,000

LESSON 39

Power Builder A   **1.** 5.5   **2.** 0.86   **3.** 0.099   **4.** 0.435
5. 0.0149   **6.** 0.4567   **7.** 4.53   **8.** 1.23   **9.** 1.456
10. 2.111   **11.** 185.6   **12.** 55.55   **13.** 0.111
14. 0.0123   **15.** 0.0001   **16.** 0.0008   **17.** 0.000099
18. 1.234   **19.** 0.00001   **20.** 0.00123
Think It Through: 17

Power Builder B   **1.** 4.4   **2.** 0.88   **3.** 0.069   **4.** 0.135
5. 0.0444   **6.** 0.7654   **7.** 1.03   **8.** 3.33   **9.** 2.457
10. 2.222   **11.** 885.6   **12.** 11.11   **13.** 0.222
14. 0.01414   **15.** 0.001   **16.** 0.0002   **17.** 0.000999
18. 4.234   **19.** 0.000001   **20.** 0.00423
Think It Through: 10,000,000 days, or between 25,000 and 30,000 years

LESSON 40

Power Builder A   **1.** 1.05 m   **2.** 1.85 m   **3.** 12.34 m
4. 5 m   **5.** 0.75 m   **6.** 1.5 m   **7.** 2.5 m   **8.** 0.75 m
9. 40 m   **10.** 0.01 m   **11.** 2500 mm   **12.** 4800 mm
13. 500 mm   **14.** 250 mm   **15.** 5 mm   **16.** 1800 mm
17. 50 mm   **18.** 5 mm   **19.** 0.1 mm   **20.** 2500 mm
Think It Through: 150 km

Power Builder B   **1.** 2.05 m   **2.** 3.55 m   **3.** 43.21 m
4. 9 m   **5.** 0.55 m   **6.** 4.5 m   **7.** 7.5 m   **8.** 0.5 m
9. 50 m   **10.** 0.001 m   **11.** 5500 mm   **12.** 8800 mm
13. 750 mm   **14.** 450 mm   **15.** 1 mm   **16.** 1500 mm
17. 500 mm   **18.** 0.5 mm   **19.** 3.55 mm
20. 12.5 mm
Think It Through: 150,000,000 kilometers, or about the distance from the earth to the sun

LESSON 41

Power Builder A   **1.** 60 buns   **2.** 96 in.
3. 108 cookies   **4.** 144 in.   **5.** 132 chocolates
6. 192 in.   **7.** 300 bottles   **8.** 180 in.   **9.** 168 in.
10. 264 eggs   **11.** 8 feet   **12.** 5 feet   **13.** 10 dozen
14. 15 feet   **15.** 13 dozen   **16.** 60 feet   **17.** 20 dozen
18. 16 feet   **19.** 25 feet   **20.** 60 dozen
Think It Through: 720, 360, 1080

Power Builder B   **1.** 48 in.   **2.** 144 in.   **3.** 72 rolls
4. 60 doughnuts   **5.** 300 in.   **6.** 156 eggs   **7.** 192 in.
8. 204 bottles   **9.** 288 pens   **10.** 216 in.   **11.** 20 dozen
12. 60 feet   **13.** 9 feet   **14.** 14 dozen   **15.** 24 dozen
16. 30 feet   **17.** 40 dozen   **18.** 16 dozen   **19.** 26 feet
20. 120 feet
Think It Through: 7 days; 360 hours

LESSON 42

Power Builder A   **1.** 23   **2.** 11   **3.** 21   **4.** 73   **5.** 21
6. 101   **7.** 21   **8.** 21   **9.** 102   **10.** 111   **11.** 101
12. 103   **13.** 213   **14.** 108   **15.** 102   **16.** 102
17. 1001   **18.** 2002   **19.** 404   **20.** 909
Think It Through: 1024; 512; 256

Power Builder B   **1.** 33   **2.** 11   **3.** 42   **4.** 423   **5.** 31
6. 51   **7.** 41   **8.** 42   **9.** 407   **10.** 333   **11.** 202
12. 103   **13.** 313   **14.** 81   **15.** 202   **16.** 306   **17.** 2002
18. 2012   **19.** 606   **20.** 912
Think It Through: 33; 64; 1032; 132

LESSON 43

Power Builder A   **1.** 14   **2.** 38   **3.** 12   **4.** 27   **5.** 14
6. 29   **7.** 24   **8.** 14   **9.** 13   **10.** 16   **11.** 24   **12.** 45
13. 22   **14.** 22   **15.** 26   **16.** 32   **17.** 25   **18.** 93
19. 65   **20.** 64
Think It Through: 2100

Power Builder B   **1.** 14   **2.** 49   **3.** 26   **4.** 24   **5.** 13
6. 27   **7.** 12   **8.** 13   **9.** 14   **10.** 18   **11.** 36   **12.** 18
13. 55   **14.** 45   **15.** 42   **16.** 24   **17.** 23   **18.** 39
19. 45   **20.** 54
Think It Through: 3200

LESSON 44

Power Builder A   **1.** 2   **2.** 4   **3.** 6   **4.** 16   **5.** 150
6. 0.48   **7.** 0.72   **8.** 2.25   **9.** 28   **10.** 32   **11.** 6.4
12. 0.36   **13.** 0.6   **14.** 3   **15.** 9   **16.** 50   **17.** $1\frac{1}{2}$
18. 23.5   **19.** 9.6   **20.** 22
Think It Through: $24.00

Power Builder B   **1.** 8   **2.** 12   **3.** 10   **4.** 40   **5.** 250
6. 0.52   **7.** 0.56   **8.** 0.90   **9.** 36   **10.** 36   **11.** 3.2
12. 7.2   **13.** 30   **14.** 9   **15.** 13   **16.** 64   **17.** $\frac{2}{3}$
18. 53.5   **19.** 12.8   **20.** 14
Think It Through: 31; 31; 3.1

LESSON 45

Power Builder A   **1.** 1%   **2.** 8%   **3.** 11%   **4.** 18%
5. 29%   **6.** 70%   **7.** 90%   **8.** 12.3%   **9.** 0.9%
10. 140%   **11.** 0.1   **12.** 0.03   **13.** 0.25   **14.** 0.38
15. 0.99   **16.** 0.5   **17.** 0.666   **18.** 0.001   **19.** 0.0125
20. 1.14
Think It Through: neither—both equal $\frac{1}{1000}$

Power Builder B 1. 5% 2. 9% 3. 22% 4. 81%
5. 99% 6. 60% 7. 70% 8. 55.55% 9. 0.99%
10. 550% 11. 0.2 12. 0.01 13. 0.35 14. 0.83
15. 0.91 16. 0.40 17. 0.9999 18. 0.003
19. 0.02125 20. 2.0
Think It Through: $\frac{1}{100}$%, or 1 part in 10,000 is impure

LESSON 46

Power Builder A 1. $33\frac{1}{3}$% 2. 50% 3. 10% 4. 1%
5. $133\frac{1}{3}$% 6. 110% 7. 201% 8. $133\frac{1}{3}$% 9. 250%
10. 510% 11. $4 12. $25 13. $8 14. $45 15. $88
16. $135 17. $40 18. $3.50 19. $353.50 20. $350
Think It Through: 25%; 12.5%; 37.5%; 6.25%

Power Builder B 1. 50% 2. $33\frac{1}{3}$% 3. 1% 4. 10%
5. 150% 6. 210% 7. 401% 8. $233\frac{1}{3}$% 9. 450%
10. 601% 11. $5 12. $30 13. $18 14. $35
15. $198 16. $105 17. $90 18. $10.50
19. $1060.50 20. $650
Think It Through: 21%: 10% of $1.00 = $0.10;
10% of $1.10 = $0.11; increase $0.21

LESSON 47

Power Builder A 1. $2.50 2. $5.00 3. $7.50
4. $10.00 5. $8.00 6. $1.60 7. $2.40 8. $3.20
9. $5 10. $10 11. $20 12. $12 13. $1.90
14. $3.80 15. $13.00 16. $75 17. $15.12
18. $30.24 19. $9.00 20. $72.72
Think It Through: I LOVE MENTAL MATH

Power Builder B 1. $4.50 2. $9.00 3. $13.50
4. $18.00 5. $12 6. $24 7. $36 8. $48 9. $15
10. $30 11. $60 12. $15 13. $6.90 14. $13.80
15. $15.00 16. $45.00 17. $5.16 18. $10.32
19. $0.03 20. $57.20
Think It Through: FIGURING IS FUN

LESSON 48

Power Builder A 1. $33\frac{1}{3}$% 2. 50% 3. 25%
4. 12.5% 5. 37.5% 6. 62.5% 7. 87.5% 8. 112.5%
9. 20% 10. 60% 11. $10 12. $5 13. $15 14. $30
15. $45 16. $35 17. $17.50 18. $8 19. $4 20. $2
Think It Through: The better deal is (a), $40 vs. $38 reduction.

Power Builder B 1. $33\frac{1}{3}$% 2. $66\frac{2}{3}$% 3. 25%
4. 12.5% 5. 6.25% 6. 18.75% 7. 37.5% 8. 75%
9. 87.5% 10. 62.5% 11. $120 12. $60 13. $180
14. $360 15. $540 16. $22.50 17. $11.25
18. $1.84 19. $0.92 20. $2.40
Think It Through: The best buy is (a), $5 vs. $3 vs. $4.70 reduction.

LESSON 49

Power Builder A 1. $60 2. $6 3. $66 4. $54
5. $57 6. $70 7. $56 8. $63 9. $6.50 10. $3.25
11. $7.50 12. $15.00 13. $11.25 14. $18.75
15. $500 16. $625 17. $4.00 18. $2.00
19. $1.00 20. $1.00
Think It Through: 212-1212

Power Builder B 1. $1800 2. $180 3. $1980
4. $1620 5. $1710 6. $2.40 7. $0.48 8. $0.24
9. $2.64 10. $2.16 11. $300 12. $320 13. $8
14. $2 15. $6.48 16. $3.24 17. $9.72 18. $16.20
19. $1.62 20. $0.81
Think It Through: 323-2323

LESSON 50

Power Builder A 1. $3 2. $4.50 3. $14.50
4. $2500 5. $62.50 6. $28 7. $111 8. $1600
9. $2400 10. $40 11. $6.75 12. $7 13. $3.70
14. $150 15. $3.75 16. $4400 17. $75,000
18. $3000 19. $2.20 20. $175
Think It Through: $99

Power Builder B 1. $1.20 2. $2.00 3. $24.50
4. $1250 5. $625 6. $36 7. $200 8. $1500
9. $1400 10. $30 11. $45 12. $10.50 13. $4.80
14. $570 15. $7.50 16. $4200 17. $30,000
18. $1800 19. $2.75 20. $20
Think It Through: $337.50

UNIT ONE PROGRESS TEST

1. 322   2. 5.2   3. 601   4. 9.23   5. 3 hr 15 min
6. 590   7. 39   8. 503   9. 3 hr 45 min   10. 2.4
11. $5.31   12. 3.64   13. $4.50   14. 393   15. 351
16. 171   17. $5.63   18. 8 hr 15 min   19. 673
20. $0.90   21. 33   22. $18.22   23. 7.2   24. 29.2
25. 4.5   26. 225   27. 2.746   28. $4.15   29. 73
30. 0.33   31. 545   32. 6 hr 55 min   33. 9425   34. 355
35. 903   36. 68   37. 3.40   38. $24.12   39. 333
40. 102

UNIT TWO PROGRESS TEST

1. 4.03   2. 234   3. 1.7   4. 720   5. 328   6. $1.90
7. 500   8. 40   9. 8 hr   10. 656   11. 2800   12. $5.95
13. 3.98   14. 1350   15. 80   16. 228   17. 426   18. 90
19. 2.5   20. 5.02   21. 3 hr   22. 24.09   23. $9.96
24. 508   25. 7.03   26. 180,000   27. 70   28. 30 hr
29. 247   30. 3000   31. 6558   32. $21.87   33. $1.02
34. 50 hr   35. 13.44   36. 900   37. 5800   38. 1400
39. $7.97   40. 60

UNIT THREE PROGRESS TEST

1. $\frac{4}{10}$ or $\frac{2}{5}$ 2. $9\frac{1}{10}$ 3. $1\frac{1}{8}$ 4. $\frac{5}{6}$ 5. $3\frac{5}{8}$ 6. 5
7. $3\frac{2}{3}$ ft   8. $3\frac{1}{5}$ 9. 8 for $6.89   10. $3\frac{4}{9}$ 11. $\frac{5}{8}$ 12. $\frac{4}{9}$
13. $13\frac{1}{4}$ ft   14. $8\frac{5}{12}$ 15. 5 for $0.39   16. $\frac{5}{8}$ 17. $4\frac{2}{5}$
18. 27   19. $3\frac{1}{4}$ 20. $2\frac{2}{8}$ or $2\frac{1}{4}$ 21. $7\frac{1}{3}$ ft
22. 9 for $1.67   23. $2\frac{3}{4}$ 24. $\frac{5}{10}$ or $\frac{1}{2}$ 25. $2\frac{5}{6}$ 26. $2\frac{11}{12}$
27. $\frac{5}{10}$ or $\frac{1}{2}$ 28. $3\frac{3}{5}$ 29. $4\frac{6}{10}$ or $4\frac{3}{5}$ 30. $\frac{1}{6}$ 31. $\frac{5}{8}$
32. $2\frac{1}{3}$ 33. $2\frac{1}{3}$ 34. $5\frac{5}{8}$ ft   35. $1\frac{3}{7}$ 36. $7\frac{1}{6}$
37. $2\frac{4}{8}$ or $2\frac{1}{2}$ 38. 6   39. 8 for $4.00   40. 25

UNIT FOUR PROGRESS TEST

1. $5\frac{1}{3}$ 2. 340   3. 600   4. 52   5. 1800   6. 1.05 m
7. 5021   8. 20   9. 340   10. $1\frac{1}{2}$ 11. 4200   12. 0.534
13. 3600   14. 330   15. 0.2463 m   16. 770   17. 34
18. 1800   19. 28   20. 4.6   21. 300   22. 21
23. 42.561 m   24. 490   25. 110   26. 4.15   27. 2700
28. $1\frac{1}{2}$ 29. 40 m   30. 270   31. 40   32. $20
33. 0.0527   34. 640   35. 4   36. 0.1256   37. 672
38. 540   39. 4.273   40. 3.6

UNIT FIVE PROGRESS TEST

1. 12   2. $6   3. 4.8   4. 43%   5. $15   6. 106
7. 96 eggs   8. 12.5%   9. $1.35   10. 3003   11. 90%
12. $45   13. 8   14. $21   15. 212   16. 156 inches
17. $198   18. $130   19. 6.4   20. 130%   21. $7
22. 63   23. 606   24. $0.39   25. $1.80   26. $18
27. $400   28. 32   29. 60 feet   30. $85.85   31. 18.75%
32. $25   33. 4   34. 12   35. $10   36. $59.40
37. 2.5%   38. 6 dozen rolls   39. $63   40. $45

CUMULATIVE TEST, FORM A

1. 571   2. 6.6   3. 56,000   4. 613   5. 50   6. 803
7. 1.58   8. $2\frac{2}{3}$ 9. 5 hr 50 min   10. 136   11. 2600
12. 3.4   13. $\frac{7}{8}$ 14. $8.94   15. 700   16. $2\frac{5}{9}$
17. $11\frac{7}{12}$ ft   18. 316   19. 7476   20. 70   21. $8.50
22. $\frac{4}{10}$ or $\frac{2}{5}$ 23. $29.36   24. 416   25. 16
26. 12 for $0.70   27. 920   28. $5\frac{1}{2}$ 29. 800   30. 6.15
31. $6\frac{1}{8}$ 32. 36   33. $4   34. $2\frac{1}{6}$ 35. 7.03   36. $700
37. $80   38. 12   39. 1900   40. 18   41. 5.416
42. 51.26 m   43. $1\frac{1}{2}$ 44. 490   45. 288 inches
46. $73.50   47. 606   48. 110%   49. 25   50. $4.50

CUMULATIVE TEST, FORM B

1. 182   2. 4.8   3. 27,000   4. 426   5. 80   6. 902
7. 3.43   8. $4\frac{3}{8}$ 9. 5 hr 55 min   10. 145   11. 27
12. 3.4   13. $\frac{7}{10}$ 14. $12.78   15. 700   16. $4\frac{1}{3}$
17. $8\frac{3}{8}$ ft   18. 450   19. 9456   20. 400   21. $120
22. $\frac{3}{8}$ 23. $9.64   24. 41.7   25. 38   26. 4 for $0.69
27. 540   28. $3\frac{1}{3}$ 29. 2400   30. 3.15   31. $6\frac{2}{6}$ or $6\frac{1}{3}$
32. 40   33. $0.84   34. $3\frac{1}{8}$ 35. 4.52   36. $1200
37. $1.80   38. 17   39. 1700   40. 10   41. 0.4172
42. 41.56 cm   43. $4\frac{1}{2}$ 44. 560   45. 240 eggs
46. $306   47. 707   48. 10%   49. 24   50. $3.15